Cognitive Psychology: Theory, Process and Methodology

Cognitive Psychology: Theory, Process and Methodology

Dawson Coffey

CLANRYE
INTERNATIONAL
www.clanryeinternational.com

Clanrye International,
750 Third Avenue, 9th Floor,
New York, NY 10017, USA

ISBN: 978-1-64726-159-7

Cataloging-in-Publication Data

Cognitive psychology : theory, process and methodology / Dawson Coffey.
p. cm.
Includes bibliographical references and index.
ISBN 978-1-64726-159-7
1. Cognitive psychology. 2. Cognitive psychology--Methodology. 3. Psychology.
4. Cognitive science. I. Coffey, Dawson.
BF201 .C64 2021
153--dc23

For information on all Clanrye International publications
visit our website at www.clanryeinternational.com

CLANRYE INTERNATIONAL

Contents

Preface

The scientific study of mental processes is known as cognitive psychology. Some of the various processes studied under this discipline are language use, attention, problem solving, memory and perception. Cognitive psychology generally sees cognition through the dual process theory. This theory states that cognition is made up of two styles of processing, intuition and reasoning. Cognitive psychology finds application in several fields such as abnormal psychology, social psychology, developmental psychology, personality psychology and economics. Components of behaviourism were integrated with cognitive psychology to form cognitive behavioural therapy. It is an intervention which seeks to improve mental health and treat issues such as depression and anxiety. The topics included in this book on cognitive psychology are of utmost significance and bound to provide incredible insights to readers. It will serve as a valuable source of reference for graduate and post graduate students.

A foreword of all Chapters of the book is provided below:

Chapter 1 - The branch of psychology which studies mental processes is known as cognitive psychology. Some of the aspects on which this area of study focuses are conscious mind, cognition, cognitive development and cognitive flexibility. This is an introductory chapter which will introduce briefly all the significant aspects of cognitive psychology and the processes associated with it.; **Chapter 2** - The organization, interpretation, and identification of sensory information for the purpose of comprehending it is known as perception. The cognitive and behavioral process of selectively focusing on a discrete aspect of information is known as attention. The topics elaborated in this chapter will help in gaining a better perspective about perception and attention as well as the basic characteristics of perception and attention.; **Chapter 3** - The faculty of the brain through which it stores, encodes and retrieves information is called memory. It is broadly categorized into long-term memory and short-term memory. This chapter discusses in detail the theories and concepts related to memory such as working memory and state-dependent memory.; **Chapter 4** - The branch of linguistics which describes the manner in which language interacts with cognition and how language forms our thoughts is known as cognitive linguistics. Some of the aspects which are dealt with under this field are lexical semantics, language acquisition and non-verbal communication. All these diverse concepts of cognitive linguistics have been carefully analyzed in this chapter.; **Chapter 5** - The usage of ad-hoc or generic methods for the purpose of finding solutions to problems is known as problem solving. The capacity of applying logic, understanding things and verifying facts is known as reasoning. The chapter closely examines the key concepts of problem solving and reasoning such as social cognition, decision-making strategies and deductive reasoning to provide an extensive understanding of the subject.; **Chapter 6** - The capacity to perceive and retain information as well as applying it for adaptive behaviors is known as intelligence. This chapter closely examines the key concepts of general intelligence such as the theories of intelligence and models of intelligence in order to provide an extensive understanding of the subject.

I would like to thank the entire editorial team who made sincere efforts for this book and my family who supported me in my efforts of working on this book. I take this opportunity to thank all those who have been a guiding force throughout my life.

Dawson Coffey

1

Introduction to Cognitive Psychology

The branch of psychology which studies mental processes is known as cognitive psychology. Some of the aspects on which this area of study focuses are conscious mind, cognition, cognitive development and cognitive flexibility. This is an introductory chapter which will introduce briefly all the significant aspects of cognitive psychology and the processes associated with it.

Cognitive psychology involves the study of internal mental processes—all of the things that go on inside your brain, including perception, thinking, memory, attention, language, problem-solving, and learning. While it is a relatively young branch of psychology, it has quickly grown to become one of the most popular subfields.

There are numerous practical applications for this cognitive research, such as providing help coping with memory disorders, increasing decision-making accuracy, finding ways to help people recover from brain injury, treating learning disorders, and structuring educational curricula to enhance learning.

Learning more about how people think and process information not only helps researchers gain a deeper understanding of how the human brain works, but it allows psychologists to develop new ways of helping people deal with psychological difficulties. For example, by recognizing that attention is both a selective and limited resource, psychologists are able come up with solutions that make it easier for people with attentional difficulties to improve their focus and concentration.

Findings from cognitive psychology have also improved our understanding of how people form, store, and recall memories. By knowing more about how these processes work, psychologists can develop new ways of helping people improve their memories and combat potential memory problems.

For example, psychologists have found that while your short-term memory is quite short and limited (lasting just 20 to 30 seconds and capable of holding between five and nine items), rehearsal strategies can improve the chances that information will be transferred to long-term memory, which is much more stable and durable.

While many cognitive psychologists specialize in research and are employed by universities or government agencies, others take a clinical focus and work directly with individuals who are experiencing challenges related to different mental processes. They may work in hospitals, mental health clinics, or private practices.

Psychologists who work in this area often focus on a particular area of interest such as memory, while others might instead choose to work directly on specific health concerns related to cognition, such as degenerative brain disorders or brain injuries.

Consider, for example, how negative thinking can interfere with your health and happiness. We all experience these negative thoughts from time to time, but some people may find themselves overwhelmed with pessimistic thinking patterns that make it difficult to function in daily life. These ruminations can lead to increased stress levels, pessimism, and self-sabotaging, and can even contribute to feelings of learned helplessness.

With the help of cognitive psychologists, people are often able to find ways to cope and even overcome such difficulties.

Therapy treatments rooted in cognitive research focus on helping people change these negative thinking patterns and replace such thoughts with more positive and realistic ones.

Impact of Cognitive Psychology on Approaches Mental Health

In addition to adding to our understanding of how the human mind works, the field of cognitive psychology has also had an impact on approaches to mental health. Before the 1970s, many mental health approaches were focused more on psychoanalytic, behavioral, and humanistic approaches.

The so-called "cognitive revolution" that took place during this period put a greater emphasis on understanding the way people process information and how thinking patterns might contribute to psychological distress. Thanks to research in this area by cognitive psychologists, new approaches to treatment were developed to help treat depression, anxiety, phobias, and other psychological disorders.

Cognitive behavior therapy and rational emotive behavior therapy are two methods in which clients and therapists focus on the underlying cognitions that contribute to psychological distress.

Therapists can help clients identify irrational beliefs and other cognitive distortions that are in conflict with reality and then aid them in replacing such thoughts with more realistic, healthy beliefs.

Being diagnosed with a brain or cognitive health problem can be frightening and sometimes confusing, but it is important to remember that you are not alone.

By working with your doctor, you can come up with an effective treatment plan to help address brain health and cognitive problems. Your treatment may involve consulting with a cognitive psychologist who has a background in the specific area of concern that you are facing, or you may be referred to another mental health professional that has training and experience with your particular illness.

You may find it helpful to learn as much as you can about your initial diagnosis and to consider putting together a list of questions you have before your next visit with your physician, cognitive psychologist, or mental health professional. This can help you feel better prepared and ready to tackle the next steps in your treatment.

As you can see, the field of cognitive psychology is both broad and diverse, yet it touches on so many aspects of daily life.

Research on cognitive psychology may at times seem academic and far-removed from the problems you face in everyday life, yet the findings from such scientific investigations play a role in how professionals approach the treatment of mental illness, traumatic brain injury, and degenerative brain diseases. Thanks to the work of cognitive psychologists, we can better pinpoint ways to measure human intellectual abilities, develop new strategies to combat memory problems, and decode the workings of the human brain—all of which ultimately has a powerful impact on how we treat cognitive disorders.

The field of cognitive psychology is a rapidly growing area that continues to add to our understanding of the many influences that mental processes have on our health and daily lives. From understanding how cognitive processes change over the course of child development to looking at how the brain transforms sensory inputs into perceptions, cognitive psychology has helped us gain a deeper and richer understanding of the many mental events that contribute to our daily existence and overall well-being.

Conscious Mind

In Sigmund Freud's psychoanalytic theory of personality, the conscious mind consists of everything inside of our awareness. This is the aspect of our mental processing that we can think and talk about in a rational way.

The conscious mind includes such things as the sensations, perceptions, memories, feeling, and fantasies inside of our current awareness. Closely allied with the conscious mind is the preconscious, which includes the things that we are not thinking of at the moment but which we can easily draw into conscious awareness.

Things that the conscious mind wants to keep hidden from awareness are repressed into the unconscious mind. While we are unaware of these feelings, thoughts, urges, and emotions, Freud believed that the unconscious mind could still have an influence on our behavior. Things that are in the unconscious are only available to the conscious mind in disguised form. For example, the contents of the unconscious might spill into awareness in the form of dreams. Freud believed that by analyzing the content of dreams, people could discover the unconscious influences on their conscious actions.

Freud often used the metaphor of an iceberg to describe the two major aspects of human personality. The tip of the iceberg that extends above the water represents the conscious mind. The conscious mind is just the "tip of the iceberg." Beneath the water is the much larger bulk of the iceberg, which represents the unconscious.

While the conscious and preconscious are important, Freud believed that they were far less vital than the unconscious. The things that are hidden from awareness, he believed, exerted the greatest influence over our personalities and behaviors.

Conscious vs. Preconscious Differences

The conscious mind involves all of the things that you are currently aware of and thinking about. It is somewhat akin to short-term memory and is limited in terms of capacity. Your awareness of yourself and the world around you are part of your consciousness.

The preconscious mind, also known as the subconscious mind, includes things that we might not be presently aware of but that we can pull into conscious awareness when needed. You might not presently be thinking about how to do long division, but you can access the information and bring it into conscious awareness when you are faced with a math problem.

The preconscious mind is a part of the mind that corresponds to ordinary memory. These memories are not conscious, but we can retrieve them to conscious awareness at any time.

While these memories are not part of your immediate awareness, they can be quickly brought into awareness through conscious effort. For example, if you were asked what television show you watched last night or what you had for breakfast this morning, you would be pulling that information out of your preconscious.

A helpful way to think of the preconscious is that it acts as a sort of gatekeeper between the conscious and unconscious parts of the mind. It allows only certain pieces of information to pass through and enter conscious awareness.

Phone numbers and social security numbers are also examples of information stored in your preconscious mind. While you do not walk around consciously thinking about this information all the time, you can quickly draw it out of your subconscious when you are asked to relate these numbers.

In Freud's iceberg metaphor, the preconscious exists just below the surface of the water.

Like the unconscious mind, Freud believed that the preconscious could have an influence on conscious awareness. Sometimes information from the preconscious surfaces in unexpected ways, like in dreams or in accidental slips of the tongue (known as Freudian slips). While we might not be actively thinking about these things, Freud believed they still served to influence conscious actions and behaviors.

Cognition

Cognition is a term referring to the mental processes involved in gaining knowledge and comprehension. These processes include thinking, knowing, remembering, judging and problem-solving. These are higher-level functions of the brain and encompass language, imagination, perception, and planning.

The study of how we think dates back to the time of the ancient Greek philosophers Plato and Aristotle. Plato's approach to the study of the mind suggested that people understand the world by first identifying basic principles buried deep inside themselves and then using rational thought to create knowledge. This viewpoint was later advocated by philosophers such as Rene Descartes and linguist Noam Chomsky. This approach to cognition is often referred to as rationalism.

Aristotle, on the other hand, believed that people acquire their knowledge through their observations of the world around them. Later thinkers including John Locke and B.F. Skinner also advocated this point of view, which is often referred to as empiricism.

During the earliest days of psychology and for the first half of the twentieth century, psychology was largely dominated by psychoanalysis, behaviorism, and humanism. Eventually, a formal field of study devoted solely to the study of cognition emerged as part of the "cognitive revolution" of the 1960s. The field of psychology concerned with the study of cognition is known as cognitive psychology.

One of the earliest definitions of cognition was presented in the first textbook on cognitive psychology published in 1967. According to Neisser, cognition is "those processes by which the sensory input is transformed, reduced, elaborated, stored, recovered, and used."

Transforming Sensory Input

As you take in sensations from the world around you, the information that you see, hear, taste and smell must first be transformed into signals that your brain can understand. The perceptual process allows you to take in sensory information and convert it into a signal that your brain can understand and act upon. For example, if you see an object flying through the air toward you, the information is taken in by your eyes and transferred as a neural signal to your brain. Your brain then sends out signals to your muscle groups so that you are able to respond and duck out of the way before the object smacks you in the head.

Reducing Sensory Information

The world is full of an endless amount of sensory experiences. To make meaning out of all this incoming information, it is important for your brain to be able to reduce your experience of the world down to the fundamentals. You cannot attend to or remember every single sentence of the psychology lecture you attend each week. Instead, the experience of the event is reduced down to the critical concepts and ideas that you need to remember to succeed in your class. Instead of remembering every detail about what the professor wore each day, where you sat during each class session and how many students were in the class, you focus your attention and memory on the key ideas presented during each lecture.

Elaborating Information

In addition to reducing information to make it more memorable and understandable, people also elaborate on these memories as they reconstruct them. Imagine that you are telling a friend about a funny event that happened last week. As you weave your tale, you might actually start adding in details that were not part of the original memory. This might also happen as you are trying to recall items on your shopping list. You may find that you add a number of items that seem like they belong on your list due to their similarity with other items you wanted to buy. In some cases, this elaboration happens when people are struggling to remember something. When the information cannot be recalled, the brain sometimes fills in the missing data with whatever seems to fit.

Storing and Recovering Information

Memory is a major topic of interest in the field of cognitive psychology. How we remember, what we remember and what we forget reveal a great deal about how the cognitive processes operate. While people often think of memory as being much like a video camera, carefully recording and cataloging life events and storing them away for later recall, research has found that memory is much more complex.

Short-term memory is surprisingly brief, typically lasting just 20 to 30 seconds. Long-term memory can be surprisingly stable and enduring, on the other hand, with memories lasting years and even decades. Memory can also be surprisingly fragile and fallible. Sometimes we forget, and other times we are subject to misinformation effects that can even lead to the formation of false memories.

Using Information

Cognition involves not only the things that go on inside our heads but also how these thoughts and mental processes influence our actions. Our attention to the world around us, memories of past events, understanding of language, judgments about how the world works, and abilities to solve problems all contribute to how we behave and interact with our surrounding environment.

Cognitive Development

Cognitive development is the construction of thought processes, including remembering, problem solving, and decision-making, from childhood through adolescence to adulthood.

It was once believed that infants lacked the ability to think or form complex ideas and remained without cognition until they learned language. It is now known that babies are aware of their surroundings and interested in exploration from the time they are born. From birth, babies begin to actively learn. They gather, sort, and process information from around them, using the data to develop perception and thinking skills.

Cognitive development refers to how a person perceives, thinks, and gains understanding of his or her world through the interaction of genetic and learned factors. Among the areas of cognitive development are information processing, intelligence, reasoning, language development , and memory.

Historically, the cognitive development of children has been studied in a variety of ways. The oldest is through intelligence tests, such as the widely used Stanford Binet Intelligence Quotient (IQ) test first adopted for use in the United States by psychologist Lewis Terman in 1916 from a French model pioneered in 1905. IQ scoring is based on the concept of "mental age," according to which the scores of a child of average intelligence match his or her age, while a gifted child's performance is comparable to that of an older child, and a slow learner's scores are similar to those of a younger child. IQ tests are widely used in the United States, but they have come under increasing criticism for defining intelligence too narrowly and for being biased with regard to race and gender.

In contrast to the emphasis placed on a child's native abilities by intelligence testing, learning theory grew out of work by behaviorist researchers such as John Watson and B. F. Skinner, who argued that children are completely malleable. Learning theory focuses on the role of environmental factors in shaping the intelligence of children, especially on a child's ability to learn by having certain behaviors rewarded and others discouraged.

Piaget's Theory of Cognitive Development

The most well-known and influential theory of cognitive development is that of French psychologist Jean Piaget (1896–1980). Piaget's theory, first published in 1952, grew out of decades of extensive observation of children, including his own, in their natural environments as opposed to the laboratory experiments of the behaviorists. Although Piaget was interested in how children reacted to their environment, he proposed a more active role for them than that suggested by learning theory. He envisioned a child's knowledge as composed of schemas, basic units of knowledge used to organize past experiences and serve as a basis for understanding new ones.

Schemas are continually being modified by two complementary processes that Piaget termed assimilation and accommodation. Assimilation refers to the process of taking in new information by incorporating it into an existing schema. In other words, people assimilate new experiences by relating them to things they already know. On the other hand, accommodation is what happens when the schema itself changes to accommodate new knowledge. According to Piaget, cognitive development involves an ongoing attempt to achieve a balance between assimilation and accommodation that he termed equilibration.

At the center of Piaget's theory is the principle that cognitive development occurs in a series of four distinct, universal stages, each characterized by increasingly sophisticated and abstract levels of thought. These stages always occur in the same order, and each builds on what was learned in the previous stage. They are as follows:

- Sensorimotor stage (infancy): In this period, which has six sub-stages, intelligence is demonstrated through motor activity without the use of symbols. Knowledge of the world is limited, but developing, because it is based on physical interactions and experiences. Children acquire object permanence at about seven months of age (memory). Physical development (mobility) allows the child to begin developing new intellectual abilities. Some symbolic (language) abilities are developed at the end of this stage.

- Pre-operational stage (toddlerhood and early childhood): In this period, which has two sub stages, intelligence is demonstrated through the use of symbols, language use matures, and memory and imagination are developed, but thinking is done in a non-logical, non-reversible manner. Egocentric thinking predominates.

- Concrete operational stage (elementary and early adolescence): In this stage, characterized by seven types of conservation (number, length, liquid, mass, weight, area, and volume), intelligence is demonstrated through logical and systematic manipulation of symbols related to concrete objects. Operational thinking develops (mental actions that are reversible). Egocentric thought diminishes.

- Formal operational stage (adolescence and adulthood): In this stage, intelligence is demonstrated through the logical use of symbols related to abstract concepts. Early in the period there is a return to egocentric thought. Only 35 percent of high school graduates in industrialized countries obtain formal operations; many people do not think formally during adulthood.

The most significant alternative to the work of Piaget has been the information-processing approach, which uses the computer as a model to provide new insight into how the human mind receives, stores, retrieves, and uses information. Researchers using information-processing theory to study cognitive development in children have focused on areas such as the gradual improvements in children's ability to take in information and focus selectively on certain parts of it and their increasing attention spans and capacity for memory storage. For example, researchers have found that the superior memory skills of older children are due in part to memorization strategies, such as repeating items in order to memorize them or dividing them into categories.

Infancy

As soon as they are born, infants begin learning to use their senses to explore the world around them. Most newborns can focus on and follow moving objects, distinguish the pitch and volume of sound, see all colors and distinguish their hue and brightness, and start anticipating events, such as sucking at the sight of a nipple. By three months old, infants can recognize faces; imitate the facial expressions of others, such as smiling and frowning; and respond to familiar sounds.

At six months of age, babies are just beginning to understand how the world around them works. They imitate sounds, enjoy hearing their own voice, recognize parents, fear strangers, distinguish between animate and inanimate objects, and base distance on the size of an object. They also realize that if they drop an object, they can pick it up again. At four to seven months, babies can recognize their names.

By nine months, infants can imitate gestures and actions, experiment with the physical properties of objects, understand simple words such as "no," and understand that an object still exists even when they cannot see it. They also begin to test parental responses to their behavior, such as throwing food on the floor. They remember the reaction and test the parents again to see if they get the same reaction.

At 12 months of age, babies can follow a fast moving object; can speak two to four words, including "mama" and "papa"; imitate animal sounds; associate names with objects; develop attachments to objects, such as a toy or blanket; and experience separation anxiety when away from their parents. By 18 months of age, babies are able to understand about 10–50 words; identify body parts; feel a sense of ownership by using the word "my" with certain people or objects; and can follow directions that involve two different tasks, such as picking up toys and putting them in a box.

Toddlerhood

Between 18 months to three years of age, toddlers have reached the "sensorimotor" stage of Piaget's theory of cognitive development that involves rudimentary thought. For instance, they understand the permanence of objects and people, visually follow the displacement of objects, and begin to use instruments and tools. Toddlers start to strive for more independence, which can present challenges to parents concerned for their safety. They also understand discipline and what behavior is appropriate and inappropriate, and they understand the concepts of words like "please" and "thank you."

Two-year-olds should be able to understand 100 to 150 words and start adding about ten new words per day. Toddlers also have a better understanding of emotions, such as love, trust, and fear. They begin to understand some of the ordinary aspects of everyday life, such as shopping for food, telling time, and being read to.

Preschool

Preschoolers, ages three to six, should be at the "preoperational" stage of Piaget's cognitive development theory, meaning they are using their imagery and memory skills. They should be conditioned to learning and memorizing, and their view of the world is normally very self-centered. Preschoolers usually have also developed their social interaction skills, such as playing and cooperating with other children their own age. It is normal for preschoolers to test the limits of their cognitive abilities, and they learn negative concepts and actions, such as talking back to adults, lying , and bullying. Other cognitive development in preschoolers are developing an increased attention span, learning to read, and developing structured routines, such as doing household chores.

School Age

Younger school-age children, six to 12 years old, should be at the "concrete operations" stage of Piaget's cognitive development theory, characterized by the ability to use logical and coherent actions in thinking and solving problems. They understand the concepts of permanence and conservation by learning that volume, weight, and numbers may remain constant despite changes in outward appearance. These children should be able to build on past experiences, using them to explain why some things happen. Their attention span should increase with age, from being able to focus on a task for about 15 minutes at age six to an hour by age nine.

Adolescents, ages 12 through 18, should be at the "formal operations" stage of Piaget's cognitive development theory. It is characterized by an increased independence for thinking through problems and situations. Adolescents should be able to understand pure abstractions, such as philosophy and higher math concepts. During this age, children should be able to learn and apply general information needed to adapt to specific situations. They should also be able to learn specific information and skills necessary for an occupation. A major component of the passage through adolescence is a cognitive transition. Compared to children, adolescents think in ways that are more advanced, more efficient, and generally more complex. This ability can be seen in five ways.

First, during adolescence individuals become better able than children to think about what is possible, instead of limiting their thought to what is real. Whereas children's thinking is oriented to the here and now—that is, to things and events that they can observe directly—adolescents are able to consider what they observe against a backdrop of what is possible; they can think hypothetically.

Second, during the passage into adolescence, individuals become better able to think about abstract ideas. For example, adolescents find it easier than children to comprehend the sorts of higher-order, abstract logic inherent in puns, proverbs, metaphors, and analogies. The adolescent's greater facility with abstract thinking also permits the application of advanced reasoning and logical processes to social and ideological matters. This is clearly seen in the adolescent's increased facility and interest in thinking about interpersonal relationships, politics, philosophy, religion, and morality.

Third, during adolescence individuals begin thinking more often about the process of thinking itself, or metacognition. As a result, adolescents may display increased introspection and self-consciousness. Although improvements in metacognitive abilities provide important intellectual advantages, one potentially negative byproduct of these advances is the tendency for adolescents to develop a sort of egocentrism, or intense preoccupation with the self.

A fourth change in cognition is that thinking tends to become multidimensional, rather than limited to a single issue. Whereas children tend to think about things one aspect at a time, adolescents can see things through more complicated lenses. Adolescents describe themselves and others in more differentiated and complicated terms and find it easier to look at problems from multiple perspectives. Being able to understand that people's personalities are not one-sided or that social situations can have different interpretations depending on one's point of view permits the adolescent to have far more sophisticated and complicated relationships with other people.

Cognitive development	
Age	Activity
One month	Watches person when spoken to.
Two months	Smiles at familiar person talking. Begins to follow moving person with eyes.
Four months	Shows interest in bottle, breast, familiar toy, or new surroundings.
Five months	Smiles at own image in mirror. Looks for fallen objects.
Six months	May stick out tongue in imitation. Laughs at peekaboo game. Vocalizes at mirror image. May act shy around strangers.
Seven months	Responds to own name. Tries to establish contact with a person by cough or other noise.
Eight months	Reaches for toys out of reach. Responds to "no."
Nine months	Shows likes and dislikes. May try to prevent face-washing or other activity that is disliked. Shows excitement and interest in foods or toys that are well-liked.
Ten months	Starts to understand some words. Waves bye-bye. Holds out arm or leg for dressing.
Eleven months	Repeats performance that is laughed at. Likes repetitive play. Shows interest in books.
Twelve months	May understand some "where is?" questions. May kiss on request.
Fifteen months	Asks for objects by pointing. Starting to feed self. Negativism begins.
Eighteen months	Points to familiar objects when asked "where is?" Mimics familiar adult activities. Know some body parts. Obeys two or three simple orders.
Two years	Names a few familiar objects. Draws with crayons. Obeys found simple orders. Participates in parallel play.
Two-and-a-half years	Names several common objects. Begins to take interest in sex organs. Gives full names. Helps to put things away. Peak of negativism.
Three years	Constantly asks questions. May count to 10. Begins to draw specific objects. Dresses and undresses doll. Participates in cooperative play. Talks about things that have happened.
Four years	May make up silly words and stories. Beginning to draw pictures that represent familiar things. Pretends to read and write. May recognize a few common words, such as own name.
Five years	Can recognize and reproduce many shapes, letters, and numbers. Tells long stories. Begins to understand the difference between real events and make-believe ones. Asks meaning of words.

Finally, adolescents are more likely than children to see things as relative, rather than absolute. Children tend to see things in absolute terms—in black and white. Adolescents, in contrast, tend to see things as relative. They are more likely to question others' assertions and less likely to accept facts as absolute truths. This increase in relativism can be particularly exasperating to parents, who may feel that their adolescent children question everything just for the sake of argument. Difficulties often arise, for example, when adolescents begin seeing their parents' values as excessively relative.

Common Problems

Cognitive impairment is the general loss or lack of development of cognitive abilities, particularly autism and learning disabilities. The National Institutes of Mental Health (NIMH) describes learning disabilities as a disorder that affects people's ability to either interpret what they see and hear or to link information from different parts of the brain. These limitations can show up in many ways, such as specific difficulties with spoken and written language, coordination, self-control, or attention. Such difficulties extend to schoolwork and can impede learning to read or write or to do math. A child who has a learning disability may have other conditions, such as hearing problems or serious emotional disturbance. However, learning disabilities are not caused by these conditions, nor are they caused by environmental influences such as cultural differences or inappropriate instruction.

Parental Concerns

As of 2004 it is widely accepted that a child's intellectual ability is determined by a combination of heredity and environment. Thus, although a child's genetic inheritance is unchangeable, there are definite ways that parents can enhance their child's intellectual development through environmental factors. They can provide stimulating learning materials and experiences from an early age, read to and talk with their children, and help children explore the world around them. As children mature, parents can both challenge and support the child's talents. Although a supportive environment in early childhood provides a clear advantage for children, it is possible to make up for early losses in cognitive development if a supportive environment is provided at some later period, in contrast to early disruptions in physical development, which are often irreversible.

Cognitive Flexibility

Cognitive flexibility refers to the brain's ability to transition from thinking about one concept to another. The quicker you are able to switch or "shift" your thinking from one dimension (e.g. color of an object) to another (e.g. shape of an object), the greater your level of cognitive flexibility. As an example, let's say you were playing a game of Texas Hold 'Em poker, but the dealer tells everyone that every other hand you'll be playing 7 Card Stud.

Mentally, you'll need to transition between the rules for Texas Hold 'Em and 7 Card Stud. Certain individuals would struggle to rapidly transition between these two card-game constructs due to the fact that they have poor cognitive flexibility or "rigidity." Rigid thinkers are poor at adapting to the introduction of novel stimuli and shifting their thinking to accommodate various changes.

Those that are able to easily alternate between playing Texas Hold 'Em and 7 Card Stud in an "every-other-hand" format, likely have significant cognitive flexibility. Cognitive flexibility not only helps when faced with unexpected situations, but it helps you update your belief system when exposed to better information. If you learn that smoking causes lung cancer, but are unable to shift your thinking to accept the more accurate information – you may be cognitively inflexible or "rigid."

Cognitive flexibility is defined as the ability to switch one's thinking (cognition) (or train of thought) as an adaptation to the demands of stimuli. In neuroscience, the term is sometimes referred to as "attention switching," "cognitive shifting," "mental flexibility," "set shifting," and "task switching." Perhaps the most helpful way to explain cognitive flexibility is to use an analogy.

Think of cognitive flexibility as being analogous to changing channels on a TV, but think of the channels as "streams-of-thought" (concepts) and the TV as your "brain." If you are stuck on one channel and can't change it – your cognition is inflexible; your stream-of-thought and/or beliefs cannot be updated or altered. However, if you possess a remote and can rapidly change the channel rapidly at whim, you are considered to have cognitive flexibility.

There are varying degrees of cognitive flexibility as well. Two people may be considered cognitively flexible, but one may be more flexible than the other. In other words, both individuals may be able to shift their thinking to adapt to new stimuli, but one may be able to accomplish this at a faster rate.

Cognitive flexibility is useful in that it helps people adapt to novel scenarios and information such as: moving to a foreign country, unexpected demands in the workplace, and/or a last-minute change of plans. There are many nuanced, technical definitions of "cognitive flexibility," but to keep things simple – think of it as the ability to shift your thinking as an adaptation to new stimuli.

Aspects of Cognitive Flexibility

Below is a list of potential elements of cognitive flexibility. It is important to understand that while most psychologists refer to cognitive flexibility as the ability to transition between multiple thoughts, some consider it to encompass concepts such as: updating old beliefs, multi-faceted thinking, and establishing commonalities between completely unrelated concepts.

- Transition "stream-of-thoughts" and attention: Cognitive flexibility most often refers to the ability to shift thoughts between multiple concepts. Let's say you're in a group of two friends and one starts talking about the rules of baseball. Suddenly the other friend starts talking about French literature. In this scenario – your ability to transition between the two concepts would be considered flexibility of cognition.

- Updating beliefs and cognition: In some cases, cognitive flexibility can refer to updating cognitive function as an adaptation to new information or stimuli. Individuals that are "set in their ways" or display rigidity of thinking have poor cognitive flexibility; these people are unable to change their thinking even when presented with novel stimuli or better information. For example, even after Copernicus suggested that the Sun was the center of the solar system (which was upgraded information), may people lacked cognitive flexibility to accept this concept.

- Multi-faceted observation: Cognitive flexibility can sometimes refer to considering multiple elements of observation simultaneously. For example, let's say you're looking at an object and notice that it's a reddish color. In addition to the color, you may consider a multitude of other descriptors such as the: shape, cost, fragility, texture, density, etc. Your ability to connect certain observable aspects may be considered cognitive flexibility by some.

- Deconstructing thoughts: When posed with a complex thought or problem, cognitive flexibility can help deconstruct the complexity into smaller chunks. The ability to shift between specific elements of a larger problem in effort to solve it is an example of cognitive flexibility. Interjection of new perspectives, simplification, and/or understanding how smaller pieces contribute to the larger problem may be considered cognitive flexibility.
- Expanded awareness: Some have suggested that cognitive flexibility is the ability to be consciously aware of all possible choices and alternatives in a specific scenario. For example, someone playing a game of poker may understand that although he has a "Full House," other players could have a superior hand (e.g. 4-of-a-Kind) or an inferior hand (e.g. a "High Card").

Measuring Cognitive Flexibility

There are many different tests and protocols utilized to measure cognitive flexibility. The ability to rapidly switch between focusing on one specific aspect of an object such as "color" to another aspect such as "shape" determines how cognitively flexible you are. Many measures of cognitive flexibility are regarded as age-specific due to the fact that they are either too simplistic or advanced for other age groups.

A-not-B Task

This is a cognitive flexibility test typically administered to children. During this test, children are visually presented with an object that is hidden at "Location A." The children are then allowed to look for the object at the hidden "Location A" – which is generally within arm's reach.

The hiding of the object at Location A is repeated a few times until the child becomes focused on how to find it. Next, the same object is hidden in a new area called "Location B" – a distinct location separate from Location A (also within arm's reach). Individuals under 1 years of age will typically look again in Location A.

Children over 1 years of age are able to display "cognitive flexibility" and learn to find the object at the novel Location B. This is a cognitive flexibility task reserved for infants and would be far too simplistic for older children, teens, and adults.

Dimensional Change Card Sorting (DCCS) Task

The Dimensional Change Card Sorting task is a test used to measure cognitive flexibility in children. During this task, a child will be instructed to sort cards by a specific descriptor (e.g. shape) and during this sorting process, are interrupted and instructed to sort the cards to fit a secondary characteristic (e.g. size). Researchers have determined that children between 3 and 5 are unable to adjust to integrate the secondary characteristic into their sorting process.

However, children 5 years of age are able to integrate the novel, secondary characteristic into their sorting; this displays cognitive flexibility. This is a significantly easier task for children over the age of 5 due to the fact that their brain has undergone significantly more development than younger infants.

Multiple Classification Card Sorting Task

The Multiple Classification Card Sorting Task is a cognitive flexibility test administered to children. During the test, various cards are shown to a child, and the child is instructed to sort them based on multiple characteristics (e.g. color and shape). The child will then place them into 4 distinct piles based on the characteristics: red squares, red triangles, purple squares, purple triangles. Studies have suggested that this is a challenging task for most children, but becomes easier once a child reaches age 11.

Evidence highlights that 7 year olds have a difficult time sorting the cards based on multiple characteristics. This suggests that up to a certain age, children are unable to simultaneously focus on two characteristics of a single object. There appears to be a significant jump in cognitive flexibility between age 7 and 11.

Wisconsin Card Sorting Test

Another popular test to measure cognitive flexibility is the Wisconsin Card Sorting Test (WCST). This test focuses on elements of abstract reasoning and incorporates problem-solving. During the WCST, an individual is presented with cards with displays that differ in elements of: color, shapes, and quantities.

The individual is then handed another set of cards and instructed to match the new cards with the already-presented cards. This is another test administered primarily to children. Individuals between ages 9 and 11 typically have developed enough cognitive flexibility to properly complete the test.

Stroop Test (Color-Word Naming Test)

Many adults are familiar with the Stroop Test to measure cognitive function and flexibility. In the Stoop Test, an individual is presented with 3 different types of cards: a color card, a word card, and a combo "color-word" card. Their goal is to identify the colors on the color card, the words on the word card, and then solely the colors on the "color-word" card. This is a cognitive flexibility test primarily reserved for individuals over the age of 11.

- Color card: Displays segments of various colors. Individuals are instructed to identify these colors as rapidly as possible.
- Word card: Displays the names of colors printed in black and white. Individuals are instructed to read the names of these colors as rapidly as possible.
- Color-Word card: Displays the names of colors printed in the ink of an entirely distinct color. In other words, the color of a word does not match up with the text. For example, a person may see the word "Black" with all letters printed in purple ink. When a person sees the Color-Word card, they are instructed to name only the color of the ink, while selectively ignoring the text. In the example of seeing "Black" printed in purple ink, a person would therefore respond with "purple" as quickly as possible.

Neural Mechanisms of Cognitive Flexibility

To determine the specific regions of the brain associated with cognitive flexibility, researchers used fMRI (functional magnetic resonance imaging) scans. The fMRI scans revealed that a variety of cortical networks are activated to facilitate cognitive flexibility. These networks include: the anterior cingulate cortex, basal ganglia, posterior parietal cortex, and the prefrontal cortex.

- Anterior cingulate cortex.
- Basal ganglia.
- Posterior parietal cortex.
- Prefrontal cortex.

It should be noted that the regions associated with cognitive flexibility are likely subject to variation based on the specific task used to measure it. In other words, certain parts of your brain may light up during the Stroop Test that wouldn't be as active during a separate test of cognitive flexibility. Some research has documented that the dorsolateral prefrontal cortex modulates interference.

Most experts believe that the prefrontal cortex is the driving force behind cognitive flexibility. The specific regions within the prefrontal cortex that are activated during a cognitive flexibility task are likely task-dependent. The basal ganglia is known to become active during selection of responses, whereas the posterior parietal cortex is active as we update preexisting information about how to perform a task.

It may be too simplistic to assume that the aforementioned areas are solely responsible for cognitive flexibility. Some evidence suggests that any form of brain damage – regardless of the specific region, could reduce cognitive flexibility.

Age and Cognitive Flexibility

Generally adults ages 25 and up are thought to display the greatest degree of cognitive flexibility. The human brain is fully developed by the mid-20s, but up until the mid-20s, humans haven't reached their full cognitive capacity. Young children display a significant degree of cognitive inflexibility due to lack of cortical development.

For this reason, children are administered different cognitive flexibility measures such as the A-not-B test (ages 1+), Dimensional Change Card Sorting task (ages 5+), Multiple Classification Card Sorting task (ages 7+), and the Wisconsin Card Sorting task (ages 9 to 11). Adults generally are administered a test too difficult for children to perform called the "Stroop Test."

Adolescents' cognitive flexibility continues to improve, and some evidence suggests that they learn faster from negative "reward prediction errors" compared to adults. The ability to learn quicker from reward prediction errors means that they may display heightened cognitive flexibility in certain capacities compared to adults.

Following peak brain development in the mid-20s, it is thought that cognitive flexibility can be maintained and/or enhanced for a long period of time. There is a transition between mid-life adulthood and elderly adulthood in which the cognition declines and neurodegeneration sets in. The elderly tend to have significantly reduced cognitive flexibility compared to younger adults.

Importance of Maintaining Cognitive Flexibility

Cognitive flexibility is immensely important for shifting attention and thoughts quickly. Those with low levels of cognitive flexibility are unable to shift from one concept to another, and often become "stuck" in a single train of thought or aspect of focus (i.e. centration). Being cognitively stuck is akin to watching just one TV channel or reading one book for the rest of your life; you'll have a difficult time adapting to changes and novel stimuli.

What is helpful, is to be able to rapidly shift your thinking between concepts and alter your perspective to accommodate new information. With cultural evolution continuing to outpace biological evolution, cognitive flexibility helps you update your old belief system as an adaptation to novel stimuli. Just think of all the people that weren't able to learn how to use a computer or cell phone; these individuals may be stuck in their ways and still fail to understand the perspectives of a newer generation.

In addition to improving a person's ability to adapt when faced with novel stimuli, cognitive flexibility is associated with improved brain functioning. It allows your brain to function more efficiently, with various regions operating in orchestra. Those with high levels of cognitive flexibility tend to have superior comprehension and fluency associated with reading, higher levels of fluid intelligence, and an expanded sense of awareness.

Individuals with low levels of cognitive flexibility are generally "stuck in their ways" and dislike the intake of novel stimuli. These are people that have a difficult time adapting to change, whether it be behavioral, psychological, environmental, technological, etc. If your goal is to maintain peak mental performance, engaging in activities that increase cognitive flexibility may provide substantial benefit.

Application of Cognitive Psychology

Cognitive psychology has been applied to many other aspects of psychology. Many psychologists who do not call themselves cognitive psychologists do use cognitive approaches to a wide range of psychological problems. Here are some examples.

Depression

Antidepressants are commonly used to improve the mood of people with depression. However, most psychiatrists suggest their patients also have counseling along with their medications. Why? The reason is that they need to develop positive patterns of thought and behavior. Otherwise, when they're taken off the antidepressants, they'll return to their depressed state. To avoid this, they need to change the way they think about and respond to depressed feelings.

Aggressive and Anti-Social Behavior

Cognitive psychology has produced several different social information processing models. These are models of how people think and behave in response to others. As it turns out, children who develop the ability to process social information well become adults who behave in more socially-acceptable ways. Kenneth Dodge identified five steps in the process of evaluating and interpreting others' behavior. They include:

- Encoding social cues

- Interpreting social cues
- Searching for a response
- Evaluating responses
- Carrying out the response.

As you learn and become aware of this process, you're better able to make better choices in your social behavior. These concepts can be used to help people curb their aggressive behavior as they learn to take their time and think out each step as they come to it.

Education

Jean Piaget was a famous psychologist who studied and wrote about cognition from a developmental standpoint. His cognitive development stages outline the way people's thought processes change throughout their lives.

Piaget's four stages of cognitive development have been used extensively to guide teachers in helping their students progress at rates that are appropriate for their level of cognitive development. Piaget's theory was based on biological readiness for each stage, and teachers must take readiness into account when creating learning experiences for their students.

Cognitive psychology has also influenced education in other ways. For example, the idea of metacognition is used to help students assess their learning and develop better learning strategies. Cognitive psychology also distinguishes between declarative knowledge and procedural knowledge. In other words, the first step is to know how to think about doing something and the second step is to develop the skills to do it.

Also, cognitive research has shown how knowledge is organized in the brain. By knowing how knowledge is naturally organized, teachers can supply a useful framework for the information they give their students. And, as students learn cognitive strategies for setting goals and assessing their study habits, their learning improves.

Using Cognitive Strategies in Learning

Whether you're a college student or just an adult who enjoys learning, using the right cognitive strategies can help you comprehend and remember the information better. These strategies help you understand the material better and enhance your memory of it. Some of the cognitive strategies you can use include summarizing or annotating readings, predicting outcomes, and reflecting on what you've learned.

Benefits

The benefits of cognitive psychology are easy to understand. Cognitive psychology can:

- Help you understand yourself and others better.
- Learn more effectively.
- Make better life choices.
- Change unwanted behaviors.
- Diminish mood problems.
- Understand past traumas differently.
- Remember past experiences and put them in perspective with your current life.

Cognitive Therapy

Cognitive therapy was developed during the 1960s by Aaron Beck. Cognitive therapy is based on cognitive psychology. CT is similar to cognitive behavioral therapy (CBT), and sometimes the terms are used interchangeably. However, there are some differences, starting with the fact that CBT is a part of many different types of therapy while CT is just one type of therapy.

In cognitive therapy, the patient and the therapist work together to target thoughts, emotions, behaviors, and physical responses. The goal is to make changes in the mental processes in the here and now. Cognitions are uncovered and examined. You then challenge those cognitions and decide if you want to hold onto them or replace them with other more realistic and positive cognitions.

Cognitive therapy is used in specific ways for different types of disorders. And, unlike CBT, cognitive therapy focuses on the mental processes behind the behavior rather than on the behavior itself. Cognitive therapists assume that if the cognitions that lead to behavior can be changed, the behavior will change more easily.

Still, cognitive therapy does address what to do about unwanted behaviors. The main theme is that if you think differently, you're more likely to respond differently. So, thinking behaviors are targeted. You come to understand that you not only choose your behaviors, but you also choose the thoughts that lead to those behaviors.

A cognitive therapist can help you with mental health issues such as depression, anxiety, and anger management. Instead of focusing on what's happening to you, you concentrate on how you can think differently to have a different outcome. When you take charge of your thoughts, you can also change the way you respond to your feelings. For example, if you think about how you can overcome depression rather than about how bad you feel, you can make positive changes, such as taking care of your physical health, that diminish your depression.

You can talk to a cognitive therapist about any mental health problem that you don't know how to solve. Through CT, you can examine your thoughts and make the changes that make sense to you. Therapists are available at BetterHelp to assist you with cognitive therapy. Whether you choose cognitive therapy or some other form of treatment, you can get the help you need to resolve your mental health issues and build a better life.

Behaviorism

The central idea in behaviorism can be stated simply: A science of behavior is possible. Behaviorists have diverse views about what this proposition means, and particularly about what science is and what behavior is, but every behaviorist agrees that there can be a science of behavior.

Many behaviorists add that the science of behavior should be psychology. This causes contention because many psychologists reject the idea that psychology is a science at all, and others who regard it as a science consider its subject matter something other than behavior. Most behaviorists have come to call the science of behavior behavior analysis. The debate continues as to whether behavior analysis is a part of psychology, the same as psychology, or independent of psychology, but professional organizations, such as the Association for Behavior Analysis, and journals, such as The Behavior Analyst, Journal of the Experimental Analysis of Behavior, and Journal of Applied Behavior Analysis, give the field an identity.

Since behaviorism is a set of ideas about this science called behavior analysis, not the science itself, properly speaking behaviorism is not science, but philosophy of science. As philosophy about behavior, however, it touches topics near and dear to us: why we do what we do, and what we should and should not do. Behaviorism offers an alternative view that often runs counter to traditional thinking about action, because traditional views have been unscientific.

Objective Psychology

Some nineteenth-century psychologists were uneasy with introspection as a scientific method. It seemed too unreliable, too open to personal bias, too subjective. Other sciences used objective methods which produced measurements that could be checked and duplicated in laboratories around the world. If two trained introspectors disagreed over their findings, the conflict would be hard to resolve; with objective methods, however, one might note differences in procedure that could produce different results.

One of the early pioneers in objective psychology was the Dutch psychologist F. C. Donders (1818–89), who was inspired by an intriguing astronomy problem: how to arrive at the exact time when a star is in a certain position in the sky. When a star is viewed through a powerful telescope, it appears to travel at considerable speed. Astonomers trying to make accurate time measurements were having difficulty estimating to the fraction of a second. An astronomer would listen to a clock ticking once a second while watching a star, and count ticks. As the star crossed a line marked in the telescope (the "moment of transit"), the astronomer would mentally note its position at the tick just before transit, mentally note its position at the tick just after transit, and then estimate the fraction of the distance between the two positions that lay between the position just before transit and the line. The problem was that different astronomers watching the same moment of transit obtained different time estimates. The astronomers tried to get around this variation by finding an equation, called the "personal equation," for each astronomer that would compute the correct time from the particular astronomer's time estimates.

Donders reasoned that the time estimates varied because no two astronomers took the same time to judge the exact moment of transit, and he believed they were actually making their judgments by different mental processes. Donders thought that this "judgment time" might be a useful objective measure. He began doing experiments in which he measured people's reaction times – the times required to detect a light or sound and then press a button. He found that it took a certain reliable amount longer to press the correct one of two buttons when one or the other of two lights came on than to press a single button when a single light came on. By subtracting the shorter simple reaction time from the longer choice reaction time, Donders argued that one could objectively measure the mental process of choice. This seemed a great advance over introspection because it meant that psychologists could do laboratory experiments with the same objective methods as the other sciences.

Other psychologists developed other methods that seemed to measure mental processes objectively. Gustav Fechner (1801–87) attempted to measure subjective intensity of sensation by developing a scale based on the just-noticeable difference – the physical difference between two lights or sounds that a person could just detect. Hermann Ebbinghaus (1850–1909) measured the time it took him to learn and later relearn lists of nonsense syllables (consonant–vowel–consonant combinations with no meaning) to produce objective measures of learning and memory. Others used the method developed by I. P. Pavlov (1849– 1936) to study learning and association by measuring a simple reflex transferring to new signals arranged in the laboratory. These attempts held the common promise that by following objective methods psychology could become a true science.

Comparative Psychology

At the same time that psychologists were trying to make psychology an objective science, psychology was also being influenced by the theory of evolution. No longer were human beings seen as separate from other living things. The recognition was growing that not only do we share anatomical traits with apes, monkeys, dogs, and even fish, but we share with them also many behavioral traits.

Thus arose the notion of the continuity of species – the idea that even if species clearly differ from one another, to the extent that they share a common evolutionary history, they also resemble one another. Darwin's theory taught that new species came into existence only as modifications of existing species. If our species evolved like any other species, then it too must have arisen as a modification of some other species. It was easy to see that we and the apes shared common ancestors, that apes and monkeys shared common ancestors, that monkeys and tree shrews shared common ancestors, that tree shrews and reptiles shared common ancestors, and so on.

Comparative thinkers reasoned that, just as we could see the origins of our own anatomical traits in other species, so we could see the origins of our own mental traits. Thus the notion of making comparisons among species in order to learn more about our own, coupled with the assumption that our mental traits would appear in other species in simpler or rudimentary form, gave rise to comparative psychology.

Comparisons between our species and others became common. Darwin himself wrote a book called The Expression of the Emotions in Men and Animals. At first, evidence of seemingly human mentality in other animals consisted of casual observations of wild and domestic creatures, often just anecdotes about pets or farm animals. With a little imagination one could see a dog that learned to open the garden gate by lifting the latch as having observed and reasoned from its owner's example. One could imagine further that the dog's sensations, thoughts, feelings, and so on must resemble ours. George Romanes (1848–94) took this line of reasoning to its logical conclusion, even claiming that our own consciousness must form the basis of our guesses at whatever dim consciousness occurs in ants.

This "humanizing the beast" or anthropomorphism seemed too speculative to some psychologists. In the last part of the nineteenth and early part of the twentieth century, comparative psychologists began to replace the loose anecdotal evidence with rigorous observation by conducting experiments with animals. Much of this early research relied on mazes, because any creature that moves about, from human to rat to fish to ant, can be trained to solve a maze. One could measure the time the creature took to traverse the maze and the number of errors it made, and one could see these decline as the maze was learned. Carrying on the attempt to humanize the beast, these early researchers frequently added speculations about the animals' mental states, thoughts, and emotions. Rats were said to show disgust on making an error, confusion, hesitation, confidence, and so on.

The problem with these claims about animal consciousness was that they depended too much on individual bias. If two people introspecting could disagree over whether they were feeling angry or sad, it was even more true that two people could disagree over whether a rat was feeling angry or sad. Since the observations were so subjective, making more observations was no help in resolving either disagreement. John B. Watson (1879–1958), the founder of behaviorism, considered inferences about consciousness in animals to be even less reliable than introspection and concluded that neither could serve as the method of a true science.

In 1913, Watson published "Psychology as the behaviorist views it," soon considered the manifesto of early behaviorism. Taking his lead from objective psychology, he articulated the growing unease among psychologists over introspection and analogy as methods. He complained that introspection, unlike methods in physics or chemistry, depended too much on the individual.

If you fail to reproduce my findings it is due to the fact that your introspection is untrained. The attack is made upon the observer and not upon the experimental setting. In physics and in chemistry the attack is made upon the experimental conditions. The apparatus was not sensitive enough, impure chemicals were used, etc. In these sciences a better technique will give reproducible results. Psychology is otherwise. If you can't observe 3–9 states of clearness in attention, your introspection is poor. If, on the other hand, a feeling seems reasonably clear to you, your introspection is again faulty. You are seeing too much. Feelings are never clear.

If introspection was unreliable, analogies between animals and humans were even more so. Watson complained that the emphasis on consciousness forced him into the absurd position of attempting to construct the conscious content of the animal whose behavior we have been studying. On this view, after having determined our animal's ability to learn, the simplicity or complexity of its methods of learning, the effect of past habit upon present response, the range of stimuli to which it ordinarily responds, the widened range to which it can respond under experimental conditions, – in more general terms, its various problems and its various ways of solving them, – we should still feel that the task is unfinished and that the results are worthless, until we can interpret them by analogy in the light of consciousness we feel forced to say something about the possible mental processes of our animal. We say that, having no eyes, its stream of consciousness cannot contain brightness and color sensations as we know them, – having no taste buds this stream can contain no sensations of sweet, sour, salt and bitter. But on the other hand, since it does respond to thermal, tactual and organic stimuli, its conscious content must be made up largely of these sensations. Surely this doctrine which calls for an analogical interpretation of all behavior data may be shown to be false.

Psychologists trapped themselves into such fruitless efforts, Watson argued, because of their definition of psychology as the science of consciousness. This definition was to blame for the unreliable methods and baseless speculations. It was to blame for psychology's failure to become a true science.

Instead, Watson wrote, psychology should be defined as the science of behavior. He described his disappointment when, seeing psychology defined by Pillsbury at the beginning of a textbook as the science of behavior, he found that after a few pages the book ceased referring to behavior and reverted instead to the "conventional treatment" of consciousness. In reaction, Watson wrote, "I believe we can write a psychology, define it as Pillsbury, and never go back upon our definition: never use the terms consciousness, mental states, mind, content, introspectively verifiable, imagery.

Avoiding the terms relating to consciousness and mind would free psychologists to study both human and animal behavior. If continuity of species could lead to "humanizing the beast," it could equally well lead to the opposite (bestializing the human?); if ideas about humans could be applied to animals, principles developed by studying animals could be applied to humans. Watson argued against anthropocentrism. He pointed to the biologist studying evolution, who "gathers his data from the study of many species of plants and animals and tries to work out the laws of inheritance in the particular type upon which he is conducting experiments. It is not fair to say that all of his work is directed toward human evolution or that it must be interpreted in terms of human evolution". To Watson, the way seemed clear to turn psychology into a general science of behavior that covered all species, with humans as just one of the species.

This science of behavior Watson envisioned would use none of the traditional terms referring to mind and consciousness, would avoid the subjectivity of introspection and animal–human analogies, and would study only objectively observable behavior. Yet even in Watson's own time, behaviorists debated over the correctness of this recipe. It was unclear what objective meant or exactly what constituted behavior. Since these terms were left open to interpretation, behaviorists' ideas about what constitutes science and how to define behavior have varied.

Of post-Watsonian behaviorists, the best known is B. F. Skinner (1904–90). His ideas of how to achieve a science of behavior contrasted sharply with those of most other behaviorists. Whereas the others focused on natural-science methods, Skinner focused on scientific explanation. He argued that the way to a science of behavior lay through development of terms and concepts that would allow truly scientific explanations. He labeled the opposing view methodological behaviorism and styled his own view radical behaviorism.

Whatever their disagreements, all behaviorists agree with Watson's basic premises that there can be a natural science of behavior and that psychology could be that science. The idea that behavior can be treated scientifically implies that, just as the other sciences cast out hidden essences, forces, and causes, so behavior analysis (or psychology if they are the same) omits such mysterious factors. This omission raises controversy paralleling the reaction to Darwin's naturalistic account of evolution. Whereas Darwin offended by leaving out the hidden hand of God, behaviorists offend by leaving out another hidden force: the power of individuals to direct their own behavior. Just as Darwin's theory challenged the cherished idea of God the Creator, so behaviorism challenges the cherished idea of free will. We will discuss hidden causes more fully in chapter, but because the challenge to free will often arouses antagonism, we take it up now.

Free Will versus Determinism

The idea that there can be a science of behavior implies that behavior, like any scientific subject matter, is orderly, can be explained, with the right knowledge can be predicted, and with the right means can be controlled. This is determinism, the notion that behavior is determined solely by heredity and environment.

Many people find determinism objectionable. It appears to run counter to long-standing cultural traditions that assign the responsibility for action to the individual, rather than to heredity and environment. These traditions have changed to some extent: delinquency is blamed on bad environment; famous artists acknowledge debts to parents and teachers; and some behavioral traits, such as alcoholism, schizophrenia, handedness, and IQ are acknowledged to have a genetic component. Yet the tendency remains to assign credit and blame to individuals, to assert that behavior depends not just on heredity and environment but on something more, that people have freedom to choose their actions.

The name for the ability to choose is free will. It implies a third element besides heredity and environment, something within the individual. It asserts that despite inheritance and despite all environmental impacts, a person who behaves one way could have chosen to behave another way. It asserts something beyond merely experiencing that one has choice – it could seem to me that I can eat the ice cream or not, and yet my eating the ice cream could be entirely determined by past events. Free will asserts that choice is no illusion, that individuals themselves cause behavior.

Philosophers have tried to reconcile determinism and free will. Positions have emerged called "soft determinism" and "compatibilist" theories of free will. A soft determinism attributed to Donald Hebb, for example, holds that free will consists of behavior's dependence on inheritance and past environmental history, factors less visible than one's present environment. But, since such a view still considers behavior to result solely from inheritance and environment, past and present, it implies that free will is only an experience, an illusion, and not a causal relation between person and action. A compatibilist theory of free will proposed by philosopher Daniel Dennett defines free will as deliberation before action. As long as you deliberate over eating the ice cream (Will it make me fat? Could you offset its effects with exercise later? Can you be happy if you are always dieting?), my eating the ice cream is freely chosen. This is compatible with determinism because deliberation itself is behavior that might be determined by heredity and past environment. If deliberation plays any role in the behavior that follows, it would act only as a link in a chain of causality extending back into earlier events. This definition, however, deviates from what people conventionally mean by free will.

Philosophers call the conventional idea of free will – the idea that choice really can be free of past events – libertarian free will. Any other definition, like those of Hebb and Dennett, that is compatible with determinism presents no problem for behaviorism or a science of behavior. Only libertarian free will conflicts with behaviorism. The history of the concept in Jewish and Christian theology suggests that it exists precisely in order to deny the sort of determinism that behaviorism represents. Parting with the philosophers, therefore, we will refer to libertarian free will as "free will."

Arguments for and against Free Will

Proving free will (in other words, disproving determinism) would require that an act go counter to prediction even though every possible contributing factor is known. Since such perfect knowledge is impossible in practice, the conflict between determinism and free will can never be resolved by evidence. If it seems that middle-class children from good homes who become drug addicts must have chosen freely to do so because nothing in their backgrounds would account for the behavior, the determinist can insist that further investigation would reveal the genetic and environmental factors that lead to such addictions. If it seems that Mozart's musical career was entirely predictable on the basis of his family background and the way society in Vienna worked in his day, the free-will advocate can insist that little Wolfgang freely chose to please his parents with musical efforts rather than to play with toys like the other children. If evidence cannot persuade, then whether a person accepts determinism or free will may depend on the consequences of believing one or the other, and these may be social or aesthetic.

Social Arguments

Practically, it appears that denial of free will might undermine the whole moral fabric of our society. What will happen to our judicial system if people cannot be held responsible for their actions? We are already having trouble when criminals plead insanity and diminished competence. What will happen to our democratic institutions if people have no free choice? Why bother to have elections if choice among candidates is not free? Belief that people's behavior can be determined might encourage dictatorship. For these reasons, perhaps it is good and useful to believe in free will, even if it cannot be proved.

Behaviorists must address these arguments; otherwise, behaviorism risks being labeled a pernicious doctrine. We will address them in Part Three when we discuss freedom, social policy, and values. A brief survey now will give an idea of the general direction taken later.

The perceived threat to democracy derives from a false assumption. Although it is true that democracy depends on choice, it is false that choice becomes meaningless or impossible without free will. The idea that choice would disappear arises from an oversimplified notion of the alternative to free will. If an election offers a person two different ways to vote, which vote actually occurs depends not only on the person's long-term history (background, upbringing, or values) but also on events right before the election. Campaigning goes on for precisely this reason. I can be swayed by a good speech, and without it I might have voted for the other candidate. People need not have free will for elections to be meaningful; their behavior need only be open to influence and persuasion (shorter-term environmental determinants).

We favor democracy not because we have free will but because we find that, as a set of practices, it works. People in a democratic society are happier and more productive than under any known monarchy or dictatorship. Instead of worrying over the loss of free will, we may more profitably ask what it is about democracy that makes it better. If we can analyze our democratic institutions to discover what makes them work, we might be able to find ways to make them even more effective. Political freedom consists of something more practical than free will: It means having choices available and being able to affect the behavior of those who govern. A scientific understanding of behavior could be used to increase political freedom. In this way, the knowledge gained from a science of behavior could be put to good use; nothing requires that it be abused. And after all, if we really do have free will, presumably no one need worry about the use of such knowledge anyway.

What about morals? Jewish and Christian theology incorporated free will as the means to salvation. Without such teaching, will people still be good? One way of answering this question is to point to that part of humanity, by far the majority, that lacks this commitment to the notion of free will. Do Buddhists and Hindus in China, Japan, and India behave less morally? In the USA, the rise of public education has increasingly moved moral training from church and home into the schools. As American society leans more heavily on schools to produce good citizens, behavior analysis is already helping. Far from destroying morals, the science of behavior may be used to educate children into good, happy, and effective citizens.

As for the justice system, it exists to deal with society's failures, and we need not regard justice as a purely moral issue. We will always need to "hold people responsible for their behavior" in the practical sense that actions are assigned to individuals. Once the courts have established that someone has transgressed, then practical issues arise as to how to protect society from this person and how to make it unlikely that the person will behave so in the future. Jailing criminals has done little to prevent repeat offenses. A science of behavior could help both to prevent crime and to treat it more effectively.

Aesthetic Arguments

Critics of the notion of free will often point to its illogic. Even theologians who promoted the idea have puzzled over its paradoxical conflict with an omnipotent God. Saint Augustine put the matter clearly: If God does everything and knows everything before it happens, how is it possible for a person to do anything freely? Just as with natural determinism, if God determines all events (including our actions), then it is only our ignorance – here, of God's will – that allows the illusion of free will. The common theological solution is to call free will a mystery; somehow God gives us free will despite His omnipotence. From a scientific viewpoint, this conclusion is unsatisfactory because it defies logic and leaves the paradox unresolved.

In its conflict with determinism, godly or natural, free will seems to depend on ignorance. Indeed, it can be argued that free will is simply a name for ignorance of the determinants of behavior. The more we know of the reasons behind a person's actions, the less likely we are to attribute them to free will. If a boy who steals cars comes from a poor environment, we are inclined to attribute the behavior to the environment, and the more we know about how he was abused and neglected by his family and society the less likely we are to say that he chose freely. When we know that a politician has accepted a bribe, we no longer consider that politician's positions to be taken freely. When we learn that an artist had supportive parents and a great teacher, we wonder less over his talent.

The other side of this argument is that no matter how much we know, we still cannot predict exactly what a person will do in a given situation. This unpredictability has sometimes been considered evidence of free will. The weather, however, is also unpredictable, but we never regard weather as the product of free will. Many natural systems exist, the momentary behavior of which we cannot predict in advance but which we never consider free. Why would we set a higher standard for a science of behavior than for the other natural sciences? It seems illogical, and it is, because the argument from unpredictability contains a logical error. Free will does imply unpredictability, but this in no way requires the converse, that unpredictability implies free will.

In a way, it should even be false that free will implies unpredictability. My actions may be unpredictable by another person, perhaps, but if my free will causes my behavior, we should know perfectly well what you are going to do. This requires that you know my will, because it is difficult to see how a will that was unknown could be free. If you decide to go on a diet, and you know this is my will, then you ought to predict that you will be go on the diet. If you know my will and my will causes my behavior, we should be able to predict my behavior perfectly.

The notion that free will causes behavior also raises a thorny problem. How can a nonnatural event like free will cause a natural event like eating ice cream? Natural events can lead to other natural events, because they can be related to one another in time and space. Sexual intercourse leads to a baby just about nine months later. The phrase leads to implies that the cause can be placed in time and space. By definition, however, nonnatural things and events cannot be placed in time and space. (If they could be placed in time and space, then they would be natural.) How, then, can a nonnatural event lead to a natural event? When and where does willing take place, that it can lead to my eating ice cream? The murkiness of such hypothetical connections led to Newton's Hypotheses non fingo. Science admits unsolved puzzles, because puzzles may ultimately yield to further thought and experimentation, but the connection between free will and action cannot be so illuminated. It is a mystery. Science's aim of explaining the world excludes mysteries that cannot be explained. The mysterious nature of free will, for example, runs counter to the theory of evolution. First, it raises the problem of discontinuity. If animals lack free will, how did it suddenly arise in our species? It would have to have been presaged in our nonhuman ancestors. Second, even if animals could have free will, how could such a nonnatural thing evolve? Natural traits evolve by modification from other natural traits. One can imagine even the evolution of a natural mechanical system that could behave unpredictably from moment to moment. But no conceivable way exists for natural selection to produce a nonnatural free will. This may be a powerful reason that some religious groups oppose the theory of evolution; conversely, it is an equally powerful reason to exclude free will from scientific accounts of behavior.

In fact, the whole reason for our discussing these arguments against free will is really to show that scientific accounts of behavior excluding free will are possible. The arguments aim to defend the science of behavior against the claim that human behavior cannot be understood because people have free will. Behavior analysis cautions against the use of the concept in arenas where it has unfortunate consequences, such as in the judicial system and government. Behavior analysis omits free will, but it places no ban on using the concept in everyday discourse or in the spheres of religion, poetry, and literature; clerics, poets, and writers often talk of free will and free choice. A science of behavior might seek to explain such talk, but in no way forbids it. In this book, however, we explore how to understand behavior without mysterious concepts like free will.

Skinner Operant Conditioning

Operant conditioning is a method of learning that occurs through rewards and punishments for behavior. Through operant conditioning, an individual makes an association between a particular behavior and a consequence.

By the 1920s, John B. Watson had left academic psychology, and other behaviorists were becoming influential, proposing new forms of learning other than classical conditioning. Perhaps the most important of these was Burrhus Frederic Skinner. Although, for obvious reasons, he is more commonly known as B.F. Skinner.

Skinner's views were slightly less extreme than those of Watson. Skinner believed that we do have such a thing as a mind, but that it is simply more productive to study observable behavior rather than internal mental events.

The work of Skinner was rooted in a view that classical conditioning was far too simplistic to be a complete explanation of complex human behavior. He believed that the best way to understand behavior is to look at the causes of an action and its consequences. He called this approach operant conditioning.

Skinner is regarded as the father of Operant Conditioning, but his work was based on Thorndike's law of effect. According to this principle, behavior that is followed by pleasant consequences is likely to be repeated, and behavior followed by unpleasant consequences is less likely to be repeated.

Skinner introduced a new term into the Law of Effect - Reinforcement. Behavior which is reinforced tends to be repeated (i.e., strengthened); behavior which is not reinforced tends to die out-or be extinguished (i.e., weakened).

Skinner studied operant conditioning by conducting experiments using animals which he placed in a '*Skinner Box*' which was similar to Thorndike's puzzle box.

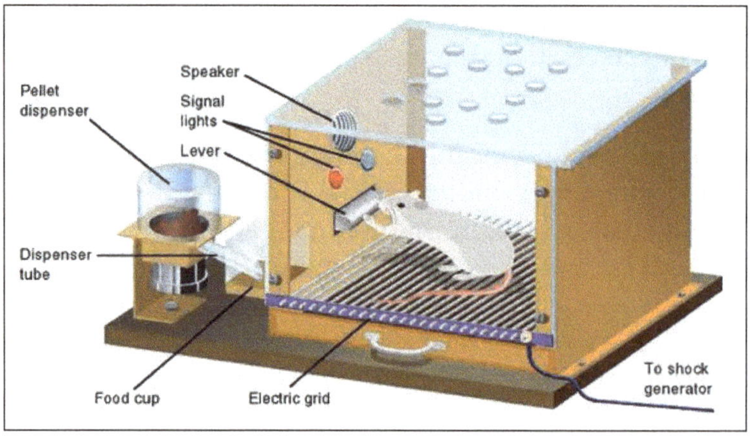

Skinner identified three types of responses, or operant, that can follow behavior.

- Neutral operants: responses from the environment that neither increase nor decrease the probability of a behavior being repeated.
- Reinforcers: Responses from the environment that increase the probability of a behavior being repeated. Reinforcers can be either positive or negative.
- Punishers: Responses from the environment that decrease the likelihood of a behavior being repeated. Punishment weakens behavior.

We can all think of examples of how our own behavior has been affected by reinforcers and punishers. As a child you probably tried out a number of behaviors and learned from their consequences.

For example, if when you were younger you tried smoking at school, and the chief consequence was that you got in with the crowd you always wanted to hang out with, you would have been positively reinforced (i.e., rewarded) and would be likely to repeat the behavior.

If, however, the main consequence was that you were caught, caned, suspended from school and your parents became involved you would most certainly have been punished, and you would consequently be much less likely to smoke now.

Positive Reinforcement

Skinner showed how positive reinforcement worked by placing a hungry rat in his Skinner box. The box contained a lever on the side, and as the rat moved about the box, it would accidentally knock the lever. Immediately it did so a food pellet would drop into a container next to the lever.

The rats quickly learned to go straight to the lever after a few times of being put in the box. The consequence of receiving food if they pressed the lever ensured that they would repeat the action again and again.

Positive reinforcement strengthens a behavior by providing a consequence an individual finds rewarding. For example, if your teacher gives you £5 each time you complete your homework (i.e., a reward) you will be more likely to repeat this behavior in the future, thus strengthening the behavior of completing your homework.

Negative Reinforcement

The removal of an unpleasant reinforcer can also strengthen behavior. This is known as negative reinforcement because it is the removal of an adverse stimulus which is 'rewarding' to the animal or person. Negative reinforcement strengthens behavior because it stops or removes an unpleasant experience.

For example, if you do not complete your homework, you give your teacher £5. You will complete your homework to avoid paying £5, thus strengthening the behavior of completing your homework.

Skinner showed how negative reinforcement worked by placing a rat in his Skinner box and then subjecting it to an unpleasant electric current which caused it some discomfort. As the rat moved about the box it would accidentally knock the lever. Immediately it did so the electric current would be switched off. The rats quickly learned to go straight to the lever after a few times of being put in the box. The consequence of escaping the electric current ensured that they would repeat the action again and again.

In fact Skinner even taught the rats to avoid the electric current by turning on a light just before the electric current came on. The rats soon learned to press the lever when the light came on because they knew that this would stop the electric current being switched on.

These two learned responses are known as Escape Learning and Avoidance Learning.

Punishment (Weakens Behavior)

Punishment is defined as the opposite of reinforcement since it is designed to weaken or eliminate a response rather than increase it. It is an aversive event that decreases the behavior that it follows.

Like reinforcement, punishment can work either by directly applying an unpleasant stimulus like a shock after a response or by removing a potentially rewarding stimulus, for instance, deducting someone's pocket money to punish undesirable behavior.

There are many problems with using punishment, such as:

- Punished behavior is not forgotten, it's suppressed - behavior returns when punishment is no longer present.
- Causes increased aggression - shows that aggression is a way to cope with problems.
- Creates fear that can generalize to undesirable behaviors, e.g., fear of school.
- Does not necessarily guide toward desired behavior - reinforcement tells you what to do, punishment only tells you what not to do.

Schedules of Reinforcement

Imagine a rat in a "Skinner box." In operant conditioning, if no food pellet is delivered immediately after the lever is pressed then after several attempts the rat stops pressing the lever (how long would someone continue to go to work if their employer stopped paying them?). The behavior has been extinguished.

Behaviorists discovered that different patterns (or schedules) of reinforcement had different effects on the speed of learning and extinction. Ferster and Skinner (1957) devised different ways of delivering reinforcement and found that this had effects on,

- The Response Rate - The rate at which the rat pressed the lever (i.e., how hard the rat worked).
- The Extinction Rate - The rate at which lever pressing dies out (i.e., how soon the rat gave up).

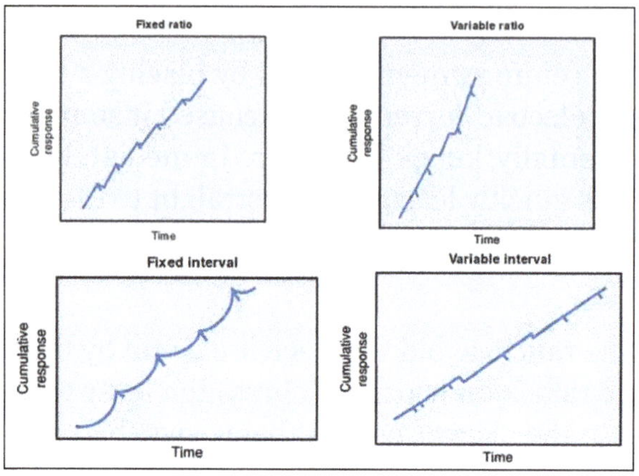

Skinner found that the type of reinforcement which produces the slowest rate of extinction (i.e., people will go on repeating the behavior for the longest time without reinforcement) is variable-ratio reinforcement. The type of reinforcement which has the quickest rate of extinction is continuous reinforcement.

Continuous Reinforcement

An animal/human is positively reinforced every time a specific behavior occurs, e.g., every time a lever is pressed a pellet is delivered, and then food delivery is shut off.

- Response rate is SLOW.
- Extinction rate is FAST.

Fixed Ratio Reinforcement

Behavior is reinforced only after the behavior occurs a specified number of times. e.g., one reinforcement is given after every so many correct responses, e.g., after every 5th response. For example, a child receives a star for every five words spelled correctly.

- Response rate is FAST.
- Extinction rate is MEDIUM.

Fixed Interval Reinforcement

One reinforcement is given after a fixed time interval providing at least one correct response has been made. An example is being paid by the hour. Another example would be every 15 minutes (half hour, hour, etc.) a pellet is delivered (providing at least one lever press has been made) then food delivery is shut off.

- Response rate is MEDIUM.
- Extinction rate is MEDIUM.

Variable Ratio Reinforcement

Behavior is reinforced after an unpredictable number of times. For examples gambling or fishing.

- Response rate is FAST.
- Extinction rate is SLOW (very hard to extinguish because of unpredictability).

Variable Interval Reinforcement

Providing one correct response has been made, reinforcement is given after an unpredictable amount of time has passed, e.g., on average every 5 minutes. An example is a self-employed person being paid at unpredictable times.

- Response rate is FAST.
- Extinction rate is SLOW.

Behavior Modification

Behavior modification is a set of therapies/techniques based on operant conditioning. The main principle comprises changing environmental events that are related to a person's behavior. For example, the reinforcement of desired behaviors and ignoring or punishing undesired ones.

This is not as simple as it sounds — always reinforcing desired behavior, for example, is basically bribery.

There are different types of positive reinforcements. Primary reinforcement is when a reward strengths a behavior by itself. Secondary reinforcement is when something strengthens a behavior because it leads to a primary reinforcer.

Examples of behavior modification therapy include token economy and behavior shaping.

Token Economy

Token economy is a system in which targeted behaviors are reinforced with tokens (secondary reinforcers) and later exchanged for rewards (primary reinforcers).

Tokens can be in the form of fake money, buttons, poker chips, stickers, etc. While the rewards can range anywhere from snacks to privileges or activities. For example, teachers use token economy at primary school by giving young children stickers to reward good behavior.

Token economy has been found to be very effective in managing psychiatric patients. However, the patients can become over reliant on the tokens, making it difficult for them to adjust to society once they leave prison, hospital, etc.

Staff implementing a token economy programme have a lot of power. It is important that staff do not favor or ignore certain individuals if the programme is to work. Therefore, staff need to be trained to give tokens fairly and consistently even when there are shift changes such as in prisons or in a psychiatric hospital.

Behavior Shaping

A further important contribution made by Skinner (1951) is the notion of behavior shaping through successive approximation. Skinner argues that the principles of operant conditioning can be used to produce extremely complex behavior if rewards and punishments are delivered in such a way as to encourage move an organism closer and closer to the desired behavior each time.

To do this, the conditions (or contingencies) required to receive the reward should shift each time the organism moves a step closer to the desired behavior.

According to Skinner, most animal and human behavior (including language) can be explained as a product of this type of successive approximation.

Educational Applications

In the conventional learning situation, operant conditioning applies largely to issues of class and student management, rather than to learning content. It is very relevant to shaping skill performance.

A simple way to shape behavior is to provide feedback on learner performance, e.g., compliments, approval, encouragement, and affirmation. A variable-ratio produces the highest response rate for students learning a new task, whereby initially reinforcement (e.g., praise) occurs at frequent intervals, and as the performance improves reinforcement occurs less frequently, until eventually only exceptional outcomes are reinforced.

For example, if a teacher wanted to encourage students to answer questions in class they should praise them for every attempt (regardless of whether their answer is correct). Gradually the teacher will only praise the students when their answer is correct, and over time only exceptional answers will be praised.

Unwanted behaviors, such as tardiness and dominating class discussion can be extinguished through being ignored by the teacher (rather than being reinforced by having attention drawn to them). This is not an easy task, as the teacher may appear insincere if he/she thinks too much about the way to behave.

References

- Cognitive-psychology: verywellmind.com, Retrieved 2 April, 2019
- What-is-the-conscious-mind: verywellmind.com, Retrieved 12 June, 2019
- What-is-cognition: verywellmind.com, Retrieved 15 January, 2019
- Cognitive-Development: healthofchildren.com, Retrieved 5 May, 2019
- What-is-cognitive-flexibility: mentalhealthdaily.com, Retrieved 26 July, 2019
- Understanding-behaviourism: blackwellpublishing.com, Retrieved 16 August, 2019

2

Perception and Attention

The organization, interpretation, and identification of sensory information for the purpose of comprehending it is known as perception. The cognitive and behavioral process of selectively focusing on a discrete aspect of information is known as attention. The topics elaborated in this chapter will help in gaining a better perspective about perception and attention as well as the basic characteristics of perception and attention.

Perception

The perceptual process allows us to experience the world around us. Take a moment to think of all the things you perceive on a daily basis. At any given moment, you might see familiar objects in your environment, feel the touch of objects and people against your skin, smell the aroma of a home-cooked meal and hear the sound of music playing in your next door neighbor's apartment. All of these things help make up our conscious experience and allow us to interact with the people and objects around us.

Hans Solcer

Perception is our sensory experience of the world around us and involves both recognizing environmental stimuli and actions in response to these stimuli. Through the perceptual process, we gain information about properties and elements of the environment that are critical to our survival. Perception not only creates our experience of the world around us; it allows us to act within our environment.

Perception includes the five senses; touch, sight, sound, smell, and taste. It also includes what is known as proprioception, a set of senses involving the ability to detect changes in body positions and movements. It also involves the cognitive processes required to process information, such as recognizing the face of a friend or detecting a familiar scent.

Steps in the Perceptual Process

Manuel Orero Galen

The perceptual process is a sequence of steps that begins with the environment and leads to our perception of a stimulus and action in response to the stimulus. This process is continual, but you do not spend a great deal of time thinking about the actual *process* that occurs when you perceive the many stimuli that surround you at any given moment.

The process of transforming the light that falls on your retinas into an actual visual image happens unconsciously and automatically. The subtle changes in pressure against your skin that allow you to feel object occur without a single thought.

In order to fully understand how the perception process works, we'll start by breaking down each step.

The Environmental Stimulus

Stanislaw Pyte

The world is full of stimuli that can attract our attention through various senses. The environmental stimulus is everything in our environment that has the potential to be perceived.

This might include anything that can be seen, touched, tasted, smelled, or heard. It might also involve the sense of proprioception, such as the movements of the arms and legs or the change in position of the body in relation to objects in the environment.

For example, imagine that you are out on a morning jog at your local park. As you perform your workout, there are a wide variety of environmental stimuli that might capture your attention. The tree branches are swaying in the slight breeze; a man is out on the grass playing fetch with his Golden Retriever; a car drives past with the windows rolled down and the music blaring; a duck splashes in a nearby pond. All of these things represent environmental stimuli and serve as a starting point for the perceptual process.

The Attended Stimulus

Mark Newman

The attended stimulus is the specific object in the environment on which our attention is focused. In many cases, we might focus on stimuli that are familiar to us, such as the face of a friend in a crowd of strangers at the local coffee shop. In other instances, we are likely to attend to stimuli that have some degree of novelty.

From our earlier example, let's imagine that during your morning jog you focus your attention on the duck floating in the nearby pond. The duck represents the attended stimulus. During the next step of the perceptual process, the visual process will progress.

The Image on the Retina

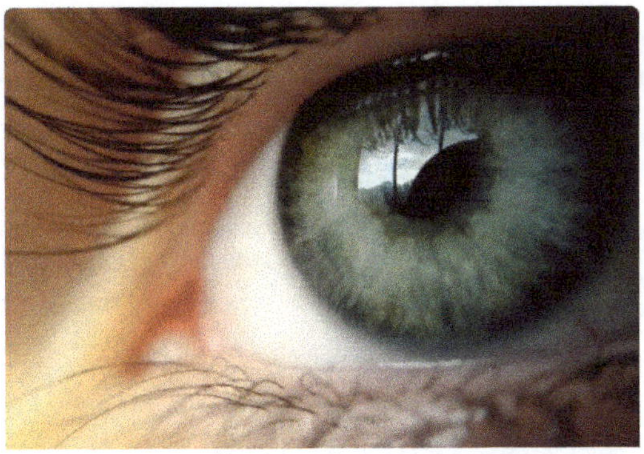

Caelan Stulken

Next, the attended stimulus is formed as an image on the retina. The first part of this process involves the light actually passing through the cornea and pupil and onto the lens of the eye. The cornea helps focus the light as it enters the eye, and the iris of the eye controls the size of the pupils in order to determine how much light to let in. The cornea and lens act together to project an inverted image onto the retina.

As you might already be aware, the image on the retina is actually upside down from the actual image in the environment. At this stage of the perceptual process, this is not terribly important. The image has still not been perceived, and this visual information will be changed even more dramatically in the next step of the process.

Transduction

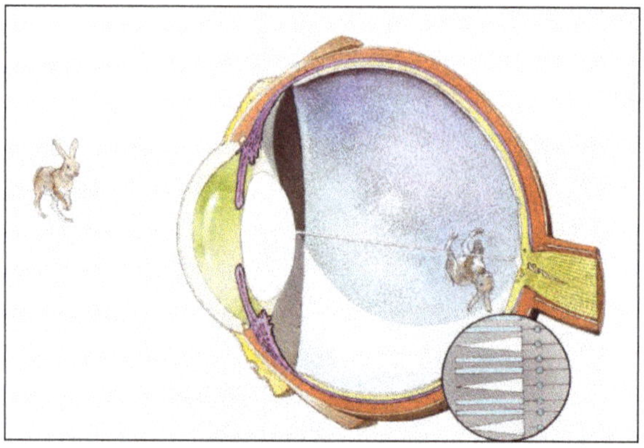

Dorling Kindersley

The image on the retina is then transformed into electrical signals in a process known as transduction. This allows the visual messages to be transmitted to the brain to be interpreted.

The retina contains many photoreceptor cells. These cells contain proteins known as rods and cones. Rods are primarily for seeing things in low light, while cones are associated with detecting color and shapes at normal light levels.

The rods and cones contain a molecule called retinal, which is responsible for transducing the light into visual signals that are then transmitted via nerve impulses.

Neural Processing

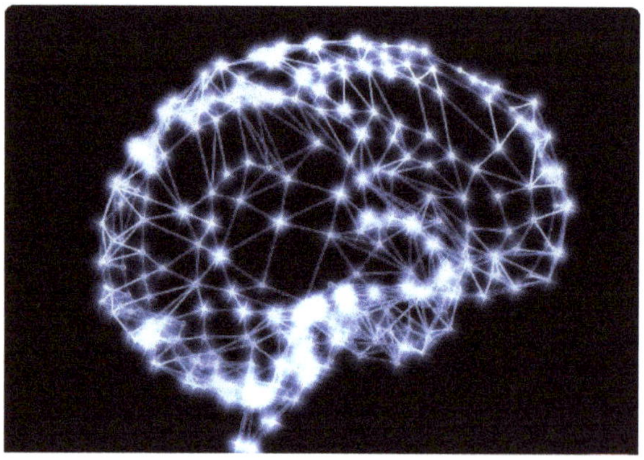

The electrical signals then undergo neural processing. The path followed by a particular signal depends on what type of signal it is (i.e. an auditory signal or a visual signal).

Through the series of interconnecting neurons located throughout the body, electrical signals are propagated from the receptors cells to the brain. In our previous example, the image of a duck floating in the pond is received as light on the retina, which is then transduced into an electrical signal and then processed through the neurons in the visual network.

In the next step of the perceptual process, you will actually perceive the stimuli and become aware of its presence in the environment.

Perception

Jordan Siemens

In the next step of the perception process, we actually perceive the stimulus object in the environment. It is at this point that we become consciously aware of the stimulus.

Let's consider our previous example, in which we imagined that you were out for a morning jog in the park. At the perception stage, you have become aware that there is something out on the pond to perceive.

Now, it is one thing to be *aware* of stimuli in the environment, and quite another to actually become fully consciously aware of what we have perceived. In the next stage of the perceptual process, we will sort the perceived information into meaningful categories.

Recognition

Tim Robberts

Perception doesn't just involve becoming consciously aware of the stimuli. It is also necessary for our brain to categorize and interpret what it is we are sensing. Our ability to interpret and give meaning to the object is the next step, known as recognition.

Continuing our example, it is at the recognition stage of the perceptual process that you realize that there is a duck floating on the water. The recognition stage is an essential part of perception since it allows us to make sense of the world around us. By placing objects in meaningful categories, we are able to understand and react to the world around us.

Action

Katie Huisman

The final step of the perceptual process involves some sort of action in response to the environmental stimulus. This could involve a variety of actions, such as turning your head for a closer look or turning away to look at something else.

The action phase of perceptual development involves some type of motor activity that occurs in response to the perceived and recognized stimulus. This might involve a major action, like running toward a person in distress, or something as subtle as blinking your eyes in response to a puff of dust blowing through the air.

Basic Characteristics of Perception

Perception can be defined as the meaningful interpretation of information received by the senses. In other words, it is a process in which the sensory experience is organised, interpreted and made meaningful.

Some important characteristics of perception are as follows:

Perception is a Selective Process

We do not perceive each and everything in the world or around us. We attend to only a part of the stimuli around us. We select only a limited range of stimuli to which we attend. Attention is a basic process in perception. It makes our perception selective in nature. What we select would depend upon our needs, interests, and motives or on the nature of stimuli to which we are exposed.

Perception Requires Sensation

Perception is intimately related to sensation. In order for perception to occur, we must first experience some sensation.

Perception Involves Organisation

Perception is not merely a collection of present sensations and memory traces of past experiences. It is a meaningful and integrated organization of past and present knowledge.

Perception Involves Past Experience

Perception involves past experience also. The present information can be meaningfully understood only when we integrate our past and interpret it in terms of present or future consequences.

Change is the basis of Perception

Perception is always a response to some change or difference in the environment. If the world were uniformly the same we would experience no perception. E.g., change in the weather, style of dress, food, etc. is easily perceived. Any change in the normal routine is perceived quickly.

Perception is Objective as well as Subjective

We all perceive certain things as the same e.g., table, chair, etc. are perceived by every one of us in a more or less similar manner. This is objective perception. In many cases our perception is considerably influenced by our thoughts, motives, interests, etc. Such perception is subjective in nature, e.g., an ambiguous event may be perceived differently by different individuals.

Perception has Affective Aspect

Our perception often induces emotions in us. When we perceive an old friend we feel happy. When we perceive a snake we are afraid. Thus, perception produces feelings and emotions.

Form Perception

Gestalt psychology attempts to understand psychological phenomena by viewing them as organised and structured wholes rather than the sum of their constituent parts. Thus, Gestalt psychology dissociates itself from the more 'elementistic'/reductionistic/decompositional approaches to psychology like structuralism (with its tendency to analyse mental processes into elementary sensations) and it accentuates concepts like emergent properties, holism, and context.

In the 30s and 40s Gestalt psychology was applied to visual perception, most notably by Max Wertheimer, Wolfgang Köhler, and Kurt Koffka who founded the so-called gestalt approaches to form perception. Their aim was to investigate the global and holistic processes involved in perceiving structure in the environment (e.g. Sternberg 1996). More specifically, they tried to explain human perception of groups of objects and how we perceive *parts* of objects and form *whole* objects on the basis of these. The investigations in this subject crystallised into "the gestalt laws of perceptual organization." Some of these laws, which are often cited in the HCI or interaction design community, are as follows:

Law of Proximity

The law of proximity posits that when we perceive a collection of objects, we will see objects close to each other as forming a group. In figure, we perceive the MTV logo and the logo for the Europe Music Awards as forming a group in the top left corner and the logos of the sponsors as forming a group in the bottom right corner. The white space separating the two groups of logos is used to indicate 'grouping', and the proximity of the logos of each groups is thus used to this end. Thus, a semantic separation of 'organisers' from 'sponsors' is achieved via structuring the graphical layout in accordance with this simple principle of perceptual organisation.

A real-world example of the law of proximity from MTV Music Awards 2002

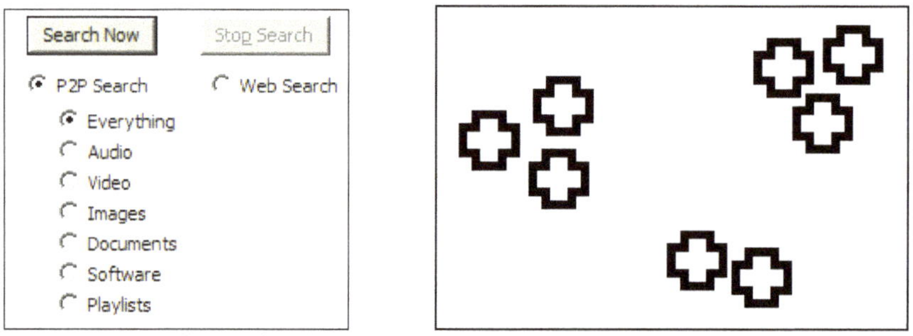

A typical "text-book way" of exemplifying the law of proximity

Figure above is a typical textbook example, exemplifying how the law of proximity groups the items into 3 groups as opposed to 8 individual items.

Law of Similarity

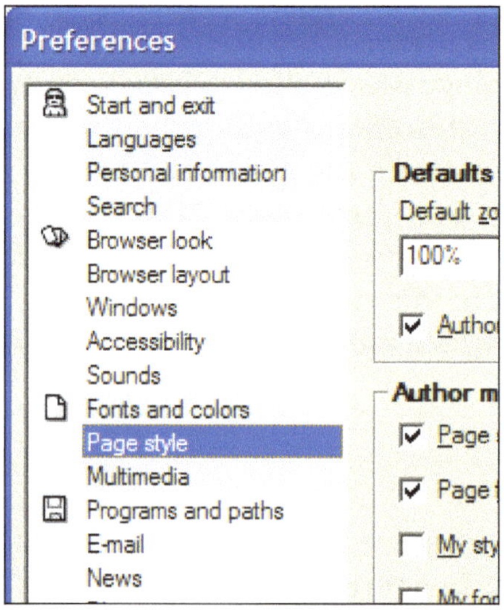

The "preferences window" of the Opera browser

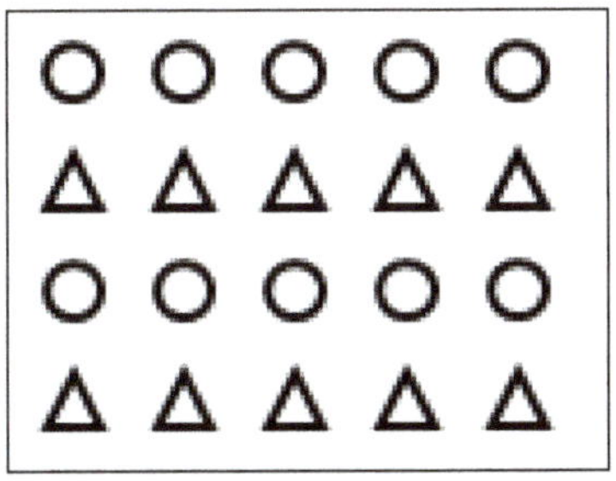

A typical textbook example of the law of similarity

The law of similarity captures the idea that elements will be grouped perceptually if they are similar to each other. In the "preferences window" of the Opera browser, colour is used to make the user group the menu items on the basis of their background colour. The grey background of the first four menu items thus "tie them together". Figure. is a typical textbook example of the principle of similarity, whereby we see the circles and triangles as forming four horizontal rows (or at least some configuration where triangles and circles are grouped depending on their shape). Objects similar to each other thus tend to be seen as a unit.

Law of Prägnanz (Figure-ground)

The logo of visitnorway. com

The logo of the Gnome Desktop Environment

The logo of the Macintosh

Edgar Rubin, a Danish psychologist, was the first to systematically investigate the figure-ground phenomenon. The phenomenon captures the idea that in perceiving a visual field, some objects take a prominent role (the figures) while others recede into the background (the ground). The visual field is thus divided into these two basic parts. This effect is often used by smart logo makers, as figure 3.A, B, and C suggest: The logo of visitnorway.com can be viewed as both three separate elements of blue, green and navy colour. It may, however, also be viewed as a person stretching his/her arms into the air. Similarly, the logo of the Gnome Desktop Environment can be viewed as both a "G" and a footprint. Lastly, the Macintosh logo can be viewed as a regular happy face and a happy face in profile (looking at a computer screen).

Common to these logos is that you can focus on only one "interpretation" at a time; you cannot observe both the figure and ground at the same time, as ground will *become* figure when shifting the focus.

It should be noted that the figure-ground is most often exemplified using the Rubin Face/Vase Illusion, named after Edgar Rubin.

Law of Symmetry

CSC Finland's logo

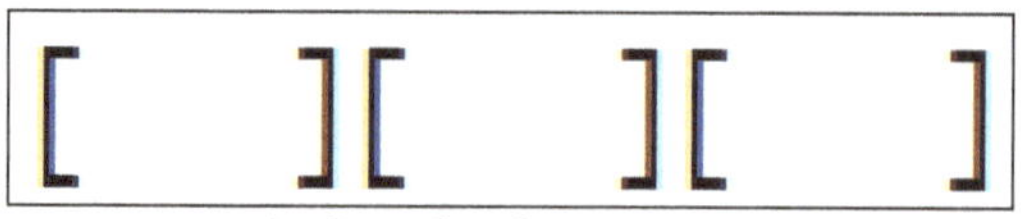

A typical textbook example of the law of symmetry

The law of symmetry captures the idea that when we perceive objects we tend to perceive them as symmetrical shapes that form around their centre. Most objects can be divided in two more or less symmetrical halves and when for example we see two unconnected elements that are symmetrical, we unconsciously integrate them into one coherent object (or percept). The more alike objects are, they more they tend to be grouped.

In the above, CSC Finland's logo is perceived as an integral whole although the two constituent geometrical shapes seem to be pointing in different directions and have differing colours.

A typical textbook example of the law of symmetry, consists of a configuration of a number of brackets. When perceiving the configuration, we see three pairs of symmetrical brackets as opposed to 6 individual brackets, or two pairs and two singles. This happens despite what is suggested by some of the brackets immediate proximity to each other.

Law of Closure

IBM's logo

Half of the book cover of Paul Thagard's book, "Coherence in Thought and Action"

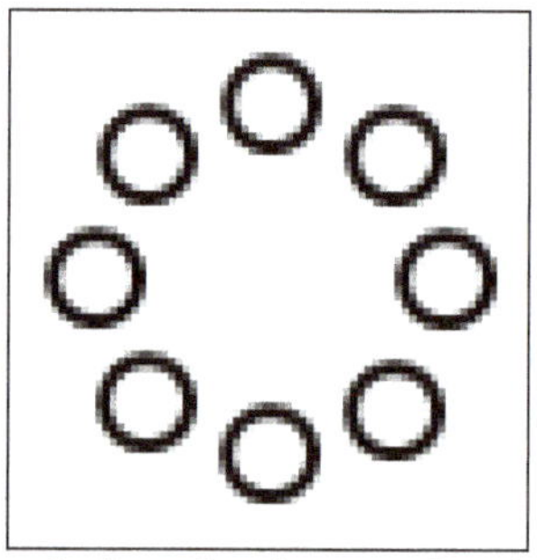

A typical textbook example of the law of closure

The law of closure posits that we perceptually close up, or complete, objects that are not, in fact, complete. In the above, we perceive the letters 'I', 'B', and 'M' although the shapes we see, in fact, are only lines of white space of differing length hovering above each other. Similarly, we see the figure on Paul Thagard's book as forming a three-dimensional box although all we see, in fact, is 24 dissimilar red shapes (count for yourself!) on a dark red background. Figure. is the typical textbook example of the law of closure; we perceive a circle and not 8 individual circles.

The Gestalt approach can be said to be a "bottom-up" theory as it starts from the bottom (the aspects of the stimuli that influence perception) and work its way up to higher-order cognitive processes. An example of another bottom-up theory (of perception) that is well-known in the HCI community is James Gibson's theory of "direct perception".

Attention

Attention in psychology is the concentration of awareness on some phenomenon to the exclusion of other stimuli.

Attention is awareness of the here and now in a focal and perceptive way. For early psychologists, such as Edward Bradford Titchener, attention determined the content of consciousness and influenced the quality of conscious experience. In subsequent years less emphasis was placed on the subjective element of consciousness and more on the behaviour patterns by which attention could be recognized in others. Although human experience is determined by the way people direct their attention, it is evident that they do not have complete control over such direction. There are, for example, times when an individual has difficulty concentrating attention on a task, a conversation, or a set of events. At other times an individual's attention is "captured" by an unexpected event rather than voluntarily directed toward it.

Attention has to do with the immediate experience of the individual; it is a state of current awareness. There are, of course, myriad events taking place in the world all the time, each impinging upon a person's senses. There are also events taking place within the body that affect attention, just as there are representations of past events stored in one's memory but accessible to awareness under appropriate circumstances.

While it might be expected that current awareness is the totality of all those events at any given moment, clearly this is not the case. Within this vast field of potential experiences, an individual focuses upon—or attends to—some limited subset of the whole. This subset constitutes the subjective field of awareness. It is possible to determine the reason for this limitation. Control and coordination of the many inputs and stored experiences and the organization of appropriate patterns of response are the province of the brain. The brain has impressive processing capabilities, but it has a limited capacity. A person cannot consciously experience all the events and information available at any one time. Likewise, it is impossible to initiate, simultaneously, an unlimited number of different actions. The question becomes one of how an appropriate subset of inputs, intermediate processes, and outputs are selected to command attention and engage available resources.

Attention, then, may be understood as a condition of selective awareness which governs the extent and quality of one's interactions with one's environment. It is not necessarily held under voluntary control. Some of the history of attention and the methods by which psychologists and others have come to characterize and understand it are presented in the discussion that follows.

The Influence of Behaviourism

During this period the development of the psychological school of behaviourism marginalizedthe study of attention. Behaviourism's principal advocate, John B. Watson, was interested primarily in stimulus–response relations. Attention seemed an unnecessary concept in a system of this kind, which rejected mentalistic notions, such as volition, free will, introspection, and consciousness. If used at all, the term *attention* was operationally defined in terms of discriminative responses to external stimuli. Ultimately, however, it became apparent that behaviourism failed to explain situations in which multiple stimuli compete with one another for attention. This led to a new emphasis on notions of attitude and expectancy and to a renewed interest in attention.

Relation to Information Theory

Interest in attention revived in the 1940s, when engineers and psychologists became involved in problems of man-machine interaction in various military contexts. Faced with this new range of problems, such as helping soldiers stay alert when they were watching radar systems, applied psychologists found no help in existing academic theories and sought a new communications theory. As the occupational psychologist D.E. Broadbent expressed it, "attention had to be brought back into respectability." Gradually the individual came to be viewed as a processor of information.

Paradoxical as it may seem, attention appears to depend on both the unexpectedness of events and on their familiar association. Information theory suggests that the significance of any event can only be estimated in terms of what else might have happened; hence, its tendency to attract attention is considered a function of its statistical improbability. The degree of novelty, which is estimated according to the number of times an event has been experienced previously, provides a measure of its surprise value. Thus an event that has never been experienced before has a high surprise value and should attract attention, even if it lacks any specific associations or consequences.

The attempts to apply information theory to a diversity of psychological problems met in the end with limited success. Nevertheless, the view of the human brain as an informationprocessor, a type of computer, was becoming more prevalent, and the notion that one might be able to quantify the gain or flow of information proved attractive. Information itself was defined as that which reduces or removes uncertainty. The process of removing uncertainty was seen as a series of binary (yes or no) choices. The unit of information that expressed this primitive choice between two alternatives, or halving the residual uncertainty, was called the bit (short for the term *binary digit*). In the terms of this theory, humans are seen as a communication channel, through which information is transmitted at the rate of so many bits per second. Attempts were made to measure the capacity of this communication channel in many areas of human activity, but the experimental results were found to be too inconsistent to be useful. Cognitive psychologists ultimately abandoned information theory, recognizing the incalculable effect of past experience on the information carried by any bit.

Aspects of Attention

Selective Attention

Is an individual able to attend to more than one thing at a time? There is little dispute that human beings and other animals selectively attend to some of the information available to them at the expense of the remainder. One reason advanced for this is the limited capacity of the brain, which cannot process all available information simultaneously, yet everyday experience shows that people are able to do several things at the same time. When driving an automobile, they can apparently watch the road, turn the steering wheel, change gears, and apply the brakes simultaneously if necessary. This is not to say, however, that people attend to all these activities simultaneously. It may be that only one of them, such as the road or its traffic, is at the forefront of awareness, while the others are dealt with relatively automatically. Another kind of evidence indicates that when two stimuli are presented at the same time, often only one is perceived while the other is completely ignored. In those instances when both are perceived, the responses made to them tend to be in succession, not together.

The conclusion reached and embodied in theories of the 1950s was that somewhere in the system was a bottleneck. Views differed as to where the bottleneck occurred. One of the most influential of the psychological models of selective attention was that put forward by Broadbent in 1958. He postulated that the many signals entering the central nervous system in parallel with one another are held for a very short time in a temporary "buffer." At this point the signals are analyzed for features such as their location in space, their tonal quality, their size, their colour, or other basic physical properties. They then pass through a selective "filter" that allows only those signals with the appropriate properties to proceed along a single channel for further analysis. Part of the lower-priority information held in the buffer will fail to pass this stage before the time limit on the buffer expires. Items lost in this way have no further effect on behaviour. The original theory held that signals from only one source at a time could proceed. Subsequent work cast doubt on this explanation, and it was later modified by Anne Treisman, to suggest that the filter does not completely block, but simply attenuates, the nonattended signals.

With the notion of attenuation, rather than exclusion, of nonattended signals came the idea of the establishment of thresholds. Thus threshold sensitivity might be set quite low for certain priority classes of stimuli, which, even when basically unattended and hence attenuated, may nevertheless be capable of activating the perceptual systems. Examples would be the sensitivity displayed to hearing one's own name spoken or the mother's sensitivity to the cry of her child in the night. This latter example demonstrates how processing at some level occurs even in sleep. Before attention can be said to be deployed on the activating event, however, the brain must return to a state of wakefulness. Some theorists have considered that there is no real need to postulate an early filter at all. They suggest that all signals reach central brain structures, which are, according to current circumstances, weighted to take account of particular properties. Some have a high weighting, for example, in response to one's own name; others are weighted according to the immediate task or interest. Among the concurrently active structures, that with the highest weighting gains awareness and is most directly responded to.

Some critics of the above theories consider that they overemphasize the serial elements in attention. Apart from the everyday instances of tasks performed in parallel, as in the example of driving, they point to experimental evidence for highly demanding combinations of concurrent activities. As early as 1887 the French philosopher Frédéric Paulhan reported the ability to write one poem while reciting another. More recently it has been shown that some music students can sight read and play piano music while at the same time repeating aloud a prose passage. Of course it can still be held that, when two such tasks are being performed together, one of them is being done automatically and essentially without direct attention. An alternative explanation might be that attention alternates between them in a rapid, and frequently imperceptible, way. An analogous situation occurs when many users access a mainframe computer simultaneously. In practice, the computer is servicing their demands in very rapid alternation, yet each user remains relatively unaware that the interactive process is not absolutely continuous.

The Intensity of Attention

These theories have been criticized for dealing with only the passive aspects of attention—certainly there is more to attention than mere selection. Such critics point out that there is also the question of the degree or intensity with which attention is applied to a particular task or situation. These "intensive" aspects of attention may be regarded as a subset of the broader dimension of arousal; that is to say, they relate to the continuum of awareness that extends from sleep (or even coma) to alert wakefulness. The topic of arousal is discussed later; for the present it is sufficient to note that the level of arousal can be determined by the demands of the task or activity in which the individual is engaged or by internal states; these are sometimes manifested as instinctive drives and frequently accompanied by high emotions, ranging from keen excitement to unpleasant stress. In the case of some drive states, the high arousal may be directed to the satisfaction of a particular need. The consequences for attention can be the allocation of a high priority, or weighting, to all stimuli that relate to satisfaction of the need.

By contrast, the level of arousal associated with a particular task varies from moment to moment as the task demands change; in other words, it is very much dependent upon overall stimulus load. One of the consequences of high-demand tasks is that spare capacity decreases. At full load, virtually all attention must be concentrated on the main task, leaving little attention available for perceptual monitoring of the surroundings.

In recent years the direction of attention in response to task demands has often been spoken of in terms of the deployment of mental effort. The implication is that the intensive aspects of attention correspond to effort rather than just wakefulness. Effort, like arousal, is subject to task demands and available capacity. It is regarded as being mobilized in response to such demands, although the degree of voluntary control of effort is limited. Effort is not simply to be equated with the amount of work required by a task. Much mental activity takes place without the investment of a large amount of conscious effort.

Memory and Habituation

Attempts to accommodate the selective and intensive aspects of attention and its links with both awareness and more automatic processes have led to the formulation of a number of "two-process" theories of attention. One of the most influential was that advanced by the American psychologists Richard M. Shiffrin and Walter Schneider in 1977 on the basis of experiments involving visual search. Their theory of detection, search, and attention distinguishes between two modes of processing information: controlled search and automatic detection. Controlled search is highly demanding of attentional capacity and is usually serial in nature. It is easily established and is largely under the individual's control in that it can be readily altered or even reversed. It is strongly dependent on the stimulus load. It has been suggested that it uses short-term memory. By contrast, automatic detection, or automatic processing, operates in long-term memory and is dependent upon extensive learning. It comes into operation without active control or attention by the individual, it is difficult to alter or suppress, and it is virtually unaffected by load.

The vast subject of memory is beyond the scope of this survey of attention, but a few pointers to the interactions that take place between what is attended to, how it is perceived and recognized, and factors that govern its subsequent recall are relevant. Memorizing is not simply a matter of repetition; attention plays a role in organizing material in ways that can influence its later recall. One example, known as the Von Restorff effect, is that, in any given number of items to be learned, an item that is notably different from the rest in size, colour, or other basic characteristics will be more readily recalled than the others. Unfortunately there is a price to be paid for this improvement; other "standard" items will be less well-recalled than they otherwise would have been.

It is also important to realize that what is actually perceived is not a neutral, objective representation of what exists in the external world. It is coloured by past experiences and current expectations, to the extent that substantial distortions can occur to make a perceived item fit those experiences and expectations. Perceptions are frequently formed on the basis of quite limited cues; the art of camouflage utilizes this characteristic to the benefit of both humans and other animals in certain situations. It seems that even the culture within which a person lives determines the way he perceives the world. Following a study of the Hopi and Shawnee languages, the linguist Benjamin Whorf concluded that what these Native American peoples perceived was itself different from the perceptions of English-speaking Americans, by virtue of the way their languages were structured.

Broadly speaking, the two types of attention can be characterized as focal and automatic. Someone who is focally attentive is highly aware, consciously in control, and selective in handling sensory phenomena. A person in such a state also uses the brain for short-term storage. (Indeed, some focal attention is almost certainly necessary for storing information in the memory at all.) Focal attention is flexible but makes great demands on brain capacity. Automatic attention makes fewer demands but is relatively inflexible, as it cannot cope with the unexpected. The focal and automatic modes may be illustrated by a driving example: a new driver has to attend to gear shifting in a focal way (actively thinking about it), while an experienced driver changes gears automatically (not needing to think about it).

An important aspect of the control process in many circumstances is rehearsal. In this sense rehearsal means the mental repetition of incoming information. One consequence of rehearsal is that input items spend an extended period of time in the short-term memory store. It is also generally the case that what is attended to and rehearsed eventually ends up being stored in long-term memory. This suggests a close relationship between the conditions for awareness and those for storage in memory. Evidence for learning during sleep has sometimes been cited as contradicting this assertion that people remember only those things of which they were consciously aware at the time they occurred. It is now generally accepted, however, that the original evidence for sleep learning was suspect. In subsequent studies, when more stringent electrophysiological measures were made to ensure that individuals were in fact asleep, no clear evidence for learning during sleep could be found. There has been an indication that some type of conditioning may be possible during sleep, but, generally, awareness appears to be necessary for learning to take place.

As already noted, one of the conditions for becoming aware, or selectively engaged, is when current expectations are violated. Just as people learn skills to the point where they become automatic, they also encode current experience into patterns of expectation that, as long as they continue to be fulfilled, need not engage focal processing resources. On entering a room, a person may be aware of the regular one-second tick of a grandfather clock, but the ticking soon fades from awareness as other things command attention. One is likely to remain unaware of it unless it stops (meaning that established expectations are violated) or unless other demands upon attention drop to the point where the person has sufficient spare focal capacity to become at least partially aware of the sound.

The process of habituation occurs when a person's response to novelty wanes with the repeated and regular presentation of the same signal. Habituation represents a progressive loss of behavioral responsivity to a stimulus as its lack of adaptive significance is recognized. The unchanging repetition of the signal facilitates this recognition and confirms the inappropriateness of deploying further attention upon the signal. Generally, a shorter time interval between signals means a more rapid drop in responsiveness. If, however, the signals hold special significance for the individual, they will continue to be attended to and responded to even though they may be repetitive. For example, a person who counts the ticks of the clock to check its accuracy will not become habituated to the ticking sound. In other circumstances where stimuli have special signal properties, habituation may take place but only very slowly. Other factors, such as loudness, brightness, or intensity, can affect the magnitude of response to a signal and the rate at which habituation takes place. Although response enhancement and resistance to habituation are associated with increased stimulus intensity, they can also occur in reaction to faint signals. These observations of changes in attention with time and signal properties raise the wider question of how attention behaves over long periods of time.

Sustained Attention: Vigilance

Sustained attention, or vigilance, as it is more often called, refers to the state in which attention must be maintained over time. Often this is to be found in some form of "watchkeeping" activity when an observer, or listener, must continuously monitor a situation in which significant, but usually infrequent and unpredictable, events may occur. An example would be watching a radar screen in order to make the earliest possible detection of a blip that might signify the approach of an aircraft or ship. It is especially difficult to detect infrequent signals of this nature.

Vigilance is difficult to sustain. No single theory explains vigilance satisfactorily, probably because of its complexity. In the first place, there is a distinction between sustaining attention in a detection task, where the overall workload is high, and sustaining it when little is happening except for the occasional looked-for events. Under both conditions performance can decline over time. Much depends on the allocation of neural resources to deal with the task. These resources are somewhat limited by the processing capacity already mentioned. When the task is complex, detection difficult, time limited, and a series of decisions required using variable data, the brain may not succeed in coping. Long, boring, and for the most part uneventful tasks result in lowered performance with regard to both speed and accuracy in detecting looked-for events. If the task is interesting or is taking place in a stimulating environment, the individual will be better able to sustain attention and maintain performance.

The frequency of task-relevant events holds a significant influence on vigilance performance. Generally speaking, the more frequent the events are, the better the performance, while long periods of inactivity constitute the worst case for performance. Surprisingly, the ratio of signals to nonsignal stimuli makes little difference to performance. The magnitude of the signal, however, is significant. During the course of a watch, expectancies develop about the frequency with which signals appear. If a signal occurs after an atypical interval, it is less likely to be detected. Performance can be improved (up to a point) by increasing task complexity, and in some vigilance situations the introduction of a secondary task can actually improve performance on the primary task. Performance is also enhanced when the individual receives feedback on the vigilance effort. Performance tends to dwindle in a noisy environment, particularly if the noise is high-pitched and loud and the task is difficult. Lack of sleep also impairs performance. Conversely, vigilance can be improved—or at least lapses prevented—by short periods of rest or by conversation or other mild forms of diversion. Monetary or other rewards tend to improve performance, as do some stimulant drugs.

The Neurophysiology of Attention

Physiological Changes

The external manifestations of attention are accompanied by physiological changes, particularly within the brain and nervous system. Functional magnetic resonance imaging(fMRI), a research and diagnostic method developed in the early 1990s, has been used to study many brain activities, including attention. The method detects changes of blood flow in the brain, including the concentration or pooling of blood in areas of increased neural activity.

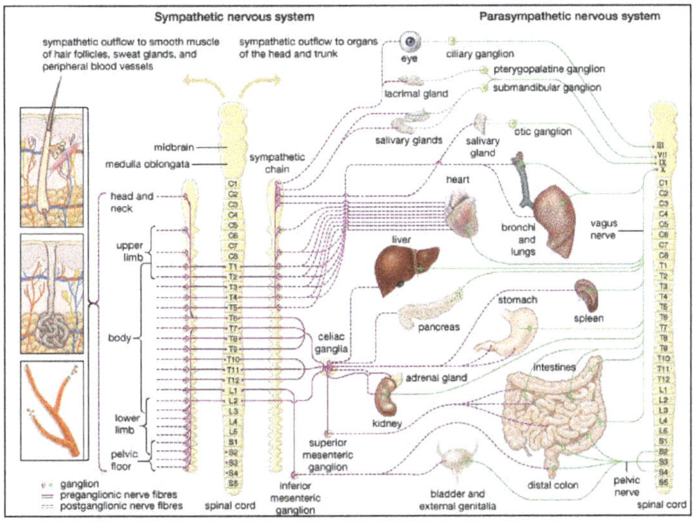

Schematic representation of the autonomic nervous system, showing distribution of sympathetic and parasympathetic nerves to the head, trunk, and limbs

Other physiological changes can be studied by examining responses to novel stimuli. Growing out of Pavlov's research, the orienting response to novel stimuli has come to be characterized by a broad complex of physiological changes. These include changes in heart rate, in the electrical conductivity of the skin, in the size of the pupils of the eyes, in the pattern of respiration, and in the level of tension in the muscles. If the novel signal is an interesting one, the heart transiently slows down; if it is startling, the heart transiently speeds up.

Most of the other types of change reflect similar reactions. Thus, the startling signal increases the level of skin conductance and the size of the pupils of the eyes, causes respiration to pause or briefly become irregular, and increases tension in certain muscles. Closer inspection reveals many more changes: for example, in the size of blood vessels and consequently in blood circulation, in digestive processes, and in other bodily functions.

The majority of the physiological responses indicate that these changes are regulated by the autonomic nervous system. They prepare the individual to respond to new and potentially threatening situations. Senses become temporarily more responsive to signals from the outside world. Overall, the pattern is one of preparing the individual to take in information rapidly and efficiently and to give priority to those systems that might need to respond promptly to that information. The endocrine system will release hormonal agents that further facilitate the preparatory process. Once the novel signal has been fully assessed and classed as nonthreatening or of no continuing importance, the defenses are "stood down." As might be predicted from the behavioral evidence, repetitive signals lead to habituation of the physiological responses as novelty dissipates.

One of the crucial factors in this process is the evaluation of the signal and the assessment of its significance. Physiologically, this entails shifting the level of arousal and focusing available resources (attention) on the demands the signal makes.

Nonvisual sensory inputs travel to the brain via primary sensory pathways that converge on a central relay structure, the thalamus. Visual stimuli go straight from the retina to the thalamus via single-synapse (monosynaptic) connections. From the thalamus, signals are sent to relatively specific and localized receiving areas in the higher (cortical) levels of the brain. On their way from the sensory receptors to the thalamus, the signals pass an area of the brainstem and midbrain to which the sensory pathways have lateral connections. This area, called the reticular formation, is important in changing the overall level of arousal (when it is damaged, the individual may be unarousable). It has interconnections with the higher brain centres, and it projects pathways to the cerebral cortex. Unlike the primary sensory projections, which are limited to specific sensory modalities, many of the reticular formation cells respond to signals from any of the sensory modalities.

When this ascending reticular activating system is operating, the individual is alert, aroused, and attentive. Reduction of its activity results in somnolence or inattentiveness; extreme reduction (for example, by anesthesia or concussion) may lead to confusion or unconsciousness, even though the senses still pass messages to the brain over the direct pathways. The reticular system seems to account physiologically for the sustained, tonic shifts in an individual's level of involvement with the environment, including the control of sleep-wakefulness. One nonspecific route to the cerebral cortex via the thalamus, the diffuse thalamic projection system, appears concerned with moment-to-moment fluctuations in the focus of attention. Collectively, the primary sensory pathways, associated areas of the cerebral cortex, and the more diffuse projection systems cooperate in the process of registering the incoming sensory signal, evaluating its contents, and mobilizing brain resources in response to the demands made.

Electrical Changes

Inevitably this account is an oversimplification. In the human brain, other structures, particularly the hypothalamus, are involved in regulating states of sleep and wakefulness, while limbic structures, such as the hippocampus, take part in arousal when rewards, punishments, or other emotional factors are involved. Much of our understanding of these systems and their interactions comes from the study of animal brains and from observing what happens in the human brain when things go wrong. There is, however, another important source of information about what is taking place in the healthy human brain when it processes incoming information. This is through the associated electrical changes that take place within the brain; these changes can be recorded from electrodes attached to the scalp. Such recording, known as electroencephalography, involves amplification of the very weak neuroelectric signals, often followed by computer analysis and display. Electroencephalography enables observation of the minute patterns of voltage fluctuation that take place as the brain cells process information and relay messages.

Often the patterns of these intrinsic brain rhythms are modified by attention to external events or by thinking and other internal activity. The clearest effect of this kind is the inhibition (blocking) of so-called alpha rhythms, usually when the eyes are opened or when the person is thinking about a task, especially one involving visual imagery. Alpha rhythms, or waves, are more or less regular electric oscillations at a frequency of about 10 cycles per second (hertz), seen principally in the hindmost (visual) part of the brain. They tend to be most prominent when the mind is relatively blank and the eyes are closed. Absence of rhythmic features in the electroencephalogram (EEG) is generally regarded as evidence of arousal as long as there are signs of less rhythmic (asynchronous) activity. A total lack of electric discharge is a serious sign of brain morbidity.

Buried within the fluctuating pattern of voltage changes are more consistent patterns that accompany the registration and evaluation of each discrete piece of sensory information. These changes are referred to as evoked potentials or, more precisely, as event-related potentials (ERPs). They extend over the period of half a second or so immediately following the onset of the signal concerned. ERPs are composed of a relatively consistent pattern of positive and negative electrical peaks that vary systematically when the properties of the signal that elicits them change. The whole waveform is divided into components, which are roughly approximate to its peaks and troughs, though not exactly, because there is overlap between adjacent components. Each component has its own pattern of distribution over the brain and varies according to the properties of the eliciting signal.

This succession of ERP components constitutes a convenient and meaningful indicator of the various aspects of information processing being carried out on the signal. Moreover, because recording of such electrical potentials using electroencephalography offers no insult to the brain or serious interference with the performance of a wide range of tasks, many aspects of processing can be studied in healthy as well as disordered brains. Among the components of the ERP are several related to attention in its various forms. For example, about 100 milliseconds after a novel sound is heard, a prominent negative component is produced, which, if the sound becomes repetitive, diminishes (habituates). The closer together in time the sounds occur, the smaller the component becomes. Components with similar characteristics, but varying slightly in time, are found following novel visual and tactile stimuli. In situations where the individual must pay particular attention to a signal, these electrically negative components become larger. Conversely, if the individual is not paying attention—but is, perhaps, reading a book when the sound occurs—the component is smaller. This physiological sign of selective attention can be shown to be larger to all stimuli in an attended channel than in a nonattended channel. For example, if an individual who is hearing different voices speaking simultaneously in each ear is told to listen for a particular word spoken by one voice only, all words spoken by the "attended" voice elicit a larger 100-millisecond component than those spoken by the other voice. Only the designated word, however, elicits a later prominent, electrically positive component, occurring about 300 milliseconds after it is spoken. These responses appear to offer physiological support for the behavioral view that there is an early filtering for broad characteristics, followed by a later one of the more complex task-relevant properties.

Although such an explanation is plausible, the indications are that selection is not a simple serial process taking place at two discrete stages. When the task is relatively simple, looked-for properties can be distinguished substantially earlier than 100 milliseconds. There is also evidence of a more sustained, electrically negative change that can begin before 100 milliseconds and continue for perhaps several hundred milliseconds. This overlaps several components, supporting the idea that much processing must take place in parallel. Another component with attentional properties occurs just after 200 milliseconds when the incoming signal and current expectations are mismatched.

In addition to the transient electrical links that are associated with selective attention, there are longer electrical changes that occur during preparatory states when one anticipates making a rapid response to an expected signal. When the signal that requires the rapid response (the imperative stimulus) is preceded at a short but fixed interval by a warning or "get-ready" signal, the warning signal triggers in the cerebral cortex a slowly rising negative voltage, which reaches its maximum by the time the imperative signal arrives. (A race starter saying "on your marks, get set," may be a warning signal; the following pistol shot, an imperative stimulus.) When the response has been made, the voltage returns to its normal level. This slow potential change, contingent on the association of the two stimuli and the individual's intended response to the imperative second stimulus, has been termed the contingent negative variation (CNV). It appears as a correlate of focal attention, and it has been suggested that one of its functions may be to prime the appropriate areas of the cerebral cortex for the expected stimuli. The expectation must be focal—i.e., in the forefront of conscious awareness. If the preparation and response are well learned or the individual is distracted, the CNV is reduced. Conversely, if the individual concentrates on the task or is highly motivated to perform it well, the CNV increases in size. The CNV offers links with two-process theories of attention in that it seems to provide a physiological distinction between the more-demanding focal, flexible mode (large CNV) and the less-demanding automatic mode (small CNV). If the priming view of the CNV is correct, it may well indicate recruitment of the necessary resources to deal with the (imperative) task.

These descriptions of a physiological basis for attention constitute an important first step toward the integration of behavioral and neurophysiological evidence and theory. Evidence already links the cortical CNV with similar processes taking place in the brainstem reticular formation of humans and animals. Several theoretical models of selective attention based on ERP evidence have been advanced. They have in common an attempt to use systematic patterns of ERP change as an index of the cerebral mechanisms underlying cognitive processes.

In addition to electroencephalography, single-cell recording studies, carried out primarily on animals, have been performed since the 1950s. This method involves inserting thin wires (electrodes) into particular brain areas to measure changes in the electrical potential of a single neuron or nearby neurons.

All the electrical changes considered are in practice electrochemical. That is, complex chemical changes underlie the electrical correlates of attention. To take just one instance, the passage of electrical signals from nerve cell to nerve cell is dependent upon a range of neurotransmitter substances. Each of the neural systems already discussed is dependent upon the action of one—or sometimes combinations—of these neurochemicals. One transmitter substance, noradrenaline, is particularly prominent in alerting processes, along with its close relative dopamine. The total amount of another transmitter substance, acetylcholine, in the brain is found to be inversely related to the level of central nervous system activity. For example, if an individual is anesthetized, the electrical activity of the brain is reduced, and the content of acetylcholine is found to be increased.

Direct electrical stimulation of the brain, or the convulsant action of certain drugs, tends to decrease brain levels of acetylcholine. This transmitter seems to be involved in a wide range of behaviour and functions. Among those related to attentional and arousal states are stress, awakening from sleep, and exploring behaviour. Certain amino acids, such as gamma-aminobutyric acid (GABA) and glycine, appear to play an inhibitory role in the brain and nervous system. Hence they, too, may be involved in reciprocal inhibitory processes accompanying some attentional states.

Lack of Attention

Inattention and Distractibility

Limited processing capacity invariably implies a competition for attention. Humans spend their waking hours attending to one thing or another. The term *inattention* usually implies that, at a given moment, the thing being attended to is either not what it was intended to be or not what adaptively it ought to be. People will often report, "I was present, but I was not taking in what was happening." On many such occasions, internal preoccupations become the object of current attention at the expense of sensory information from the external world. Alternatively, an internal stimulus, such as a pain or hunger, might capture attention. It is also possible for irrelevant sensory information from the external world to distract individuals from their current focus of attention. When this happens, it could be because the intrusive stimulus has a high priority (such as the ringing of a telephone) or perhaps because the task engaged in is simply uninteresting.

Some individuals are more easily distracted than others, but for everyone distractibility varies with circumstances. When motivation and the level of involvement are high, an individual may totally disregard intense and persistent "outside" signals. Such inputs are either heavily filtered or dealt with only at an automatic level. Even when the competing stimulus is pain from an injury sustained, say, by an athlete in the early stages of a game, it is often scarcely noticed until the game ends and attention is no longer absorbed by the game. Nevertheless, because people's ability to focus attention varies, some report "difficulties of concentration" and may find themselves so easily distracted that they can scarcely read a book. There are indications that persons who are chronically anxious may be among those whose attention can readily be distracted by quite modest and irrelevant levels of stimuli. This feature has been noted in a number of psychiatric disorders, such as attention-deficit/hyperactivity disorder, and it has been suggested that one cause of these disorders may be a flaw in the mechanisms of attention.

Lapses of Attention

It has been established that, to conserve limited resources, whole sequences and hierarchies of actions can apparently be elicited without focal attention when they have been well learned or executed many times. There is reason, however, to suppose that at least a minimum level of focal attention may be necessary, if only to ensure that the correct sequence or hierarchy is initiated. Failures of this minimal monitoring can result in the phenomena usually classed as lapses of attention. For example, most people have experienced trivial behavioral slips such as finding themselves taking a regularly used route when they had meant to go in a different direction; attempting to switch off a light when leaving a room in daylight; or, perhaps, pouring tea into the sugar bowl instead of a cup. In each case a well-established action has been inappropriately triggered by partial cues and has slipped past the attentional monitor. Such errors typically occur because a person was "thinking about something else" or was not paying attention to the activity at hand. In many circumstances it is advantageous that automatic sequences of behaviour should be executed with only very limited reference to conscious attention. Musicians, typists, and other skilled persons are well aware that too much attention devoted to the execution of a well-learned skill can disrupt performance. Nevertheless, people cannot dispense entirely with some degree of attentional monitoring if they are to avoid errors. Another kind of lapse entails being unable to remember whether one has performed a particular action as part of a highly automated sequence: "Did you or did we not put the sugar in my tea?" Yet another occurs when an automatic action triggers another unwanted or inappropriate action: "you meant to take off only my shoes but took off my socks as well." Most lapses have in common that they occur when attention has been claimed by an internal preoccupation or external distraction.

Types of Attention

Attention is your brain function that allocates cognitive processing resources to focus on information or stimuli. It deals with how you stimuli. It deals with how you mentally process specific information present in your environment that you are experiencing through your five senses.

Your attention span is your ability to keep your mind focused on something through careful observing or listening. It can be just momentarily such as turning around after hearing a loud noise, or it may be for a sustained period of time such as playing a video game.

Attention is often the beginning to other cognitive functions. You first must pay attention to something before you can process it for meaning and understanding.

There are several types of attention that you use during the course of your daily activities. The type of attention you use will vary depending on your need and circumstances.

- Does the task need your undivided attention?
- Do you need to concentrate on one thing while ignoring other things that may be going on at the same time?
- Do you have to do two activities at the same time?
- Depending on your needs and circumstances you may employ one of the following four types of attention.
- Sustained attention is the ability to focus on one specific task for a continuous amount of time without being distracted.
- Selective attention is the ability to select from many factors or stimuli and to focus on only the one that you want while filtering out other distractions.
- Alternating attention is the ability to switch your focus back and forth between tasks that require different cognitive demands.
- Divided attention is the ability to process two or more responses or react to two or more different demands simultaneously. Divided attention is often referred to as multi-tasking.

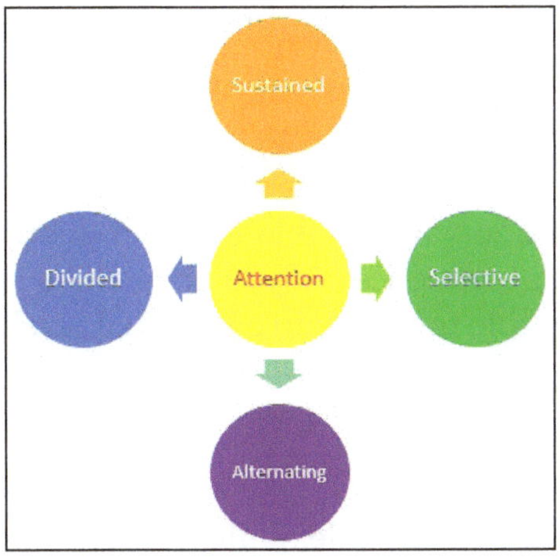

The first two types (sustained and selective) are needed when you have to focus on one thing at a time.

- Sustained attention is used when you need to focus on one specific task or activity for a long period of time (playing a video game).
- Selective attention is used to focus on one activity in the midst of many activities (listening to a friend at a loud party).

The other two types of attention (alternating and divided) are needed when a person has to focus on multiple things at once.

- Alternating attention is used to alternate back and forth between tasks or activities (reading a recipe and preparing a meal).
- Divided attention is used to complete two or more tasks simultaneously (talking on the phone while surfing the web).

Sustained Attention

Sustained attention is the ability to focus on one specific task for a continuous amount of time without being distracted. Sustained attention is probably what you think of when you hear the words "attention", "focus", "concentration", or "vigilance." You use sustained attention when you continuously maintain focus on one task or concentrate on an activity for a prolonged period of time without getting distracted. Examples of sustained attention may include listening to lecture, reading a book, playing a video, or fixing a car.

It can be challenging to maintain this type of attention for a significant amount of time without becoming distracted. Therefore, your level of sustained attention will often vary. You may be intensely focused one minute and then your attention may begin to lapse. However, a key aspect of sustained attention is the ability to re-focus on the task after a distraction arises.

Selective Attention

Selective attention is the ability to select from the various factors or stimuli that are present and to focus on only the one that you want. Every day, you are constantly exposed to a number of environmental factors or stimuli, but your brain naturally responds by selecting a particular aspect or factor to focus on. Selective attention basically allows you to be able to "select" what you want to pay attention to. You may need to use selective attention when attending a loud party and you are focusing on one person's voice, or if you are trying to study in a noisy room.

When employing selective attention you are able to avoid distractions from both external (e.g. noise) and internal (e.g. thoughts) influences. If you are good at selective attention, you are good at ignoring distractions. You are able to maintain a specified level of performance in the presence of distracting stimuli.

Alternating Attention

Alternating attention is the ability of mental flexibility that allows you to shift your focus of attention and move between tasks having different cognitive requirements. It is alternating your attention back and forth between two different tasks that require the use of different areas your brain.

You probably use alternating attention almost all the time. You constantly need to make sudden changes on your activities or actions which requires your attention to shift. You may use alternating attention when reading a recipe (learning) and then performing the tasks of recipe (doing). It could also be alternating between unrelated tasks such as cooking while helping your child with her homework.

Divided Attention

Divided attention is the ability to process two or more responses or react to two or more different demands simultaneously. It is often referred to as multi-tasking. Basically, dividing your attention between two or more tasks.

Examples of divided attention include checking email while listening in a meeting, talking with friends while making dinner, or talking on the phone while getting dressed.

Unlike alternating attention, when you are using divided attention, you do not change from one task to another completely different task. Instead, you attempt to perform them at the same time. So you are really splitting your attention, instead of alternating it. Therefore, you are only really focusing part of attention on each task.

Although divided attention is thought of as the ability to focus on two or more stimuli or activities at the same time, it is humanly impossible to concentrate on two different tasks simultaneously. Your brain can only process one task at a time. So you are really not "focused" on one task at a time, you are really continuously alternating your attention between tasks. That is why it is so difficult and dangerous to text and drive or talk and drive.

You are able to use divided attention successfully because of muscle memory and/or habit. It allows you to perform two or more tasks seemingly simultaneously such as reading music and playing an instrument, talking to a person while typing, or driving your car while listening to the radio. However, you are really not focusing on hand positions when playing the instrument or concentrating on the individual acts of driving. You are able to do the task without conscious effort or actually paying attention.

Object Recognition

Recognition-by-components is a theory of object recognition in humans that accounts for the successful identification of objects despite changes in the size or orientation of the image. Moreover, RBC explains how moderately occluded or degraded images, as well as novel examples of objects, are successfully recognized by the visual system.

The major contribution of RBC is the proposal that the visual system extracts geons (or geometricions) and uses them to identify objects. Click Here to view Geons Geons are simple volumes such as cubes, spheres, cylinders, and wedges. RBC proposes that representations of objects are stored in the brain as structural descriptions. A structural description contains a specification of the object's geons and their interrelations (e.g., the cube is above the cylinder). A perceived object is analyzed by the visual system, which parses the object into its constituent geons. Then, the interrelations are determined, which include aspects such as relative location and size (e.g., the lamp shade is left-of, below, and larger-than the fixture). The geons and interrelations of the perceived object are matched against stored structural descriptions. If a reasonably good match is found, then successful object recognition will occur. The RBC view of object recognition is analogous to speech perception. A small set of phonemes are combined using organizational rules to produce millions of different words. In RBC, the geons serve as phonemes and the spatial interrelations serve as organizational rules. Biederman (1987) estimated that as few as 36 geons could produce millions of unique objects.

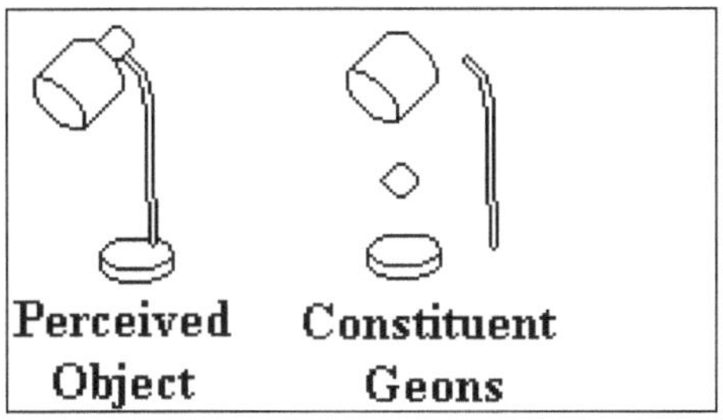

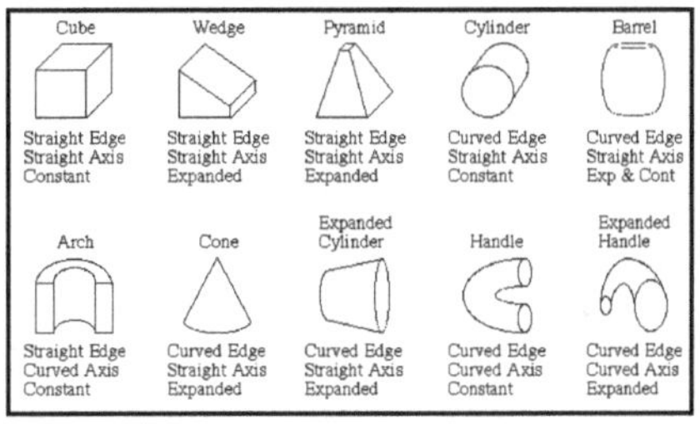

RBC was developed to account for primal recognition of objects; primal recognition is fast-acting and does not utilize higher-level cognitive processes. Higher-level processing may involve the use of shading, texture, or color in finer discriminations of objects. Additional top-down processing may also occur when environmental cues such as context are used to identify particularly difficult instances of objects (e.g., a pencil would be easier to recognize if it was partially occluded by a stack of papers on a desk than a pile of leaves in the yard).

Theoretical Predictions

There are three major facts of object recognition in humans that are predicted correctly by RBC, but are at odds with Particulate feature theory.

1. The correct spatial organization is essential for picture recognition in humans: Because RBC is based on the assumption that a small set of geons are the basis for millions of objects, organizational rules must play a large role in object recognition. It is possible to have different objects made up of the same parts, so discriminating between those objects necessarily involves a sensitivity to

spatial interrelations. This prediction of RBC stands in greatest contrast to Particulate feature theory, because PFT predicts no role for spatial organization.

If pigeons recognize objects using local features alone, then variations in the arrangement of those features would have little or no impact on the accuracy of recognition. Thus, unlike humans, the pigeon would be incapable of discriminating between the cup and the pail. The cup and the pail are comprised of two components: a cylinder and a curved handle. However, the orientation and position of the handle relative to the cylinder differs between the objects. In order to discriminate the cup from the pail, one must be able to recognize the differences in the organization of the components, a more global property of objects. Several experiments by Kirkpatrick-Steger, Wasserman, and Biederman have demonstrated that pigeons can discriminate changes in spatial organization, and that spatial organization plays a key role in picture recognition in pigeons.

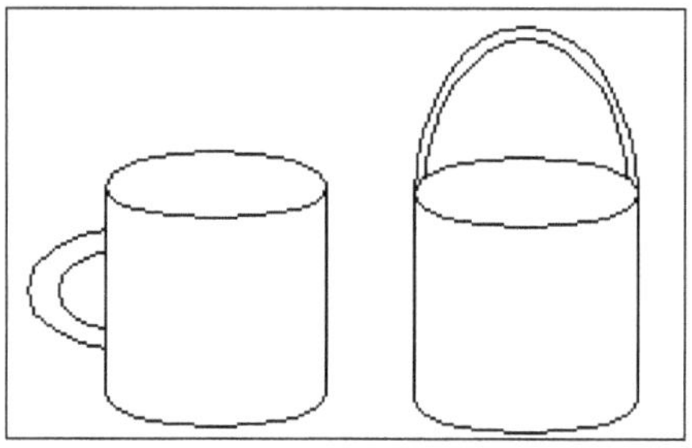

2. If a subset of only two or three geons are available and they are in the correct spatial organization, then successful object recognition will occur: RBC predicts this result because object recognition does not require an exact match between the perceived object and stored structural description. In contrast, PFT predicts a detrimental effect of deletion of parts, because the parts are the only means available for recognizing the object.

Biederman, Ju, and Clapper (1985) presented objects lacking some of their components. Human participants correctly identified objects when only 2 or 3 components were available, but not when only 1 component was presented. It is easy to identify the sailboat when only one of the sails is missing. One could also imagine that the hull and mast alone might produce moderately accurate recognition, but it is unlikely that the sailboat would be identified from the mast alone. PFT would predict that the loss of any components leads to a detriment in recognition accuracy. Kirkpatrick-Steger, Wasserman, and Biederman (1998) discovered that pigeons could recognize objects at high levels of accuracy when three of four components were available, but not when only one component was present. They also discovered that some components were recognized better than others, a result that is also consistent with research using human participants.

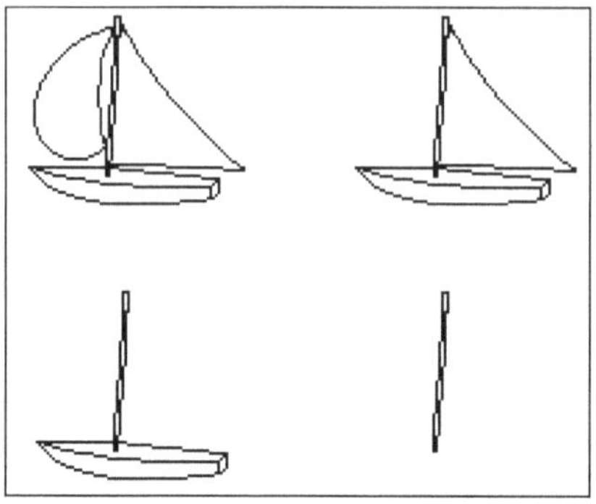

3. Object recognition in humans is largely invariant with regard to changes in the size, position, and viewpoint of the object: The visual information falling on the retina when a particular object is viewed varies drastically from occasion to occasion, depending on the distance from the image (which affects the size of the image on the retina), the vantage point from which the object is viewed, and the location of the object relative to the viewer (which affects the part of the retina that is stimulated). One of the most fundamental and essential properties of the visual system is the ability to recognize a particular object, despite great variations in the images that impose on the retina. RBC accounts for all three types of invariances. Invariances in viewpoint (rotational invariance) provide the greatest challenge to PFT.

a. Rotational Invariance: People are capable of recognizing objects from many different vantage points, even views that have never before been seen. Notice that some views of the airplane involve the display of different parts than others. If pigeons recognized simple features alone, then rotational invariance would not occur. Therefore, a model of object recognition, such as PFT, that relies on local features alone would predict that rotational invariance would not be observed. A series of experiments by Wasserman et al. demonstrated substantial, but not complete, rotational invariance in pigeons.

b. Invariance: Objects can be recognized despite variations in actual or apparent size. Because the size of an object, such as the sailboat, does not change the structural description of an object (the geons and their spatial organization), RBC predicts that recognition should be size invariant. Kirkpatrick-Steger and Wasserman (unpublished data) demonstrated generalization of responding to sizes on either size (smaller or large) of a training size in pigeons, but there was a generalization decrement at extreme sizes. Successful recognition of objects by pigeons, despite changes in size, further suggests that the mechanism of object recognition in the pigeon is similar to the mechanism of object recognition in humans. However, the finding does not discriminate between RBC and PFT, because PFT also predicts size invariance.

c. Translational Invariance: When an object is moved to a new position in the environment, a different portion of the retina is stimulated. Nonetheless, modest changes in position do not disrupt recognition accuracy in human subjects; that is, object recognition is translationally invariant. Translational invariance indicates that people do not learn to recognize an object on the basis of the absolute position in the environment or its position relative to other objects (e.g., the desk is right of the bookshelf). Kirkpatrick-Steger, Wasserman, & Biederman (1998) discovered that pigeons performed at high levels of accuracy when an object, such as the Watering Can, was displayed in a new position on the viewing screen. Thus, object recognition in both both pigeons and humans appears to be translationally invariant. However, successful translational invariance does not discriminate between RBC and PFT because the object features (and their organization) are unchanged.

Pattern Recognition

Pattern recognition is a skill of how people identify the objects in their environment which is what we do all the time in our daily life. For example, you can recognize your teachers, friends, and also which items can eat or cannot eat. Everything in the world has its own pattern. Our superiority over computers as pattern recognizers has the practical advantage that pattern recognition can serve as a test of whether a person or a computer program is trying to gain access to the Internet.

There are many kinds of the description of patterns stored in our long term memory (LTM), thus, when we observe or listen to a pattern, our mind will automatically form a description of it and compare it against the descriptions which stored in LTM. If the description closely matches with one of the descriptions in our LTM, then we are able to recognize the pattern. There are three description theories used to describe patterns which are template theories, feature theories, and structural theories.

Template theories propose that patterns are really not "described" at all. Rather, templates are holistic, or unanalyzed, entities that we compare with other patterns by measuring how much two patterns overlap. Shortly it's an analyzed pattern that is matched against alternative patterns by using the degrees of overlap as a measure of similarity.

There has some limitation with using the degree of overlap as a measure of pattern recognition. First, the comparison requires that the template be in the same position and the same orientation and be the same size as the pattern you are trying to identify. Second, is the great variability of patterns which would be difficult to construct a template for each letter that would produce a good match with all the different varieties of the letter. Third, a template theory doesn't reveal how two patterns differ. Lastly, the template theory does not allow for alternative descriptions of a pattern.

Feature theory used to describe a pattern by listing out its attributes. For example, we might describe a friend as having long blond hair, a short nose and bushy eyebrows or else can say. Gibson (1969) proposed some criteria as a basis for selecting a set of features for uppercase letters. First, the features should be critical ones, present in some members of the set but not in others, so as to provide a contrast. Second, the identity of the features should remain unchanged under changes in brightness, size and perspective. Third, the features should yield a unique pattern for each letter and the last is the number of proposed features should be reasonably small. A set of features is usually evaluated by determining how well it can predict perceptual confusions as confusable items should have many features in common.

Distinctive feature is a feature present in one pattern but absent in another aiding one's discrimination of the two patterns. For example, in child learning, when first confronted with the letters E and F, the child might not be aware of how the two differ. Learning to make this discrimination depends on discovering that a low horizontal line is present in the letter E but not in the letter F. The low horizontal line is a distinctive feature for distinguishing between an E and an F; that is, it enables us to distinguish one pattern from other. Feature theories can also be used to represent faces. If you describe a woman's face you would likely refer to features such as her nose, eyes and mouth.

Structural theory describes how features join together to create a structure which represents a guiding principle of Gestalt psychology. It emphasizes the relations among the features. Geon refers as different three dimensional shapes that combine to form three dimensional patterns. It's a limited number of simple geometric shapes or geon's for us to analyze patterns. For example, mug versus bucket.

Biederman's Component Model describe three-dimensional objects would be fairly complicated if we had to describe each of the lines and curves in the object. Like the features of letters, these components can be combined in many different ways to produce a variety of objects. For example, the mug and the pail contain the same two components in a different arrangement. Both the components and the relations among the components determine the perceived similarity of patterns. For example, the briefcase and drawer are similar because they share the same components. However, the briefcase is more similar to the pail than to the cup because of the relation between components-the handle is on top for both the briefcase and pail.

Information-Processing Stages

Sperling is responsible for the initial construction of an information-processing model of performance on a visual recognition task. Sperling was interested in measuring the number of letters that could be recognized during a brief exposure. In other words, subjects might have recognized most of the letters in the display but then forgot some before they could report what they had seen. Sperling therefore changed his procedure from a whole-report procedure to report all the letters to a partial-report procedure, which report only some of the letters.

Sperling's Model

Sperling's study of sensory memory. After the subjects had fixated on the cross, the letters were flashed on the screen just long enough to create a visual afterimage. High, medium and low tones signaled which row of letters to report. In 1963, Sperling proposed an information-processing model of performance on his visual report task. The model consisted of a visual information store, scanning, rehearsal and an auditory information store. Visual information store (VIS), a sensory store that maintains visual information for approximately one-quarter of a second. Rehearsal is repeating verbal information to keep it active in short-term memory or to transfer it into long-term memory. In Sperling's model auditory information store maintains verbal information in short-term memory through rehearsal.

Rumelhart's Model

Rumelhart proposed a detailed mathematical model of performance on a wide range of information-processing tasks, including the whole-report and partial-report procedures studied by Sperling. His model built on importance of the visual information store and the use of a parallel scan to recognize patters. More time the observer has, the more features the observer can recognize. The rate of feature recognition in Rumelhart's model is influenced by both the clarity of the information and the number of items in the display. As the number of items increases, the amount of attention that can be focused on each item declines, and this slows the rate of recognizing that particular item. Detection paradigm was designed by Estes and Taylor.

Word superiority effect is a finding that accuracy in recognizing a letter is higher when the letter is in a word than when it appears alone or is in a non-word.

Word Recognition

One of the great challenges for psychologists interested in word recognition has been to explain the reasons for the word superiority effect. Interaction activation model was proposed by McClelland and Rumelhart. It's a theory that process that both feature knowledge and word knowledge combine to provide information about the identity of letters in a word. Exeltatory connection is a positive association between concepts that belong together, as when a vertical line provides support for the possibility that a letter is a K and inhibitory connection is a negative association between concepts that do not belong together, as when the presence of a vertical line provides negative evidence that a letter is a C.

Neural Network Models

The interactive activation model was the first step for McClelland and Rumelhart in their development of neural network models of cognition. It's a theory in which concepts (nodes) are linked to other concepts through excitatory and inhibitory connections to approximate the behavior of neural networks in the brain. Nodes are the format for representing concepts in a semantic network. Activation rule is determines how inhibitory and excitatory connections combine to determine the total activation of a concept.

Visual Attention

Attention serves at least four different purposes in the visual system, including data reduction / stimulus selection, stimulus enhancement, feature binding, and recognition.

Data reduction / stimulus selection: Systems controlling perception cognition and action all exhibit capacity limitations. The brain is unable to simultaneously process everything in the continuous influx of information from the environment. One of the most critical roles for visual attention is to filter visual information. Research shows that visual attention can perform this function by actively suppressing irrelevant stimuli or by selecting potentially relevant stimuli. In either case, attention makes it possible to use limited resources for the processing of some stimuli rather than others.

Stimulus enhancement: The inputs to the visual system are noisy and ambiguous and attention can act to enhance the signal or the amplitude of neuronal activity in the sensory pathways at the initial stages of visual processing. It can enhance or alter the processing of the attended stimulus, allowing for ambiguity resolution and noise reduction. As we will discuss later, stimulus enhancement can be a consequence of allocating attention to a stimulus directly (e.g. space and object-based attention) or of directing attention to some attribute of the stimulus (e.g. color, "feature-based attention"). This allows the observer to be an active seeker and processor of information. Behaviorally, stimulus enhancement is observable in faster reaction times and higher accuracy. Physiologically, we see enhanced activity of neuronal populations that process the stimulus.

Binding: Early stages of visual processing appear to involve decomposition of the signal into separable dimensions like color and orientation, with these dimensions being processed to some degree in different neural areas. This functional decomposition has raised the question of how we integrate this compartmentalized informSation into the perception of a unified world. This problem, or set of problems, is referred to as the "binding problem". The role of visual attention in resolving the binding problem can be described in at least two ways: Attention may permit the generation of stimulus representation (e.g. arbitrary conjunctions of features) that are not "hard-wired" in the visual system and Attention may resolve ambiguities that arise when multiple stimuli fall into a single receptive field, perhaps by dynamically altering the selectivity or spatial extent of the receptive field of a neuron.

Recognition: Closely related to its role in binding is attention's role in object recognition. We define visual recognition here as the ability to identify the perceived stimulus not merely to be aware of the presence of a stimulus. Since object recognition mechanisms cannot simultaneously handle every object in the field, attention serves to deliver digestible subsets of the input for recognition. As a consequence of these acts of attention, representations of attended objects differ from those of unattended objects.

The functions described above are predominantly concerned with spatial visual processing, but attention plays similar roles in temporal processing (e.g. avoiding confusions between stimuli that appear in rapid succession) and in the management of different visual tasks (e.g. allowing the system to switching between searching for a target at one moment and perhaps tracking several objects at the next moment).

How does Attention Select Stimuli Across Space and Time?

As noted, an important function of visual attention is to avoid information overload by attempting to select the most relevant information. For example, object recognition processes can only operate on a small number of objects (perhaps 1-4) at any one time. Thus, you cannot read two streams of prose at the same time, even if the print is big enough to avoid acuity limits. Selective attention mechanisms serve to deliver a limited subset of the visual input to subsequent, limited-capacity processes.

Visual selective attention is a spatio-temporal phenomenon. You attend to one stimulus and then you attend to something else. Here we will discuss the spatial aspects of selection, while the next topic will discuss the temporal aspects.

Spatial Selective Attention

Broadly speaking, the allocation of attention is controlled by "bottom-up" stimulus-based factors and "top-down" user-driven factors. The interplay of these factors has been studied extensively using visual search tasks in which observers look for a target item among some number of distractor items. When the display is visible until response, reaction time (RT) is the measure of greatest interest. If the display is flashed briefly, accuracy is the critical measure. In either case, the slope function relating the response measure to set size is the index of search efficiency. When RT is independent of set size (e.g., slope ≈0) we term the search "efficient", and infer that whatever property distinguishes targets from distractors can be processed in parallel across the visual field. Steep slopes (e.g., > 20 ms/item) suggest "inefficient" search, and we infer that processing of the target property is subject to an attentional bottleneck. There is a longstanding debate as to whether items are selected one at a time (serial processing) or if all items are processed simultaneously (parallel processing). The answer need not be exclusively one or the other. For example, items could be selected one after another, in series, while; at any one moment, several of those items might be undergoing processing in parallel.

Bottom-up salience can be thought of as the tendency of a stimulus to attract attention without regard to the observer's desires. A limited set of stimulus attributes computed in parallel across the visual field can drive bottom-up selection. These "preattentive" attributes include obvious early vision properties such as color and motion, as well as more complex attributes (e.g., various cues to depth). For a review, see Wolfe and Horowitz. The bottom-up salience of an item will be determined by its difference from neighboring items and by the heterogeneity of other items in the field. Thus, a vertical line will be very salient in a homogeneous field of lines tilted 45° to the left. It will be less salient if presented in a mix of horizontal, 45° left and 45° right lines and still less salient if 30° left and right lines are added to the mix. Many computational models of search embody these rules in calculating a "salience map".

The observer can also exert top-down control over selection. Thus, it is possible to select the green items in a heterogeneous array of colors that give no bottom-up advantage to green. In models such as Guided Search, the deployment of attention is determined by some weighted combination of bottom-up and top-down signals. "Attentional capture" is a popular paradigm for studying the interaction of the observer's top-down desires with attention-grabbing demands of salient stimuli. Typically, observers will be asked to do a task in the presence of an irrelevant but salient distractor. Under some circumstances, this singleton will attract attention against the goals of the observer. Under other circumstances, top-down control is adequate to block the influence of the singleton. A full assessment of when a stimulus will and will not capture attention is beyond our scope but it is hard to do better than Sully who wrote: "One would like to know the fortunate (or unfortunate) man who could receive a box on the ear and not attend to it".

Top-down and bottom-up guidance operate essentially automatically. Once you establish your goals (e.g. look for things that are red and vertical), your "search engine" does the rest, at a rate of approximately 25 to 50 ms per item. It is also possible to select items volitionally (e.g. moving attention from item to item around a circle of letters). This is much slower with rates on the order of 3-5 Hz. This is similar to the speed of response to an "endogenous" attention cue (e.g. the word "left" telling the observer to move attention to the left) and to the rate of saccadic eye movements. The faster speed of deployment under control of top-down and bottomup guidance is on the same scale as the speed of response to exogenous attentional cues (e.g. a flashed onset cue at a location to the left).

When we shift attention (e.g., during a difficult search), what are the units of selection? Visual selective attention is often described in terms of a "spotlight" metaphor. This metaphor captures important spatial properties of attention. The intensity of attention falls off in a gradient from the focal point. Attention can be tightly focused on a small area, leading to large performance benefits, or distributed over a large area, with smaller performance benefits (zoom lens" model, 17, 18). The spotlight metaphor presumes that attention selects things by selecting locations. While this approach can explain a body of data, there is also evidence that attention selects objects in a manner more like the "fill" operation in a graphics program than like a flashlight in a dark room. In a classic demonstration, cueing one end of a rectangle led to better performance at the other end of that rectangle (within-object), compared to an equally distant location that was in a separate rectangle. As another example, we can select one of two perceptual objects, which share the same location. Moreover, we can attend to objects which change location constantly during a trial (multiple object tracking, 21). This notion of object selection suggests that the visual scene is initially parsed into some version of objects and it is to these entities that attention is directed. Note that the nature of this parsing may be complex, since it is be possible to attend to "objects" (e.g. the nose) that are parts of other "objects" (e.g. the face).

As with most dichotomies in the study of attention, it is probably unwise to argue that attention is either purely object-based or space based. Compromise positions that acknowledge both aspects may be closer to the truth. For example, the "grouped array hypothesis" argues that an object can be conceived of as a structured array of locations. This approach maintains the idea that location is fundamental to selection, while acknowledging that the structure of the visual world influences what is selected. Alternatively, He and Nakayama's proposal that attention is directed to surfaces also captures the roles of both space and object in selection. What ever the units of selection may be, the resolution of those units, the smallest object or area that can be attended, declines away from the fovea and is lower than the resolution of the visual system.

Can selective attention be divided among two or more objects or locations at the same time? The long-standing controversy over unity of selection is discussed in the topic on Divided Attention.

Attention can be allocated over both time and across space. Several studies have shown that observers can use cues that indicate the time at which a target is likely to appear, and these cues generate both facilitation and inhibition. The effect of spatial and temporal cues appears to be approximately additive.

An important problem in temporal attention is how to segment rapid streams of events. This problem has been extensively studied using the Rapid Serial Visual Presentation paradigm (RSVP). Imagine flipping through the channels on a television, looking for a specific program without knowing what channel it is on. In RSVP, the "channels", typically streams of letters, objects or scenes are presented at fixation and flash by at a rapid rate (10 Hz, 100 msec per frame is typical), and the observer must monitor the stream for one or more specific targets (e.g. the identity of two letters among a series of numbers). RSVP studies have yielded two important phenomena, which tell us about how the visual system segments events in time: the attentional blink and repetition blindness.

Attentional Blink

When observers search for two targets in an RSVP sequence of distractors, their capacity to detect the second target presented within 500 ms after the first target is severely impaired, a phenomenon known as "attentional blink". T2 can be accurately reported if T1 is not present or not part of the task. However, even when T2 is not reportable by the observer, evidence suggests that it receives considerable processing. An unreported T2 can semantically prime a third target. Similarly, a semantically related T1 can increase the chances that T2 will be correctly reported.

Recent evidence suggests that AB is a consequence of the cognitive strategy by which the visual system ensures the episodic distinction between separately presented targets. In many cases, AB does not occur if the second target T2 immediately follows the first target T1 (phenomenon known as "Lag-1 sparing"). More tellingly, AB is not observed if several target items are presented in direct succession. In such cases, two or more stimuli seem to be aggregated into a single event. Therefore, it seems that AB depends on the presence of a distractor or a mask in the position immediately after T1. On this view, the appearance of T1 triggers the opening of an "attentional gate", which can remain open if multiple targets are presented. Once a distractor appears, however, the system attempts to shut the gate, resulting in the inadvertent inhibition of an inopportunely timed T2.

Repetition Blindness

The problem of distinguishing between repetitions of the same stimulus is related to the problem of segregating events in time. When two identical items are presented in the same RSVP stream, observers often have difficulty reporting the second occurrence, a phenomenon termed repetition blindness (RB). As with AB, the lag between the two repeated items is critical for the occurrence of RB. The magnitude of the effect typically decreases as the lag increases. It has been hypothesized, and supported by a variety of studies, that RB occurs when items are recognized as "types" (e.g. the word "CAT") but not individuated as instances, or tokens, of the same type (e.g. this instance of the word CAT). Rather than a literal 'blindness' RB may represent the assimilation of T1 and T2 into a single instance of the item.

Although AB and RB seem to be phenomenologically similar, they are distinguishable experimentally. For example, when targets and distractors become more distinct, the AB effect decreases, but this is not the case with the RB effect. Thus, AB and RB seem to reflect distinct processes in temporal attention.

Role of Inhibition in Attentional Processes

While attention is often thought of as enhancing processing of the attended stimulus, inhibition of unattended stimuli is also an important mechanism. Inhibitory mechanisms can serve to reduce ambiguity, protect capacity-limited mechanisms from interference, and prioritize selection for new objects. Here we provide four illustrations of the role of inhibition in attention: negative priming, inhibition of return, visual marking, and inhibition of distractor locations.

Negative Priming

Imagine two overlapping stimuli, one red, one green. You are asked to respond to the shape of the green stimulus on each trial. What happens to the red stimulus? Clearly, it falls on the retina and makes some impression on the visual system. Its fate can be assessed by presenting the red stimulus from this trial as the green, to-be-responded-to stimulus on the next trial. As many studies have documented, you will be slower to respond to that previously ignored shape. This phenomenon, termed "negative priming" is hypothesized to reflect the active suppression of the representations of ignored items (e.g. red distractors in the prime display). Negative priming has been observed for time scales from a few seconds up to as much as a month. The ignored prime and subsequent probe stimuli can be quite different from each other (e.g. a picture prime and a word probe). However, it is possible to account for negative priming effects without assuming that the prime item is actively inhibited. One alternative is response competition at retrieval. When an old item that was to be ignored is now the current target for response, the old "ignore" signal interferes with the present "respond" signal.

Inhibition of Return

Previously ignored stimuli are not the only representations that might be purposefully inhibited. The phenomenon of "inhibition of return" (IOR) shows that actively attended items are also suppressed once attention is deployed elsewhere. It is proposed that this serves to bias the attentional system toward novelty and away from perseveration on salient but irrelevant stimuli, thereby facilitating attentional "foraging". In a classic IOR paradigm, attention would be attracted to an object or location and then redirected elsewhere. If observers are then asked to respond to the initially attended item, they are slower than if the item had never been attended. Whereas negative priming can inhibit specific semantic categories, objects or actions, IOR is a phenomenon of spatial selection. As with other aspects of selective attention described above, IOR seems to operate in both space-based and object-based coordinate systems. IOR can apply to the last few attended items over a time course of seconds. Note that IOR represents a tendency not to return, not an absolute prohibition on return.

Visual Marking

While negative priming and IOR are typically revealed by impairments in the observer's performance, "visual marking" is an inhibitory process that is typically revealed by an improvement in the observer's performance. In a typical marking study, the items in a visual search array would be presented in two steps: a "preview" of half of the distractors followed by the presentation of the entire display. Typically, observers search the full display as though the previewed items were not present. For example, consider a search for a red vertical among green vertical and red horizontal distractors. Typically, this "conjunction" search is of intermediate efficiency. However, if all the green verticals are previewed, the subsequent search becomes, in effect, a highly efficient search for a red vertical among red horizontals. This effect seems to involve the inhibition of the previewed items and not merely the prioritization of new, onset stimuli. Marking is not simply a memory for old locations; if the previewed distractors change shape when the full display appears, they will compete with the new distractor stimuli. Marking is also adaptive, in that it is not observed when the preview items might contain the target.

Inhibition of Distractor Locations

Spatially focused attention ("spotlight of attention") has a specific structure, advocate some recent studies, rather then just being a spatial gradient of enhanced activity that falls off monotonically with growing distance. Behavioral and neurophysiologic evidence suggest the focus of spatial attention has not only an excitatory center but also a narrow inhibitory surround region. Due to this center surround architecture when attention is deployed to certain area of space enhancing processing of selected items there is inhibition or suppression of nearby surround distractor locations. Studies show that probe detection at distractor locations close to a search target is slowed and neuronal response reduced relative to distractor locations further away from the target.

What Happens when Observers are asked to Divide Attention across Several Stimuli?

Thus far, we have treated visual attention as a process operating on one location and object at one time. Here we consider the possibility that attention can be split between multiple stimuli or tasks, as mentioned earlier. To some extent, this is a definitional issue. Consider a search for a red letter "T" among red and black "L's". There will be top-down guidance to all red items. This is sometimes considered to be evidence for the deployment of attention to all red locations. However, this guidance to red should be distinguished from the selective attention that allows an observer to recognize one of the red items as a "T" or an "L". While most would agree that attention can be guided to all red items, there is less agreement about whether attention can be divided in a manner that permits recognition processes to work simultaneously on two or more, spatially separated letters or other objects.

Empirical data, as well as everyday experiences, tell us that our ability to perform concurrent tasks or process multiple inputs is limited. However, not all combinations of tasks are equally difficult and not all interference happens at the same processing stage. Here we can only skim the surface of the large literature on divided attention. One can ask about dividing attention within a task. Is it possible to "attend" to more than one item at a time in a visual search task or an attentional cuing task? If attention is directed to two items, is it divided or merely stretched, with some attentional resources going to the space between the intended objects of attention?

Alternatively, one can also ask about dividing attention between two tasks. Is it possible to track the motion of objects while searching for a target? Is it possible to attend to some letters and still detect the presence of an animal in a superimposed scene? Where are the bottlenecks in processing and when can different tasks coexist in the nervous system.

Dual-Tasks

In dual-task paradigms, observers perform two tasks on the same trial. Interference between the tasks has been shown to be influenced by task similarity, practice, and the difficulty of the individual tasks. Thus, two dissimilar, highly practiced and simple tasks can be performed well together, while two similar, novel and complex tasks cannot. Three different theoretical accounts have been put forth to explain dual task interference: the task-general resource view (central capacity sharing, 46); the task-specific resource view; and the central bottleneck view. The task-general resource view postulates that processing for different tasks proceeds in parallel with the central resource flexibly divided among different tasks in a graded fashion. On the other hand the task-specific resource view argues that there are task-specific resources and the occurrence of interference depends on similarity or confusability of mental representations involved in the tasks. Unlike either of the former views the central or single-channel bottleneck view proposes that certain critical mental operations must be carried out sequentially (e.g. decisions to respond) resulting in interference when two tasks require those operations at the same time.

As ever, the experimental data show that these accounts are not mutually exclusive. Thus, interference between tasks depends on the nature of the tasks, and is greatest when the tasks overlap in their processing demands as would be predicted by a crosstalk account. However concurrent tasks can interfere with each other even if there is no detectable overlap in the tasks' processing demands. Two factors are important here. The tasks themselves might require bigger amounts of processing capacity as predicted by central capacity accounts. Secondly, the two tasks might each require a complex series of responses thus placing heavy demands on the response selector at the executive level of processing.

Attention to Multiple Spatial Locations

While early investigations suggested that the spatial focus of attention must be unitary (Posner, 1980), more recent studies suggest that attention can be divided among at least two spatial locations, without also boosting intervening locations It is important that the observer have an incentive to split the attentional focus. To produce this split, it is useful if the cues for attention are highly predictive and if there is distracting information in the space between the loci worth inhibiting.

Evidence for some variety of simultaneous attention to multiple objects has been available for over 20 years in the form of studies of multiple object tracking studies. In the typical MOT experiment, the observer is presented with an array of identical items. Some of the items are designated as targets and the observer's task is to track these targets for seconds or minutes as the items move independently. Most observers can track 4-5 targets, suggesting that one can attend to multiple objects simultaneously. An important caveat here is that the processes used in tracking differ from those used in selective attention. For example, observers often fail to notice when targets change color and find it difficult to recall information about a specific target, such as its starting location or its original name. It may be that, in MOT, attention is used to index locations of targets, not the targets themselves.

Automaticity

The attentional demands of a task can change over time. When learning to drive a car, all of the novice driver's attention may be occupied with the task. Once the task has become "automatic" the same actions seem to coexist happily with at least some other tasks (though you should avoid using the cell phone, 54). While there may not be an agreed definition of "automaticity", we can provisionally define automatic visual processing as the capacity to extract visual information with minimal (or no) attention, while engaging in other independent processes (for classic reviews see. A task that can be performed in an automatic fashion does not imply that it is done pre-attentively but rather requires minimal engagement of attention. Much recent research has focused on the ability to identify the 'gist' of a scene or the presence of some category of object in the near absence of attention. In dual task studies, observers can devote their attention to a demanding search task and, nevertheless, report whether a natural scene contains an animal. What is more, given sets of similar items, observers can assess the mean and distribution of a variety of basic visual feature dimensions without the need to attend to each object (e.g. size, orientation, velocity and direction of motion, center of mass just to name a few). Gist and summary statistic seem to be extracted automatically allowing observes to make very rapid, fairly accurate judgments about quite complex scenes.

The so-called "flanker task" has been used as another example of automatic processing of stimuli. In a flanker task, observers might be asked to selectively attend to a central letter and press one key for "A" and another for "B". They are instructed to ignore flanking letters but they have trouble doing so. RTs are faster when the to-be-ignored flankers are congruent (A A A) than when they are incongruent (B A B) suggesting that some automatic process wandered off to read the flanking letters in the face of instructions to the contrary. Interestingly, it is easier to ignore the flankers if the central task is harder.

Awareness

Attention and conscious awareness seem to have an intimate, if rather ambiguous relationship. It is sometimes suggested that attention is required for awareness. However, since it seems reasonably clear that you can attend to this prose while still being aware of the presence of some sort of extended visual field, this requirement would seem to depend upon a very broad definition of attention. There is experimental evidence that although attention modulates awareness, we have some awareness of unattended stimuli. For example, it is possible to direct attention to visual stimuli that we are not aware of.

The modulation of awareness by attention can be illustrated via the phenomenon of "change blindness". In a typical change blindness demonstration, two nearly identical images are shown in succession. In a famous example devised by Ron Rensink, two scenes containing an airplane alternate with a large jet engine appearing and disappearing from frame to frame. Observers are poor at noticing this substantial change if motion transients are masked, either with an intervening gray field or by irrelevant onsets (mud splashes,). In general, quite substantial changes typically go undetected, if the do not change the overall "gist" or meaning of the scene, while the same changes are trivially easy to detect if observers are attending to the location of the change. Clearly, attention modulates the awareness of significant changes though the nature of the change in awareness remains a matter for discussion.

There is also evidence that attention can be deployed without awareness. Indeed, if attention can shift 20-30 times a second, as suggested by visual search studies, we do not have easy conscious accesses to all those acts of selection. Studies on "blindsight" patients provide a different example of attention without awareness. In blindsight, damage to the primary visual cortex results in a condition where patients report being unaware of part of the visual field. However, when asked to guess what stimuli are located in the unaware area, patients can perform at above chance levels. Furthermore, when spatially cued to the unaware area, they exhibit speeded discrimination of targets that subsequently appear in that area, demonstrating that they can attend to stimuli that they cannot.

How is Attention Implemented at the Neuronal Level?

In this topic, we examine how visual attention might be implemented in the brain. Our survey is organized by methodology.

Single–Cell Physiological Recordings

Studies utilizing single cell recordings have led to several important insights about visual attention. Attentional effects are observable as early as the lateral geniculate nucleus and the primary visual cortex as well as on a variety of subcortical structures. These results suggest that attentional effects occur at multiple loci. Perhaps more interesting are data which bear on the question of how attention improves visual processing. In some experiments attention produces larger increases in firing rates at lower levels of stimulus contrast with smaller effects at high contrast. This is the pattern expected if attention produces a contrast gain. Other experiments provide evidence for a rate gain model with the largest effects at high contrast. In different studies attention changes the shape of neuronal tuning curves (e.g. sharper orientation tuning). Finally, attention can shrink a cell's receptive field around the attended stimulus to the exclusion of distracting stimuli. This diversity of results may reflect a diversity of attentional processes, though it has been suggested that different patterns of results may result from a single attentional mechanism responding to different stimulus conditions.

Single cell methods have also been used extensively to explore a fronto-parietal network involved in the allocation of attention. The lateral intraparietal area (LIP) in the parietal lobe has been proposed as the locus of a priority map that might guide attention to objects with the features of the current target off attention. The frontal eye fields (FEF) and the dorso-lateral prefrontal cortex (DLPFC) are implicated in the executive control of the deployment of attention.

Functional Imaging

Functional Magnetic Resonance Imaging (fMRI) and Positron Emission Tomography (PET) show that attention modulates a wide range of loci in the brain. These methods can be used to map distinct combinations of brain areas to particular aspects of attention. For example, visual orienting (i.e. the ability to attentionally select a particular stimulus for action) is thought to be implemented by both dorsal and ventral system. The dorsal system is bilateral and includes the LIP, FEF, and DLPFC network described above. It appears to be involved in voluntary, goal-directed selection of stimuli and responses. The ventral system is largely right-lateralized and comprises the temporal-parietal junction and ventral frontal cortex. It is seems to be specialized for the detection of behaviorally relevant stimuli.

Event-Related Potentials

While functional imaging methods provide excellent spatial information about neural processes, their temporal resolution is poor. Event-related potentials (ERP), in contrast, have high temporal resolution, at the cost of spatial precision. Thus, ERP techniques are well suited for assessing the time course of attentional effects. For example, consider the attentional modulation of primary visual cortex. ERP results show that this modulation can be seen in the first, "feed-forward" activation of cortex by an incoming stimulus. This rules out the alternative that attentional modulation of V1 is a feedback process.

The N2pc component of the ERP signal has proven quite useful, since it is associated with the focusing of selective attention on a target item. This signal has been found to shift rapidly from one item to another during a visual search task, attesting to attention moving in a serial manner among multiple items in a display.

Neglect and Balint's Syndrome

Important information about brain mechanisms has also come from studies of localized brain damage. For example, a lesion to the right posterior parietal cortex leaves the visual system intact, but results in the patient ignoring a region of space contralateral to the lesion. It therefore represents a loss of attentional, but not visual, capabilities. This "visual neglect" is especially interesting because it implicates attention in conscious perception while also showing that quite sophisticated processing can occur in the absence of attention. For example, a word presented in the neglected region that is not consciously perceived may speed the response to a semantically-related word subsequently shown in a non-neglected region. Similarly, patients show above chance performance in a forced choice comparison task between two pictures presented in the neglected field. Studies of neglect suggest that it is caused by interhemispherical competition between the cortical circuits that control the deployment of attention. For example, damage to the right cerebral cortex may allow the attentional circuits in the left cerebral cortex to dominate. As the left cerebral cortex is responsible for processing the right visual hemifield, attention is directed more often (or even exclusively) to the right visual hemifield, causing the patient to ignore objects that occur to the left of the point of fixation.

If attentional circuits in both cerebral hemispheres are damaged, then neither may dominate, resulting in a phenomenon known as Balint's syndrome. A patient with this syndrome can perceive an isolated object regardless of where it is located, but demonstrates a striking inability to perceive more than one object at a time.

Attention Span

An attention span is a measure of the amount of time someone can stay focused on a particular task, thought, or conversation without being distracted.

Attention span is a measure for how easily distracted a person is, and longer attention spans usually make it easier for people to complete tasks and remain organized. A person's attention span also affects social interactions; some people struggle to remain focused on conversations without becoming distracted or fidgeting.

A person's attention span varies with context and the type of task. Some people are able to concentrate longer on certain kinds of tasks, such as games, reading, or conversations, than they can focus on other types of tasks. Distraction-filled environments can decrease a person's attention span. People generally have shorter attention spans in loud, chaotic environments or when they are stressed.

Some researchers have expressed concern that the proliferation of technology and social networking is decreasing people's attention spans. The need to respond quickly to texts, emails, online chats, and social networking statuses can make it difficult to focus on a single task for a long period of time. People may also have fewer opportunities to practice focusing for long periods of time and may crave more distractions and stimulation, both of which can make it more difficult to focus.

Estimates of the average attention span range from 5–20 minutes, but these are only estimates, and can vary greatly from person to person.

Attention and Mental Health

A variety of mental health conditions, including depression, anxiety, and ADHD can affect a person's ability to focus. A combination of psychotherapy, lifestyle changes, and in some cases medication can help improve a person's attention span. Some people need to institute specific strategies, such as taking frequent breaks or turning off electronics, to remain focused.

Visual Perception Theory

In order to receive information from the environment we are equipped with sense organs e.g. eye, ear, nose. Each sense organ is part of a sensory system which receives sensory inputs and transmits sensory information to the brain.

A particular problem for psychologists is to explain the process by which the physical energy received by sense organs forms the basis of perceptual experience. Sensory inputs are somehow converted into perceptions of desks and computers, flowers and buildings, cars and planes; into sights, sounds, smells, taste and touch experiences.

A major theoretical issue on which psychologists are divided is the extent to which perception relies directly on the information present in the stimulus. Some argue that perceptual processes are not direct, but depend on the perceiver's expectations and previous knowledge as well as the information available in the stimulus itself.

This controversy is discussed with respect to Gibson (1966) who has proposed a direct theory of perception which is a 'bottom-up' theory, and Gregory (1970) who has proposed a constructivist (indirect) theory of perception which is a 'top-down' theory.

Psychologists distinguish between two types of processes in perception: bottom-up processing and top-down processing.

Bottom-up processing is also known as data-driven processing, because perception begins with the stimulus itself. Processing is carried out in one direction from the retina to the visual cortex, with each successive stage in the visual pathway carrying out ever more complex analysis of the input.

Top-down processing refers to the use of contextual information in pattern recognition. For example, understanding difficult handwriting is easier when reading complete sentences than when reading single and isolated words. This is because the meaning of the surrounding words provide a context to aid understanding.

Gregory and Top Down

Processing Theory

Psychologist Richard Gregory argued that perception is a constructive process which relies on top-down processing.

Stimulus information from our environment is frequently ambiguous so to interpret it, we require higher cognitive information either from past experiences or stored knowledge in order to makes inferences about what we perceive. Helmholtz called it the 'likelihood principle'.

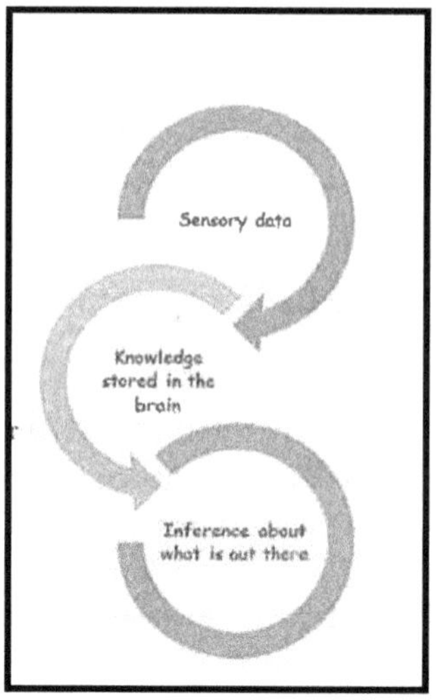

For Gregory perception is a hypothesis, which is based on prior knowledge. In this way we are actively constructing our perception of reality based on our environment and stored information.

Evidence to Support Gregory's Theory

Highly unlikely objects tend to be mistaken for likely objects
Gregory has demonstrated this with a hollow mask of a face. Such a mask is generally seen as normal, even when one knows and feels the real mask.
There seems to be an overwhelming need to reconstruct the face, similar to Helmholtz's description of 'unconscious inference'. An assumption based on past experience.

Perceptions can be Ambiguous

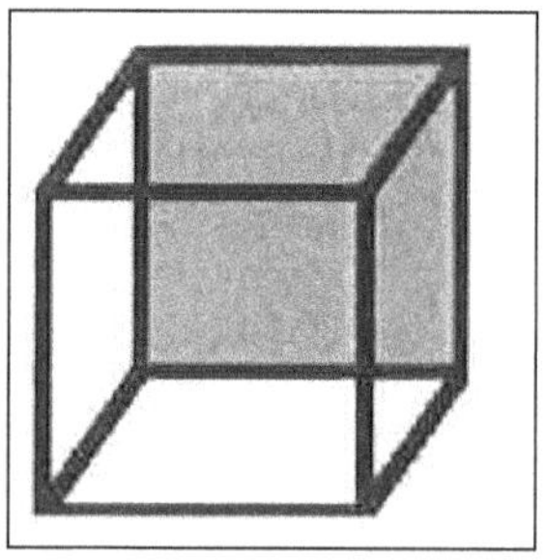

The Necker cube is a good example of this. When you stare at the crosses on the cube the orientation can suddenly change, or 'flip'.

It becomes unstable and a single physical pattern can produce two perceptions.

Gregory argued that this object appears to flip between orientations because the brain develops two equally plausible hypotheses and is unable to decide between them.

When the perception changes though there is no change of the sensory input, the change of appearance cannot be due to bottom-up processing. It must be set downwards by the prevailing perceptual hypothesis of what is near and what is far.

Perception allows behavior to be generally appropriate to non-sensed object characteristics
For example, we respond to certain objects as though they are doors even though we can only see a long narrow rectangle as the door is ajar.
What we have seen so far would seem to confirm that indeed we do interpret the information that we receive, in other words, perception is a top down process.

Critical Evaluation of Gregory's Theory

The Nature of Perceptual Hypotheses

If perceptions make use of hypothesis testing the question can be asked 'what kind of hypotheses are they?' Scientists modify a hypothesis according to the support they find for it so are we as perceivers also able to modify our hypotheses? In some cases it would seem the answer is yes. For example, look at the figure below:

This probably looks like a random arrangement of black shapes. In fact there is a hidden face in there can you see it? The face is looking straight ahead and is in the top half of the picture in the center. Now can you see it? The figure is strongly it from the side and has long hair and a beard.

Once the face is discovered, very rapid perceptual learning takes place and the ambiguous picture now obviously contains a face each time we look at it. We have learned to perceive the stimulus in a different way.

Although in some cases, as in the ambiguous face picture, there is a direct relationship between modifying hypotheses and perception, in other cases this is not so evident. For example, illusions persist even when we have full knowledge of them (e.g. the inverted face). One would expect that the knowledge we have learned (from, say, touching the face and confirming that it is not 'normal') would modify our hypotheses in an adaptive manner. The current hypothesis testing theories cannot explain this lack of a relationship between learning and perception.

Perceptual Development

A perplexing question for the constructivists who propose perception is essentially top-down in nature is 'how can the neonate ever perceive?' If we all have to construct our own worlds based on past experiences why are our perceptions so similar, even across cultures? Relying on individual constructs for making sense of the world makes perception a very individual and chancy process.

The constructivist approach stresses the role of knowledge in perception and therefore is against the nativist approach to perceptual development. However, a substantial body of evidence has been accrued favoring the nativist approach, for example: Newborn infants show shape constancy; they prefer their mother's voice to other voices; and it has been established that they prefer normal features to scrambled features as early ass minutes after birth.

Sensory Evidence

Perhaps the major criticism of the constructivists is that they have underestimated the richness of sensory evidence available to perceivers in the real world (as opposed to the laboratory where much of the constructivists' evidence has come from).

Constructivists like Gregory frequently use the example of size constancy to support their explanations. That is, we correctly perceive the size of an object even though the retinal image of an object shrinks as the object recedes. They propose that sensory evidence from other sources must be available for us to be able to do this.

However, in the real world, retinal images are rarely seen in isolation (as is possible in the laboratory). There is a rich array of sensory information including other objects, the distant horizon and movement. This rich source of sensory information is important to the second approach to explaining perception that we will examine, namely the direct approach to perception as proposed by Gibson.

Gibson argued strongly against the idea that perception involves top-down processing and criticizes Gregory's discussion of visual illusions on the grounds that they are artificial exmaples and not images found in our normal visual environments. This is crucial because Gregory accepts that misperceptions are the exception rather than the norm. Illusions may be interesting phenomena, but they might not be that informative about the debate.

Gibson and Bottom Up Processing

Gibson's bottom up theory suggests that perception involves innate mechanisms forged by evolution and that no learning is required. This suggests that perception is necessary for survival- without perception we would live in a very dangerous environment. Our ancestors would have needed perception to escape from harmful predators, suggesting perception is evolutionary.

James Gibson (1966) argues that perception is direct, and not subject to hypotheses testing as Gregory proposed. There is enough information in our environment to make sense of the world in a direct way. His theory is sometimes known as the 'Ecological Theory' because of the claim that perception can be explained solely in terms of the environment.

For Gibson: sensation is perception: what you see if what you get. There is no need for processing (interpretation) as the information we receive about size, shape and distance etc. is sufficiently detailed for us to interact directly with the environment.

Gibson (1972) argued that perception is a bottom-up process, which means that sensory information is analyzed in one direction: from simple analysis of raw sensory data to ever increasing complexity of analysis through the visual system.

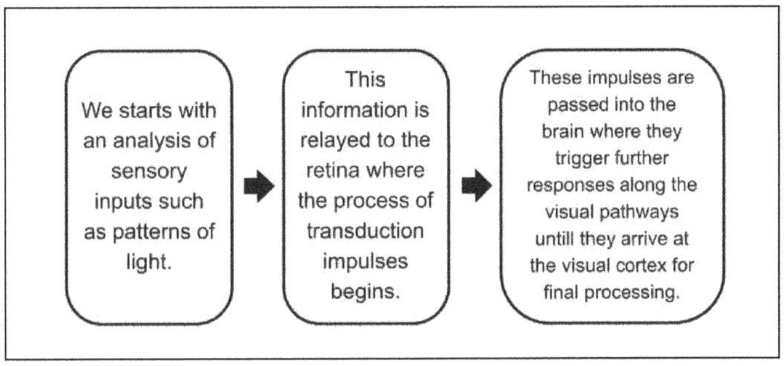

Features of Gibson's Theory

The Optic Array

The starting point for Gibson's Theory was that the pattern of light reaching the eye, known as the optic array, containing all the visual information necessary for perception.

This optic array provides unambiguous information about the layout of objects in space. Light ruys reflect off of surfaces and converge into the cornea of your eye.

Perception involves 'picking up' the rich information provided by the optic army in a direct way with little/no processing involved.

Because of movement and different intensities of light shining in different directions it is an ever changing source of sensory information. Therefore, if you move, the structure of the optic array changes.

According to Gibson, we have the mechanisms to interpret this unstable sensory input, meaning we experience a stable and meaningful view of the world.

Changes in the flow of the optic array contain important information about what type of movement is taking place. The flow of the optic array will either move from or towards a particular point.

If the flow appears to be coming from the point, it means you are moving towards it. If the optic array is moving towards the point you are moving away from it.

Invariant Features

The optic array contains invariant information that remains constant as the observer moves. Invariants are aspects of the environment which don't change. They supply us with crucial information.

Two good examples of invariants are texture and linear perspective.

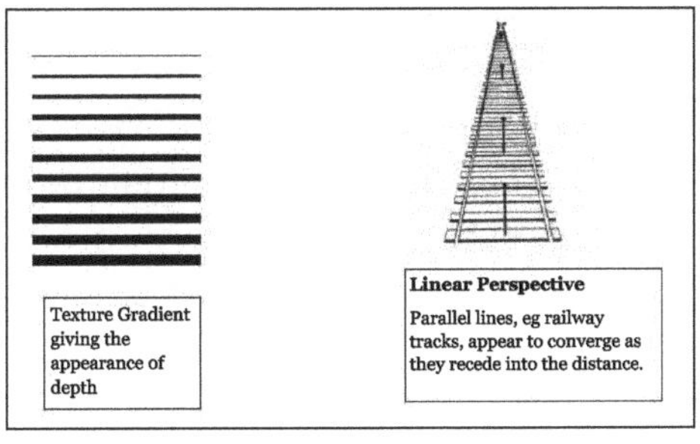

Another invariant is the horizon-ratio relation. The ratio above and below the horizon is constant for objects of the same size standing on the same ground.

Affordances

Are, in short, cues in the environment that aid perception. Important cues in the environment include:

- Optical array: The patterns of light that reach the eye from the environment.
- Relative brightness: Objects with brighter, clearer images are perceived as closer.
- Texture gradient: The grain of texture gets smaller as the object recedes. Gives the impression of surfaces receding into the distance.
- Relative size: When an object moves further away from the eye the image gets smaller. Objects with smaller images are seen as more distant.
- Superimposition: If the image of one object blocks the image of another, the first object is seen as closer.
- Height in the visual field: Objects further away are generally higher in the visual field.

Evaluation of Gibson's Direct Theory of Perception

Gibson's theory is a highly ecologically valid theory as it puts perception back into the real world. A large number of applications can be applied in terms of his theory e.g. training pilots, runway markings and road markings. It's an excellent explanation for perception when viewing conditions are clear. Gibson's theory also highlights the richness of information in optic array and provides an account of perception in animals, babies and humans.

His theory is reductionist as it seeks to explain perception solely in terms of the environment. There is strong evidence to show that the brain and long term memory can influence perception. In this case, it could be said that Gregory's theory is far more plausible.

Gibson's theory also only supports one side of the nature nurture debate, that being the nature side. Again, Gregory's theory is far more plausible as it suggests that what we see with our eyes is not enough and we use knowledge already stored in our brain, supporting both sides of the debate.

Visual Illusions

Gibson's emphasis on DIRECT perception provides an explanation for the (generally) fast and accurate perception of the environment. However, his theory cannot explain why perceptions are sometimes inaccurate, e.g. in illusions. He claimed the illusions used in experimental work constituted extremely artificial perceptual situations unlikely to be encountered in the real world, however this dismissal cannot realistically be applied to all illusions.

For example, Gibson's theory cannot account for perceptual errors like the general tendency for people to overestimate vertical extents relutive to horizontal ones.

Neither can Gibson's theory explain naturally occurring illusions. For example if you stare for some time at a waterfall and then transfer your gaze to a stationary object, the object appears to move in the opposite direction.

Bottom-up or Top-down Processing

Neither direct nor constructivist theories of perception seem capable of explaining all perception all of the time. Gibson's theory appears to be based on perceivers operating under ideal viewing conditions, where stimulus information is plentiful and is available for a suitable length of time. Constructivist theories, like Gregory's, have typically involved viewing under less than ideal conditions.

Research by Tulving et al. manipulated both the clarity of the stimulus input and the impact of the perceptual context in a word identification task. As clarity of the stimulus (through exposure duration) and the amount of context increased, so did the likelihood of correct identification.

However, as the exposure duration increased, so the impact of context was reduced, suggesting that if stimulus information is high, then the need to use other sources of information is reduced. One theory that explains how topdown and bottom-up processes may be seen as interacting with each other to produce the best interpretation of the stimulus was proposed by Neisser (1976)- known as the 'Perceptual Cycle'.

Helmholtz's Theory of Unconscious Inference

Helmholtz, in his Treatise on Physiological Optics, introduced what has become the classical, and standard, theory of perception—unconscious inference theory, a constructionist, representation a list, indirect realist theory. In developing it, Helmholtz was influenced by two findings. First, the retina, which is a two dimensional structure, could only indicate where an object was horizontally and vertically in the visual field; it could not be the basis for an explanation of three-dimensional visual perception. Something had to be added to the retinal sensations, to embellish them. Second, Müller's doctrine of specific nerve energies suggested a lack of correspondence between sensory input and subjective experience. Thus, no matter how they were stimulated, each sensory nerve, as was just mentioned, only gave a report specific to it. "It can be shown very easily," Helmholtz would later propose, "that there is no similarity whatsoever, either in kind or in degree, between the qualities of sensations and the qualities of external agents exciting and being portrayed by them". The sensory report was inadequate to represent the external world. More than that, what one perceived was not consistent with sensory stimulation. The percept therefore required mediation from within, between it and the sensory presentation, some sort of subsequent processing of the sensory input before it was delivered to consciousness as the completed percept. These mediating mechanisms, for Helmholtz, would be derived from accumulating experience and would come to serve as signs of external agents and events.

According to Helmholtz, the different nerve fibers coming from the different sensory receptors provide signs about the nature of the stimulating agent. They symbolize what is inaccessible: "the sensations have been described as being simply symbols for the relations in the external world.

They have been denied every kind of similarity or equivalence to the things they denote". At first, given that the perceiver is without prior experience, these sensory experiences, which will symbolize the object world, are without any objective meaning but, from birth, patterns of sensory experience are being ceaselessly taken up. With accumulating experience, the mind—a physiological, or brain process—builds up a store of experiences and, as a consequence, expectations are built up. One such expectation could be the possibility that the recurrence of a previously experienced sensory collage is most likely due to the same stimulating object producing those same impressions.

It is upon the basis of these expectations that an imagined world of objects (not a known world) is constructed. Consistent with his predecessor Locke, the objects of experience to Helmholtz were simply an accumulation of sensations. In the final analysis, all that we ever have knowledge of are our sensations and whatever expectations that we may build up refer to those sensations and not to the objects that produce them.

The psychic activities that lead us to infer that there in front of us at a certain place there is a certain object of a certain character, are generally not conscious activities, but unconscious ones. In their result they are equivalent to a conclusion, to the extent that the observed action on our senses enables us to form an idea as to the possible cause of this action; although, as a matter of fact, it is invariably simply the nervous stimulations that are perceived directly, that is, the actions, but never the external objects themselves. But what seems to differentiate them from a conclusion, in the ordinary sense of that word, is that a conclusion is an act of conscious thought Still it may be permissible to speak of the psychic acts of ordinary perception as unconscious conclusions, thereby making a distinction of some sort between them and the common so-called conscious conclusions.

Our ideas of things cannot be anything but symbols, natural signs for things which we learn how to use in order to regulate our movements and actions. Having learned correctly how to read those symbols, we are enabled by their help to adjust our actions so as to bring about the desired result; that is, so that the expected new sensations will arise.

Through the means of sensory experience, we act in an inaccessible world and regulate and modify those actions upon the basis of subsequent sensory feedback.

So, as a result of prior experience and unconscious association processes, incoming sensory signs or clues are automatically processed at a level that does not require conscious involvement, and which result in one's conscious experience or perception. What one perceives is thus, according to Helmholtz, due to unconscious inferences about what must have produced the present pattern of sensations. Helmholtz made his point by explaining what one's idea of a table is and to what it refers.

The idea of a single individual table which you carry in my mind is correct and exact, provided you can deduce from it correctly the precise sensations you will have when my eye and my hand are brought into this or that definite relation with respect to the table. Any other sort of similarity between such an idea and the body about which the idea exists, you do not know how to conceive. One is the mental symbol of the other. The kind of symbol was not chosen by me arbitrarily, but was forced on me by the nature of my organ of sense and of my mind.

In that regard, such unconscious inferences are, in their results, inductive and comparable to conscious inferences that are made upon the basis of analogy. The idea that a person has of external things is nothing other than symbols that one has learned to use in regulating one's actions in the world—a world that one has no access to or knowledge of, beyond unconscious conjecture.

In dealing with these processes of unconscious inference Helmholtz made three positive claims. Such inferences are, first, formed though experience. They begin as conscious inferences that through association and repetition develop into unconscious inferences. Conscious states, through repetition and by what Helmholtz called the "law of habit", are reduced until the process cannot be accessed through introspection; they sink beneath the level of consciousness. Boring called this "conscious decay under habituation," which we would today refer to as automaticity. His second point was that, due to their being unconscious, such processes are normally very difficult to resist. The associations that have been well established were practically inevitable (although they could be unlearned with further experience). The operation of such unconscious inferences is evident when one is confronted with some unfamiliar or ambiguous sensory pattern; one experiences the mind generating alternate perceptions. That is the case with a Necker cube—a two-dimensional drawing of a three-dimensional box frame. Without any conscious attempt on one's part, the perceived orientation of the frame switches and each orientation is as compelling and irresistible as the other. Optical illusions such as that, to Helmholtz, were evidence in favor of his theory. His final point, which was taken into consideration previously, was that unconscious inferences resembled conscious inferences from analogy in being inductive—an inference, indeed, but not a conscious one.

On the negative side, unconscious inferences could be wrong; we suffer illusions. The fact of illusions is taken as evidence that perception is fallible. There is nothing to guarantee us that our perceptions are veridical. At the level of the receptors after all we are provided with evidence that is insufficient for the task of perceiving depth or three dimensions. Perception of three dimensions, as Anderson expressed it, is nothing more than an educated guess. We do not know the world. We do not have direct access to it. What we do know we know only through the medium of the senses, and the medium of inferences, and, hence, perception is indirect; the world as it is will not be made available to us.

Sensation

Sensation involves the relay of information from sensory receptors to the brain and enables a person to experience the world around them.

Sensation and perception are two separate processes that are very closely related. Sensation is input about the physical world obtained by our sensory receptors, and perception is the process by which the brain selects, organizes, and interprets these sensations. In other words, senses are the physiological basis of perception. Perception of the same senses may vary from one person to another because each person's brain interprets stimuli differently based on that individual's learning, memory, emotions, and expectations.

The Senses

There are five classical human senses: sight, sound, taste, smell, and touch. Two other senses, kinesthesia and the vestibular senses, have become widely recognized by scientists. Kinesthesia is the perception of the positioning of the parts of the body, commonly known as "body awareness." Vestibular senses detect gravity, linear acceleration (such as speeding up or slowing down on a straight road), and rotary acceleration (such as speeding up or slowing down around a curve). Both kinesthesia and the vestibular senses help us to balance.

Sensory information (such as taste, light, odor, pressure, vibration, heat, and pain) is perceived through the body's sensory receptors. These sensory receptors include the eyes, ears, mouth, nose, hands, and feet (and the skin as a whole). Rod and cone receptors in the retina of the eye perceive light; cilia in the ear perceive sound; chemical receptors in the nasal cavities and mouth perceive smell and taste; and muscle spindles, as well as pressure, vibration, heat and pain receptors in the skin, perceive the many sensations of touch.

Specialized cells in the sensory receptors convert the incoming energy (e.g., light) into neural impulses. These neural impulses enter the cerebral cortex of the brain, which is made up of layers of neurons with many inputs. These layers of neurons in the function like mini microprocessors, and it is their job to organize the sensations and interpret them in the process of perception.

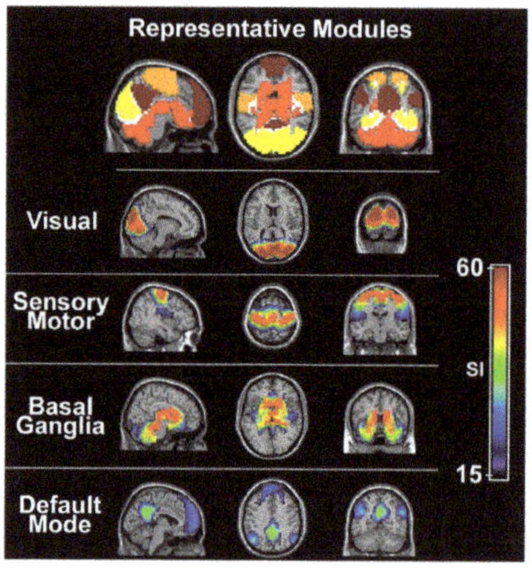

fMRI and the senses: This fMRI chart shows some of the neural activation that takes place during sensation. The occipital lobe is activated during visual stimulation

Motor Homunculus

The "motor homunculus" is a theoretical physical representation of the human body within the brain. It is a neurological "map" of the anatomical divisions of the body. Within the primary motor cortex, motor neurons are arranged in an orderly manner—parallel to the structure of the physical body, but inverted. The toes are represented at the top of the cerebral hemisphere, while the mouth is represented at the bottom of the hemisphere, closer to the part of the brain known as the lateral sulcus. These representations lie along a fold in the cortex called the central sulcus. The homunculus is split in half across the brain, with motor representation for each side of the body represented on the the opposite side of the brain.

The amount of cortex devoted to any given body region is proportional to how many nerves are in that region, not to the region's physical size. Areas of the body with greater or more complex sensory or motor connections are represented as larger in the homunculus. Those with fewer or less complex connections are represented as smaller. The resulting image is that of a distorted human body with disproportionately huge hands, lips, and face (because those regions have huge numbers of nerve endings).

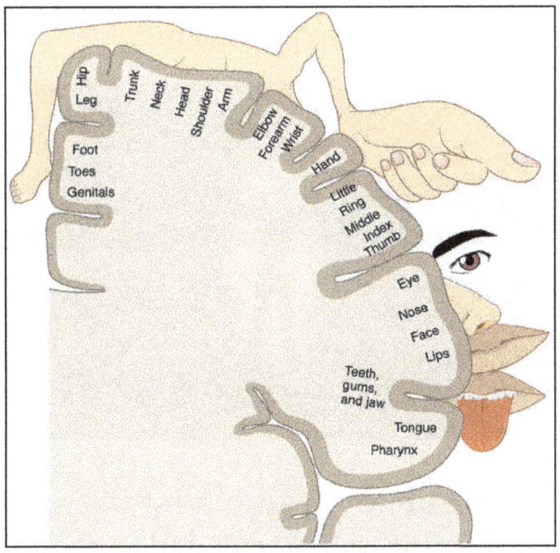

Motor Homunculus: The motor homunculus is a theoretical visualization of the locations in the cortex that correspond to motor and sensory function in the body.

Sensory Absolute Thresholds

The absolute threshold is the lowest intensity at which a stimulus can be detected.

Absolute Thresholds

A threshold is the minimum level at which a given event can occur. In neuroscience and psychophysics, there are several types of sensory threshold. The recognition threshold is the level at which a stimulus can not only be detected but also recognized; the differential threshold is the level at which a difference in a detected stimulus can be perceived; the terminal threshold is the level beyond which a stimulus is no longer detected. However, perhaps the most important sensory threshold is the absolute threshold, which is the smallest detectable level of a stimulus.

The absolute threshold is defined as the lowest intensity at which a stimulus can be detected. (Recently, signal detection theory has offered a more nuanced definition of absolute threshold: the lowest intensity at which a stimulus will be specified a certain percentage of the time, often 50%.) A classic example of absolute threshold is an odor test, in which a fragrance is released into an environment. The absolute threshold in that scenario would be the least amount of fragrance necessary for a subject to detect that there is an odor.

Smell is not the only sense with absolute thresholds: Imagine you're in a room and someone behind you slowly begins turning up the volume on the radio; the absolute threshold is the softest volume at which you would notice what they're doing. Sound thresholds can be about more than volume; they can also be about frequency. For example, humans cannot hear dog whistles. This is because dog whistles are at a frequency higher than the absolute threshold for frequency for human hearing.

Similarly, the minimum amount of light necessary to see something in the dark is the absolute threshold for vision. Every sense has an absolute threshold.

Influencing the Absolute Threshold

There are several factors that can influence the level of absolute threshold, including adaptation to the stimulus and individual motivations and expectations.

Light at the end of the tunnel: the absolute threshold for vision: In a dark space, an individual's saving grace can be the minimum amount of light needed to stimulate the eye in the dark environment and alert the brain that it is seeing light.

Sensory Adaptation

Sensory adaptation happens when our senses no longer perceive a stimulus because of our sensory receptor 's continuous contact with it. If you've ever entered a room that has a terrible odor, but after a few minutes realized that you barely noticed it anymore, then you have experienced sensory adaptation. Like thresholds, adaptation can occur with any sense, whether it's forgetting that the radio is on while you work or not noticing that the water in the pool is cold after you've been swimming for a while.

Cognitive Processes

Additionally, an individual's motivations and expectations can also influence whether a stimulus will be detected at the absolute threshold. For example, when you are in a crowded room where a lot of conversations are taking place, you tend to focus your attention on the individual with whom you are speaking. Because you are focused on one stimulus, the absolute threshold (in this case, the minimum volume at which you can hear) is lower for that stimulus than it would have been otherwise.

Expectations can also affect the absolute threshold. If you are in a dark hallway searching for the tiny glow of a nightlight, your expectation of spotting it decreases the absolute threshold for which you will actually be able to see it.

Sensory Difference Thresholds

The minimum amount of change in sensory stimulation needed to recognize that a change has occurred is known as the just-noticeable difference.

Just-noticeable Difference

The just-noticeable difference (JND), also known as the difference limen or differential threshold, is the smallest detectable difference between a starting and secondary level of sensory stimulus. In other words, it is the difference in the level of the stimulus needed for a person to recognize that a change has occurred.

Influencing the Just-noticeable Difference

The JND is usually a fixed proportion of the reference sensory level. For example, consider holding a five-pound weight (the reference level), and then having a one pound weight added. This increase in weight is significant in comparison to the reference level (a 20% increase in weight). However, if you hold a fifty pound weight (the new reference level), you would not be likely to notice a difference if one pound is added. This is because the difference in the amount of additional weight from the reference level is not significantly greater (2% increase in weight) than the reference level.

Turning Up the Volume: The difference threshold is the amount of stimulus change needed to recognize that a change has occurred.

If someone changes the volume of a speaker, the difference threshold is the amount it has to be changed in order for listeners to notice a difference.

The absolute threshold is the minimum volume of the radio we would need in order to notice that it was turned on at all. However, determining the just-noticeable difference, the amount of change needed in order to notice that the radio has become louder, depends on how much the volume has changed in comparison to where it started. It's possible to turn the volume up only slightly, making the difference in volume undetectable. This is similar to adding only one pound of weight when you're holding 50 pounds.

Sensory Adaptation

Sensory adaptation is the decrease in the responsiveness of a sensory system that is confronted with a constant stimulus.

Sensory adaptation, also called neural adaptation, is the change in the responsiveness of a sensory system that is confronted with a constant stimulus. This change can be positive or negative, and does not necessarily lead to completely ignoring a stimulus.

One example of sensory adaptation is sustained touching. When you rest your hands on a table or put clothes on your body, at first the touch receptors will recognize that they are being activated and you will feel the sensation of touching an object. However, after sustained exposure, the sensory receptors will no longer activate as strongly and you will no longer be aware that you are touching something.

This follows the model of sensory adaptation presented by Georg Meissner, which is known as "Meissner's corpuscles." Meissner's corpuscles are sensory triggers of physical sensations on the skin, especially areas of the skin that are sensitive to light and touch. These corpuscles rapidly change and adapt when a stimulus is added. Then they quickly decrease activity, and eventually cease to react to the stimulus. When the stimulus is removed, the corpuscles regain their sensitivity. For example, the constant touch of clothes on our skin leads to our sensory adaptation to the sensations of wearing clothing. Notice that when you put an article of clothing on, after a brief period you no longer feel it; however you continue to be able to feel other sensations through it. This is because the additional stimuli are new, and the body has not yet adapted to them.

In contrast, sensitization is an *increase* in behavioral responses following repeated applications of a particular stimulus. Unlike sensory adaptation, in which a large amount of stimulus is needed to incur any further responsive effects, in sensitization less and less stimulation is required to produce a large response. For example, if an animal hears a loud noise and experiences pain at the same time, it will startle more intensely the next time it hears a loud noise even if there is no pain.

There are many stimuli in life that we experience everyday and gradually ignore or forget, including sounds, images, and smells. Sensory adaptation and sensitization are thought to form an integral component of human learning and personality.

Gestalt Principles of Perception

According to Gestalt psychology, this apparent movement happens because our minds fill in missing information. This belief that the whole is greater than the sum of the individual parts led to the discovery of several different phenomena that occur during perception.

The law of closure is one example of a Gestalt law of perceptual organization. According to this principle, things in the environment often tend to be seen as part of a whole. In many cases, our minds will even fill in the missing information to create cohesive shapes.

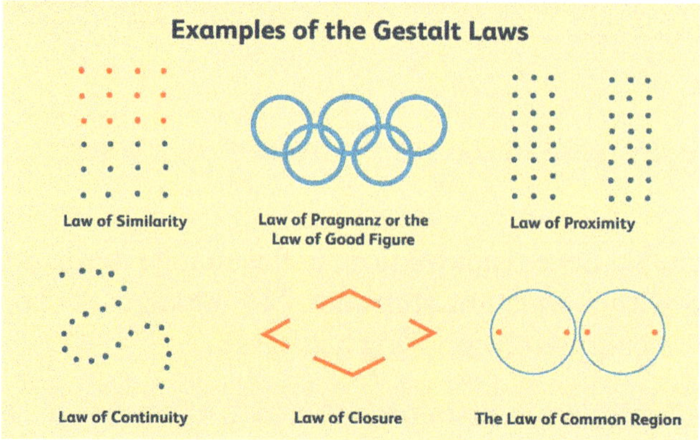

Gestalt psychology was founded by German thinkers Max Wertheimer, Wolfgang Kohler, and Kurt Koffka and focused on how people interpret the world. The Gestalt perspective formed partially as a response to the structuralism of Wilhelm Wundt, who focused on breaking down mental events and experiences to the smallest elements.

Max Wertheimer noted that rapid sequences of perceptual events, such as rows of flashing lights, create the illusion of motion even when there is none. This is known as the phi phenomenon. Motion pictures are based on this principle, with a series of still images appearing in rapid succession to form a seamless visual experience.

According to Gestalt psychology, the whole is different from the sum of its parts. Based upon this belief, Gestalt psychologists developed a set of principles to explain perceptual organization, or how smaller objects are grouped to form larger ones.

These principles are often referred to as the "laws of perceptual organization." However, it is important to note that while Gestalt psychologists call these phenomena "laws," a more accurate term would be "principles of perceptual organization." These principles are much like heuristics, which are mental shortcuts for solving problems.

Follow the links below to find more information and examples of the different Gestalt laws of perceptual organization.

Law of Similarity

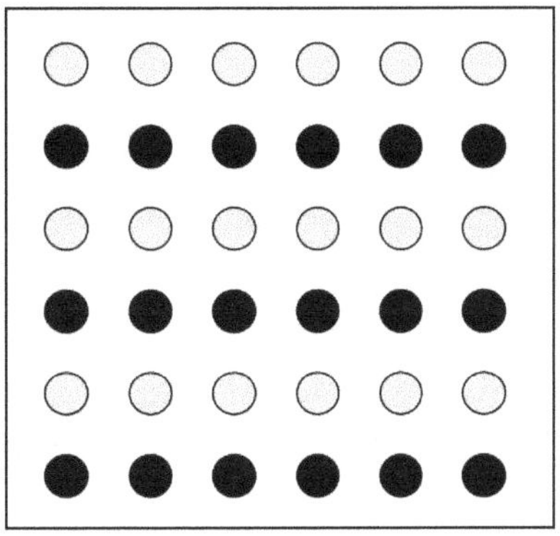

Public Domain

The law of similarity suggests that things similar things tend to appear grouped together. Grouping can occur in both visual and auditory stimuli. In the image above, for example, you probably see the groupings of colored circles as rows rather than just a collection of dots.

Law of Pragnanz

Public Domain

The word *pragnanz* is a German term meaning "good figure." The law of Pragnanz is sometimes referred to as the law of good figure or the law of simplicity. This law holds that objects in the environment are seen in a way that makes them appear as simple as possible.

You see the image above as a series of overlapping circles rather than an assortment of curved, connected lines.

Law of Proximity

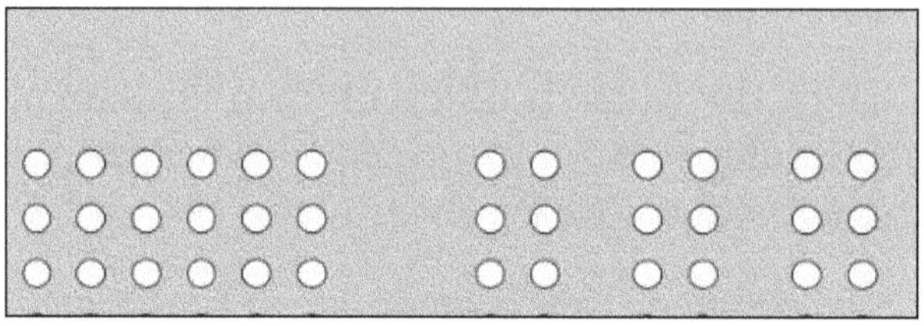

Public Domain

According to the law of proximity, things that are near each other seem to be grouped together. In the above image, the circles on the left appear to be part of one grouping while those on the right appear to be part of another. Because the objects are close to each other, we group them together.

Law of Continuity

Tobias Titz

The law of continuity holds that points that are connected by straight or curving lines are seen in a way that follows the smoothest path. Rather than seeing separate lines and angles, lines are seen as belonging together.

Law of Closure

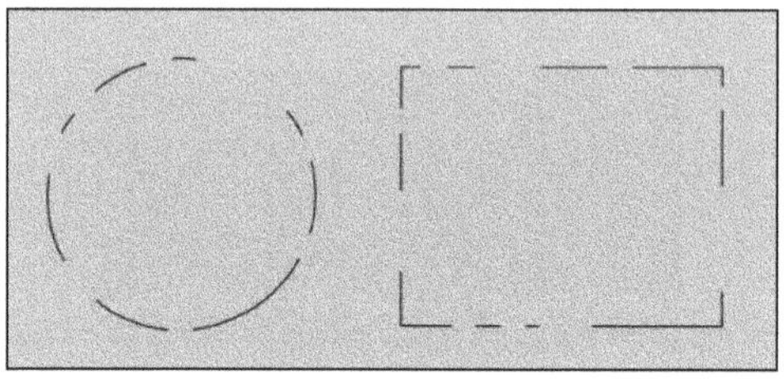

Public Domain

According to the law of closure, things are grouped together if they seem to complete some entity. Our brains often ignore contradictory information and fill in gaps in information. In the image above, you probably see the shapes of a circle and rectangle because your brain fills in the missing gaps in order to create a meaningful image.

The Law of Common Region

This Gestalt law of perceptual organization suggests that elements that are grouped together within the same region of space tend to be grouped together. For example, imagine that there are three oval shapes drawn on a piece of paper with two dots located at each end of the oval. The ovals are right next to each other so that the dot at the end of one oval is actually closer to the dot at the end of a separate oval. Despite the proximity of the dots, the two that are inside each oval are perceived as being a group rather than the dots that are actually closest to each other.

The Gestalt laws of perceptual organization present a set of principles for understanding some of the ways in which perception works. Recent research continues to offer insights into perception and how we see the world.

These principles of organization play a role in perception, but it is also important to remember that these principles can sometimes lead to incorrect perceptions of the world. For example, imagine that you are out hiking in the woods one afternoon when you spot what appears to be a moose behind a large tree. You immediately begin to leave the area to ensure you don't disturb the animal, but as you are hiking around you realize that the "moose" behind the tree is actually just two large broken tree stumps. Because of the Gestalt law of continuity, you perceived the two disconnected shapes as one continuous object, which your brain then interpreted as a moose.

It is important to remember that while these principles are referred to as laws of perceptual organization, they are actually heuristics or short-cuts. Heuristics are usually designed for speed, which is why our perceptual systems sometimes make mistakes and we experience perceptual inaccuracies.

Space and Object-based Attention

Behavioral studies of visual attention have suggested two distinct and complementary modes of selection, one involving space and the other objects. In a space-based mode, stimuli are selected by location in the visual field. Evidence for this mode has come from a variety of sources, including spatial pre-cuing tasks, in which an abrupt luminance change (a cue) summons attention to a region in space. Observers are faster to detect or identify a subsequent target that appears at the cued location than one that appears at an uncued location. The space-based mode of attention has given rise to the attention-as-a-spotlight metaphor, in which attention acts as a beam to illuminate a contiguous region of the visual field. More recently, a zoom-lens metaphor has been suggested, consistent with the finding that the region of space selected by attention can vary in size.

In contrast to the space-based mode, evidence has also been found for an object-based mode in which attention is directed to organized chunks of visual information corresponding to an object or a coherent form in the environment, even if objects overlap in space or are spatially discontinuous. All visual features of an attended object are processed concurrently, and features of an attended object are processed faster and more accurately than features of other objects. In one well-known task, observers view two overlapping objects, a box and a line. Each object varies on two feature dimensions: the box is short or tall and has a gap on its left or right side; the line is dotted or dashed and tilts to the left or right. Observers are instructed to report pairs of features. Observers are more accurate at reporting two features of the same object (e.g., the height and side of gap of the box) than two features that belong to different objects (e.g., the height of the box and the tilt of the line). The cost in accuracy cannot be attributed to spatial factors, because the two objects overlap in space; rather, the cost must be attributed to the switching of attention from one object to the other. Indeed, Vecera and Farah have shown that no additional cost is incurred if the two objects are separated in space, suggesting that spatial factors are not at play in the object-based deployment of attention.

Some studies have shown that both spatial and object factors can simultaneously influence theallocation of attention. presented displays containing two rectangles. One end of one of the rectangles is cued with a brief flicker; a target then appears, and observers make a key-press response to the appearance of the target.

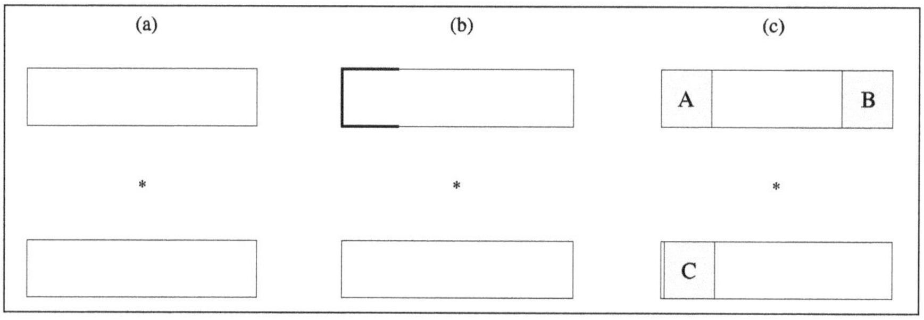

The experiment: (a) start of trial, (b) cue, (c) possible target locations.

The target appears either at the cued location, at the uncued end of the cued object, or in the uncued object. Observers show a cue validity effect: detecting a target at the cued location is fastest. This result can be interpreted in terms of ordinary space-based attention. However, although the distance from the cued location to the target is the same for the noncued target locations, observers are faster to detect targets at the uncued end of the cued object (B) than those in the uncued object (C), indicating that the cue summoned attention to the entire cued object. This object-based effect is nonetheless modulated by spatial proximity: If the two objects are moved close together, the object effect is reduced in magnitude. Further interactions between space- and objectbased attention have been found via demonstrations that object-based effects occur only within the focus of spatial attention, and the outputs of preattentive grouping processes influence the allocations of spatial attention.

Clarifying the Notion of Object-based Attention

The phrase object based is ambiguous, and a lack of clarity as to its intended meaning has resulted in some confusion in the literature. "Object-based" can be a descriptive term for experimental results: An object based effect is observed in any experimental study in which attentional allocation or performance depends not merely on the location of an object in space, but on the extent, shape, or movement of the object itself. "Object based" can also be a characterization of processes and internal representations. Object-based representations arise from processes that use object based frames of reference to transform visual features to achieve partial or complete view invariance. Object based effects do not require object-based representations or frames of reference. The distinction between object-based effects and object-based representations does not entirely remove the ambiguity in the phrase "object based." One can conceive of a continuum of senses in which attentional mechanisms and representations might be considered object based. Examples of at least four alternatives can be found in the literature. Ordered from weakest to strongest notions of object based, these alternatives are as follows:

- Grouping in a viewer-based frame: Attention might act to select the set of locations in which visual features of an object are present. The resulting segmentation has been referred to as a grouped array representation, because visual features are coded in a viewer-centered (e.g., retinotopic) array of locations, and labeled to indicate their grouping. The segmentation can be achieved via heuristics, such as the Gestalt grouping principles, or might exploit low-order statistical regularities in visual scenes. Whole-object knowledge is not required, nor are object-based frames of reference.
- Grouping and determination of principal axis: In addition to performing segmentation in a viewer-based frame, attentional processes might also determine the principal axis of an object: the axis of symmetry or elongation. Using the axis to establish a partial frame of reference, such as an up–down direction, visual features could be reinterpreted with respect to the partial frame. For example, the shape in Fig. a evokes a principal axis from which the midline of the shape can be determined, and the left–right position of visual features is then determined with respect to the midline, although the specification of which direction is "left" and which is "right" can be derived from the viewer-based frame.

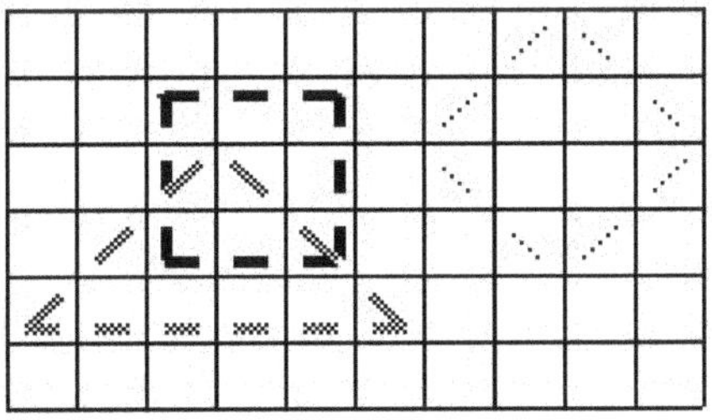

Illustration of the grouped array representation.
Grouping of the visual features is indicated by their shading.

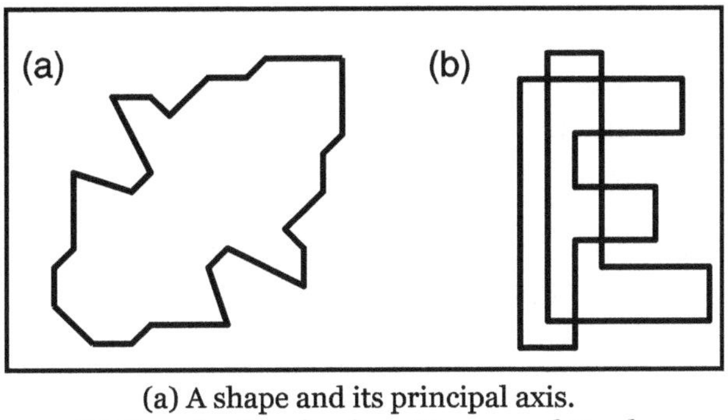

(a) A shape and its principal axis.
(b) Sample stimulus from Vecera and Farah.

- Grouping and determination of an object-based frame of reference: Attentional processes might determine not only the up–down direction of an object, but also its left–right and front–back direction, allowing for the establishment of a full-blown object-based frame of reference. It is difficult to imagine that this process could operate in a purely bottom-up fashion; most likely contact with object representations stored in long-term visual memory would be necessary.
- Grouping and determination of a structural description: For complex, articulated objects, attention might operate on a structural description of an object—a description that decomposes an object or scene into its parts, and that characterizes the relationships among the parts in terms of multiple allocentric frames of reference. Attention would then act to select a subtree of the structural description.

These alternatives vary on two dimensions: the reference frame in which object-based attention operates egocentric for (1) and (2), allocentric for (3) and (4)— and on the degree of interaction with object knowledge required for selection—from weak, low-order statistics for (1) to high-order object knowledge for (4). The key issue is the degree to which object-based attentional effects require the explicit computation of object properties, such as a principal axis, frame of reference, or structural description, and the degree to which the data mandate such computations. All four alternatives have been invoked in the literature to explain object based attentional effects.

Evidence Points to One Account of Object-based Attentional Selection

In terms of the computations required, the grouped array account of object-based selection is the simplest and can operate at the earliest point in the visual processing stream, and hence should be preferred on the grounds of parsimony. Have argued that a variety of experimental results seeming to call for more complex accounts of objectbased attention can in fact be explained in terms of the grouped array account, and object-based representations and contact with object knowledge are not required. Although the existence of multiple attentional processes raises the possibility of multiple types of object-based selection, the grouped array account can explain most, if not all, of the object-based attention literature.

A complete account of object-based attention in terms of grouped arrays requires an understanding of the cues that determine grouping and, hence, that specify objects. The Gestalt cues of similarity, closure, and connectedness are all grouping cues that can influence the allocation of attention. For example, Kramer and Jacobson reported that a target that was physically connected to adjacent flanking items was attended as a single unit or group; a target that was not connected to the flankers could be selectively attended with little influence from the surrounding flankers. Thus, grouping cues, including grouping, by similarity, connectedness, and good continuation, can determine which stimuli or visual features are attended simultaneously.

Grouping cues need not be primitive and innate; they might also be learned and influenced by familiarity with a visual environment. For example, Vecera and Farah presented displays consisting of two overlapping outline block letters, in either the upright or the inverted position. Observers were asked to determine whether an "X" in the display was contained in one of the forms or in neither of the forms. Response times were faster for upright displays than inverted displays, suggesting that familiarity with upright letter forms was at play in the allocation of object-based attention. This result seems to argue against an account that relied solely on Gestalt grouping cues for segmentation, but might nonetheless be explained by the existence of adaptive grouping mechanisms that exploit low-order statistical regularities in the environment.

Relationship between Space-based and Object-based Attention

Although many grouping cues have been identified, the relationship between these cues, which direct attention to objects, and the factors directing attention to locations in space has proved elusive. Initially, evidence for both space-based and object-based attentional selection led to a debate about whether selection was object based or space based. The current consensus is that both of these attentional modes coexist in the visual system and may influence one another. Despite this emerging consensus, many studies continue to address the relationship between these two modes of selection as if one mode of selection is more important than the other. For example, Lavie and Driver suggested a space-then-object account by demonstrating that object-based effects occur only within the focus of spatial attention. Other theorists have argued for an object-then-space relationship in which that the outputs of preattentive grouping processes influence the allocation of spatial attention.

Neither of these accounts is completely satisfactory. For example, data exist that appear inconsistent with the object-then-space account. Mack et al. demonstrated that if spatial attention is occupied at fixation by a visually demanding discrimination, grouping fails. If grouping occurred before attention, then occupying spatial attention with a demanding task should not impair object-based grouping. Similarly, a space-then-object account has difficulty explaining results from object-based attention studies. In many studies, observers are instructed to perform a discrimination on a centrally presented target item. With such instructions, spatial attention should be focused centrally, and grouping outside this central region should not influence observers' responses to this central target.

The alternative to accounts supposing primacy of either space-based or object-based attention is an interactive account in which space- and object-based attentional processing operate simultaneously, each one helping to guide the other. However, interactive accounts face a serious computational problem. Object attention requires a search to partition visual features into objects; spatial attention requires a search for salient locations in the visual field. Each of these searches entails distinct and possibly conflicting computational objectives and, hence, incompatible solutions. Consequently, the reality of interactive accounts is that they are tricky to implement: The solutions reached are often suboptimal, where each search converges but the two outcomes are inconsistent with one another and each is suboptimal within its own domain.

Thus, a significant challenge lies ahead to unify mechanisms of space- and object-based attention. The grouped array view of object-based attention provides one key insight toward a coherent theory, via its proposal of a common substrate for the two varieties of attention: a topographic, viewer-based representation of space, often referred to in the attentional modeling literature as a saliency map. Another key insight concerns the role of strategic control. Because one form of attention does not always dominate over the other, it is likely that task demands and stimulus structure influence the relative contribution of each form of attention. Thus, a complete theory of attention requires claims concerning the processes by which the flexible attentional system is configured to operate for a given task in a given environment.

Toward a Unified Theory of Space- and Object-based Attention

Rather than viewing space-based and object-based attention as two qualitatively different forms of attention, unification is possible by conceptualizing attentional processing as fundamentally aimed at grouping related locations in the visual field. One can think of space-based and object-based processes as providing weak constraints concerning which locations belong together: Space-based attention suggests that adjacent, contiguous locations be grouped; object-based attention suggests that locations containing visual features likely to belong to the same object be grouped. The attentional state is then determined by a constraintsatisfaction search that attempts to identify groupings that are consistent with as many of the suggestions as possible. Thus, the operation of attention is viewed as a single search, not two searches with distinct goals; this unification is possible via a shared representation of space.

This view suggests a weaker role for grouping processes than is ordinarily considered. Grouping processes can be heuristic and spatially local and can operate on multiple dimensions (e.g., color, shape) independently, and the global attentional state results from resolving the assorted grouping constraints with the space-based constraints.

Given the contribution of constraints from many different processes converging in attentional selection, the weighting of constraints becomes a key issue. Space-based attentional states result when spacebased constraints dominate; object-based attentional states result when object-based constraints dominate. Because the data suggest the nature of the task and the stimulus display can influence which form of attention dominates, it seems natural to suggest that the weighting of constraints is under strategic control. One particularly elegant, computationally motivated form of control might involve selection of task- and environment-specific weightings that yield optimal performance, e.g., minimal response time or maximal accuracy. For example, reinforcement learning might be used to fine-tune the operation of the attentional system to achieve optimal performance. Beyond the virtue of integrating spacebased and object-based attention, this perspective has the additional potential virtue of explaining integration of the various and diverse Gestalt grouping cues in determination of the attentional state.

References

- Perception-and-the-perceptual-process: verywellmind.com, Retrieved 28 March, 2019
- Most-important-characteristics-of-perception: shareyouressays.com, Retrieved 7 January, 2019
- Gestalt-principles-of-form-perception, human-computer-interaction: interaction-design.org, Retrieved 26 June, 2019
- Attention, science: britannica.com, Retrieved 14 February, 2019
- Types-of-attention: thepeakperformancecenter.com, Retrieved 5 August, 2019
- The-pattern-recognition-definition-psychology, psychology: ukessays.com, Retrieved 2 April, 2019
- Attention-span: goodtherapy.org, Retrieved 12 July, 2019
- Introduction-to-sensation, boundless-psychology: lumenlearning.com, Retrieved 10 January, 2019
- Gestalt-laws-of-perceptual-organization: verywellmind.com, Retrieved 21 April, 2019

3

Memory and its Types

The faculty of the brain through which it stores, encodes and retrieves information is called memory. It is broadly categorized into long-term memory and short-term memory. This chapter discusses in detail the theories and concepts related to memory such as working memory and state-dependent memory.

Cognitive psychologist Margaret W. Matlin has described memory as the "process of retaining information over time." Others have defined it as the ability to use our past experiences to determine our future path.

When they are asked to define memory, most people think of studying for a test or recalling where we put the car keys. However, memory is essential in our everyday lives. We would not be able to function in the present or move forward without relying on our memory.

Formation of Memories

The process of encoding a memory begins when we are born and occurs continuously. For something to become a memory, it must first be picked up by one or more of our senses. A memory starts off in short-term storage. We learn how to tie our shoe, for example. Once we have the process down, it goes into our long-term memory and we can do it without consciously thinking about the steps involved.

Important memories typically move from short-term memory to long-term memory. The transfer of information to long-term memory for more permanent storage can be happen in several steps. Information can be committed to long-term memory through repetition — such as studying for a test or repeatedly taking steps until walking can be performed without thinking — or associating it with other previously acquired knowledge, like remembering a new acquaintance Mrs. Emerald by associating her name with an image of the green jewel.

Motivation is also a consideration, in that information relating to something that you have a keen interest in is more likely to be stored in your long-term memory. That's why someone might be able to recall the stats of a favorite baseball player years after he has retired or where a favorite pair of shoes was purchased.

We are typically not aware of what is in our memory until we need to use that bit of information. Then we use the process of retrieval to bring it to the forefront when we need to use it. Again, much of this recall happens without having concentrate on it — particularly with common tasks such as shoe tying — but there are other types of memories that take more effort to bring to the forefront.

Memory loss is often associated with aging, but there are a number of things that can trigger short- and long-term memory loss, including injury, medications and witnessing a traumatic event.

While experts have varying definitions for short-term memory, it is generally described as the recollection of things that happened immediately up to a few days. It is generally believed that five to nine items can be stored in active short-term memory and can be readily recalled. Patients who suffer from short-term memory loss can't remember who walked into the room five minutes before, but can remember their childhood friend from 50 years ago.

Implicit memory is sometimes referred to as unconscious memory or automatic memory. Implicit memory uses past experiences to remember things without thinking about them. Musicians and professional athletes are said to have superior ability to form procedural memories.

Procedural memory, which is a subset of implicit memory, is a part of the long-term memory responsible for knowing how to do things, also known as motor skills. You don't have to delve into your memory to recall how to walk each time you take a step.

Some examples of procedural memory:

- Playing piano
- Ice skating
- Playing tennis
- Swimming
- Climbing stairs

While implicit memory requires little if any effort to recall, explicit memory — sometimes referred to as declarative memory — requires a more concerted effort to bring the surface. Declarative memory involves both semantic and episodic memory.

While most people can tick off the days of the week from the time they are in grade school — which is implicit memory — it takes explicit memory to remember that your mother's birthday is next Wednesday.

Semantic memory is not connected to personal experience. Semantic memory includes things that are common knowledge, such as the names of states, the sounds of letters, the capitals of countries and other basic facts that are not in question. Some examples of semantic memory include:

- Knowledge that the sky is blue
- Knowing how to use a knife and fork
- Remembering what dog is

Episodic memory is a person's unique recollections of a specific event or an episode. People are usually able to associate particular details with an episodic memory, such as how they felt, the time and place, and other particulars. It is not clear as to why some memories of events in our lives are committed to memory, while others don't get recorded, but researchers believe that emotions play a critical role in what we remember.

Some examples of episodic memory:

- Where you were and the people you were with when you found out about the Challenger space shuttle disaster.
- Your beach vacation last summer.
- The first time you traveled by plane.
- Your first day at a new job.
- The restaurant you went to on your first date with your spouse.

Types of Memory

Sensory Memory

Sensory memory allows an individual to remember an input in great detail but for only a few milliseconds.

Sensory memory allows individuals to retain impressions of sensory information for a brief time after the original stimulus has ceased. It allows individuals to remember great sensory detail about a complex stimulus immediately following its presentation. Sensory memory is an automatic response considered to be outside of cognitive control. The information represented in this type of memory is the "raw data" which provides a snapshot of a person's overall sensory experience. Information from sensory memory has the shortest retention time, ranging from mere milliseconds to five seconds. It is retained just long enough for it to be transferred to short-term (working) memory.

In sensory memory, no manipulation of the incoming information occurs as it is transferred quickly to working memory. The amount of information is greatly reduced during this transfer because the capacity of working memory is not large enough to cope with all the input coming from our sense organs.

Types of Sensory Memory

It is assumed that there is a subtype of sensory memory for each of the five major senses (touch, taste, sight, hearing, and smell); however, only three of these types have been extensively studied: echoic memory, iconic memory, and haptic memory.

Iconic Memory

Sensory input to the visual system goes into iconic memory, so named because the mental representations of visual stimuli are referred to as icons. Iconic memory has a duration of about 100 ms. One of the times that iconic memory is noticeable is when we see "light trails." This is the phenomenon when bright lights move rapidly at night and you perceive them as forming a trail; this is the image that is represented in iconic memory.

Light trails: In iconic memory, you perceive a moving bright light as forming a continuous line because of the images retained in sensory memory for milliseconds.

Echoic Memory

Echoic memory is the branch of sensory memory used by the auditory system. Echoic memory is capable of holding a large amount of auditory information, but only for 3–4 seconds. This echoic sound is replayed in the mind for this brief amount of time immediately after the presentation of the auditory stimulus.

Haptic Memory

Haptic memory is the branch of sensory memory used by the sense of touch. Sensory receptors all over the body detect sensations like pressure, itching, and pain, which are briefly held in haptic memory before vanishing or being transported to short-term memory. This type of memory seems to be used when assessing the necessary forces for gripping and interacting with familiar objects. Haptic memory seems to decay after about two seconds. Evidence of haptic memory has only recently been identified and not as much is known about its characteristics compared to iconic memory.

Short-term and Working Memory

Short-term memory, which includes working memory, stores information for a brief period of recall for things that happened recently.

Short-term memory is the capacity for holding a small amount of information in an active, readily available state for a brief period of time. It is separate from our long-term memory, where lots of information is stored for us to recall at a later time. Unlike sensory memory, it is capable of temporary storage. How long this storage lasts depends on conscious effort from the individual; without rehearsal or active maintenance, the duration of short-term memory is believed to be on the order of seconds.

Capacity of Short-term Memory

Short-term memory acts as a scratchpad for temporary recall of information. For instance, in order to understand this sentence you need to hold in your mind the beginning of the sentence as you read the rest. Short-term memory decays rapidly and has a limited capacity.

The psychologist George Miller suggested that human short-term memory has a forward memory span of approximately seven items plus or minus two. More recent research has shown that this number is roughly accurate for college students recalling lists of digits, but memory span varies widely with populations tested and with material used.

For example, the ability to recall words in order depends on a number of characteristics of these words: fewer words can be recalled when the words have longer spoken duration (this is known as the word-length effect) or when their speech sounds are similar to each other (this is called the phonological similarity effect). More words can be recalled when the words are highly familiar or occur frequently in the language. Chunking of information can also lead to an increase in short-term memory capacity. For example, it is easier to remember a hyphenated phone number than a single long number because it is broken into three chunks instead of existing as ten digits.

Rehearsal is the process in which information is kept in short-term memory by mentally repeating it. When the information is repeated each time, that information is re-entered into the short-term memory, thus keeping that information for another 10 to 20 seconds, the average storage time for short-term memory. Distractions from rehearsal often cause disturbances in short-term memory retention. This accounts for the desire to complete a task held in short-term memory as soon as possible.

Working Memory

Though the term "working memory" is often used synonymously with "short-term memory," working memory is related to but actually distinct from short-term memory. It holds temporary data in the mind where it can be manipulated. Baddeley and Hitch's 1974 model of working memory is the most commonly accepted theory of working memory today. According to Baddeley, working memory has a phonological loop to preserve verbal data, a visuospatial scratchpad to control visual data, and a central executive to disperse attention between them.

Phonological Loop

The phonological loop is responsible for dealing with auditory and verbal information, such as phone numbers, people's names, or general understanding of what other people are talking about. We could roughly say that it is a system specialized for language. It consists of two parts: a short-term *phonological store* with auditory memory traces that are subject to rapid decay, and an *articulatory loop* that can revive these memory traces. The phonological store can only store sounds for about two seconds without rehearsal, but the auditory loop can "replay them" internally to keep them in working memory. The repetition of information deepens the memory.

Visuospatial Sketchpad

Visual and spatial information is handled in the visuospatial sketchpad. This means that information about the position and properties of objects can be stored. The phonological loop and visuospatial sketchpad are semi-independent systems; because of this, you can increase the amount you can remember by engaging both systems at once. For instance, you might be better able to remember an entire phone number if you visualize part of it (using the visuospatial sketchpad) and then say the rest of it out loud (using the phonological loop).

Central Executive

The central executive connects the phonological loop and the visuospatial sketchpad and coordinates their activities. It also links the working memory to the long-term memory, controls the storage of long-term memory, and manages memory retrieval from storage. The process of storage is influenced by the duration in which information is held in working memory and the amount that the information is manipulated. Information is stored for a longer time if it is semantically interpreted and viewed with relation to other information already stored in long-term memory.

Transport to Long-term Memory

The process of transferring information from short-term to long-term memory involves encoding and consolidation of information. This is a function of time; that is, the longer the memory stays in the short-term memory the more likely it is to be placed in the long-term memory. In this process, the meaningfulness or emotional content of an item may play a greater role in its retention in the long-term memory.

This greater retention is owed to an enhanced synaptic response within the hippocampus, which is essential for memory storage. The limbic system of the brain (including the hippocampus and amygdala) is not necessarily directly involved in long-term memory, but it selects particular information from short-term memory and consolidates these memories by playing them like a continuous tape.

Long-term Memory

Long-term memory is used for the storage of information over long periods of time, ranging from a few hours to a lifetime.

If we want to remember something tomorrow, we have to consolidate it into long-term memory today. Long-term memory is the final, semi-permanent stage of memory. Unlike sensory and short-term memory, long-term memory has a theoretically infinite capacity, and information can remain there indefinitely. Long-term memory has also been called reference memory, because an individual must refer to the information in long-term memory when performing almost any task. Long-term memory can be broken down into two categories: explicit and implicit memory.

Explicit Memory

Explicit memory, also known as conscious or declarative memory, involves memory of facts, concepts, and events that require conscious recall of the information. In other words, the individual must actively think about retrieving the information from memory. This type of information is explicitly stored and retrieved—hence its name. Explicit memory can be further subdivided into semantic memory, which concerns facts, and episodic memory, which concerns primarily personal or autobiographical information.

Semantic Memory

Semantic memory involves abstract factual knowledge, such as "Albany is the capital of New York." It is for the type of information that we learn from books and school: faces, places, facts, and concepts. You use semantic memory when you take a test. Another type of semantic memory is called a script. Scripts are like blueprints of what tends to happen in certain situations. For example, what usually happens if you visit a restaurant? You get the menu, you order your meal, you eat it, and then you pay the bill. Through practice, you learn these scripts and encode them into semantic memory.

Episodic Memory

Episodic memory is used for more contextualized memories. They are generally memories of specific moments, or episodes, in one's life. As such, they include sensations and emotions associated with the event, in addition to the who, what, where, and when of what happened. An example of an episodic memory would be recalling your family's trip to the beach. Autobiographical memory (memory for particular events in one's own life) is generally viewed as either equivalent to, or a subset of, episodic memory. One specific type of autobiographical memory is a flashbulb memory, which is a highly detailed, exceptionally vivid "snapshot" of the moment and circumstances in which a piece of surprising and consequential (or emotionally arousing) news was heard. For example, many people remember exactly where they were and what they were doing when they heard of the terrorist attacks on September 11, 2001. This is because it is a flashbulb memory.

Semantic and episodic memory are closely related; memory for facts can be enhanced with episodic memories associated with the fact, and vice versa. For example, the answer to the factual question "Are all apples red?" might be recalled by remembering the time you saw someone eating a green apple. Likewise, semantic memories about certain topics, such as football, can contribute to more detailed episodic memories of a particular personal event, like watching a football game. A person that barely knows the rules of football will remember the various plays and outcomes of the game in much less detail than a football expert.

Implicit Memory

In contrast to explicit (conscious) memory, implicit (also called "unconscious" or "procedural") memory involves procedures for completing actions. These actions develop with practice over time. Athletic skills are one example of implicit memory. You learn the fundamentals of a sport, practice them over and over, and then they flow naturally during a game. Rehearsing for a dance or musical performance is another example of implicit memory. Everyday examples include remembering how to tie your shoes, drive a car, or ride a bicycle. These memories are accessed without conscious awareness—they are automatically translated into actions without us even realizing it. As such, they can often be difficult to teach or explain to other people. Implicit memories differ from the semantic scripts described above in that they are usually actions that involve movement and motor coordination, whereas scripts tend to emphasize social norms or behaviors.

Working Memory

Working memory is a limited capacity part of the human memory system that combines the temporary storage and manipulation of information in the service of cognition. Short-term memory refers to information-storage without manipulation and is therefore a component of working memory. Working memory differs from long-term memory, a separate part of the memory system with a vast storage capacity that holds information in a relatively more stable form. According to the multi-component model, working memory includes an executive controller that interacts with separate short-term stores for auditory-verbal and visuospatial information. The concept of working memory has proved useful in many areas of application including individual differences in cognition, neuropsychology, normal and abnormal child development and neuroimaging.

The term working memory is used most frequently to refer to a limited capacity system that is capable of briefly storing and manipulating information involved in the performance of complex cognitive tasks such as reasoning, comprehension and certain types of learning. Working memory differs from short-term memory (STM) in that it assumes both the storage and manipulation of information, and in the emphasis on its functional role in complex cognition. A range of different approaches to the study of working memory have developed with differences reflecting the interests of the researcher, whether neuropsychological, neurobiological , psychometric or oriented towards providing practical guidance on human factors. Despite very different theoretical methods and styles, there is general agreement on a need to assume a role for some form of executive controller, probably of limited attentional capacity, aided by temporary storage systems, with visual and verbal storage probably operating separately. Such a structure had in fact been proposed by Baddeley and Hitch. While accepting that this is now one of range of models, the Baddeley and Hitch multicomponent model provides a convenient structure for summarising research on working memory over the 30 years since it was first proposed.

Before moving on it is important to note that the term working memory was developed independently in the study of animal learning where it refers to the type of learning or memory thought to underpin tasks such as the radial arm maze, in which an animal has to remember which of several arms have already been visited on that day, a task which we would regard as depending on long-term memory.

The Multicomponent Model of Working Memory

In the 1960s there was a short period of consensus among researchers that human memory consisted of a system that could be divided into two principal components. One was a short-term store capable of holding small amounts of information for a few seconds. This fed into a separate long-term store holding vast amounts of information over longer time intervals. This so-called modal model could account for a range of experimental data and was able to account for selective effects of different types of brain damage on short- and long-term recall.

Baddeley and Hitch set out to test the hypothesis that the short-term store also functioned as a working memory. They did so by requiring participants to perform reasoning, comprehension or learning tasks at the same time as they were holding in STM between 0 and 8 digits for immediate recall. If STM does function as a working memory, then loading it to capacity should lead to massive disruption of cognitive processing. It did indeed cause some disruption, with time to perform a reasoning task increasing with load, but the effect was not huge, and there was no influence on error rate. Baddeley and Hitch therefore abandoned the modal model, according to which STM is a unitary store, proposing instead a multicomponent model assumes an attentional controller, the central executive aided by two subsystems, the visuospatial sketchpad concerned with visual storage and processing, and its acoustic/verbal equivalent, the phonological loop.

The Phonological Loop

This is the subsystem that is assumed to hold digit sequences for immediate recall. The fact that reasoning was slowed as number of digits increased suggests that it does play a role in reasoning, but the unchanged error rate indicates that it is not essential. It is assumed to have two basic components, a temporary speech-related/acoustic store and a subvocal articulatory rehearsal process.

The phonological store is indicated by the presence of the phonological similarity effect, whereby people are much less accurate in repeating back sequences of similar-sounding words such as man cap cat mat can, than dissimilar words such as pit day cow pen top. Similarity of meaning (huge large big wide tall) has little effect on immediate recall. On the other hand if several trials are given to learn a longer list of say 10 words, meaning becomes all-important and sound loses it power, consistent with different systems for short-term and long-term storage.

Evidence for the importance of rehearsal comes from the word length effect, whereby immediate recall of long words (e.g. Refrigerator university tuberculosis opportunity hippopotamus) is much more error-prone than for short words.

Baddeley and Hitch suggested that the memory trace of items in the short-term store would rapidly fade, but could be maintained by saying them to oneself. Long words take longer to say, allowing more fading and hence more forgetting to occur. Consistent with this interpretation, preventing subjects from saying words to themselves by requiring the continuous utterance of an item such as the word 'the', removes the word length effect. Since the initial demonstration of the word length effect other interpretations have been proposed, differing principally in the implications of the effect for whether items in the short-term store are forgotten as a result of spontaneous decay of the memory trace, or by disruption from later material.

The concept of the phonological loop has influenced a number of attempts to simulate human performance in verbal STM tasks using more detailed computational models. The first tranche of such models focused on specifying mechanisms for handling information about the serial order of items, an aspect that was left unspecified in the original account of the loop. These models tend to agree that serial ordering involves 'competitive queueing', a process whereby items are simultaneously active and compete for serial selection. The models differ principally with respect to the nature of the ordering cues that determine these activation levels. Recent attempts at computational modelling have gone further by specifying how the short-term phonological storage system interacts with long-term memory, an essential step to understanding the role of the loop in long-term learning.

Function of the Phonological Loop

Given that one accepts the evidence for a temporary verbal or phonological memory system, the question of its evolutionary significance arises. One possibility is that the phonological loop supports the acquisition of language, providing a temporary means of storing new words, while they are consolidated in phonological LTM. Evidence for this comes from the study of a patient with a very pure phonological STM deficit, who found it extremely hard to learn to link new foreign words to their meaning, while performing normally when learning to link pairs of words in her native language.

A series of studies followed up this hypothesis. One study tested eight-year-old children with specific language impairment (SLI), who had normal general intelligence but the language of six-year-olds.

They found it very difficult to repeat back nonwords such as SKITICULT. As they showed no sign of impaired hearing or speech production, their deficit was attributed to impaired phonological STM. Twin studies have shown that the deficit in nonword repetition in SLI is inheritable, but that other deficits also contribute to the disorder. Performance on nonword repetition also correlates highly with the level of vocabulary development in young normal children although as children get older, other factors such as intelligence and exposure to language become increasingly important. More recently, increasing attention has been paid to the role of the phonological loop in controlling behavior through self-instruction a function initially emphasised by the Russian psychologists, Luria and Vygotsky.

Visuospatial Sketchpad

The study of visuospatial STM has developed enormously in recent years and is very well described in the entry by Luck, who suggests that its principal function is to create and maintain a visuospatial representation that persists across the irregular pattern of eye movements that characterise our scanning of the visual world.

Another function of the sketchpad is to create and maintain visual images of the type that we might for example, use in attempting to answer questions such as whether the ears of a collie dog are floppy or pricked, in describing the route from the station to home, or that an architect might use to imagine a building he is designing. It has been shown that spatial tasks can interfere with spatial skills such as driving a car, while a more purely visual activity such as seeing a sequence of pictures or colour patches may interfere with capacity to remember objects or shapes. Such results, together with the occurrence of brain-damaged patients who show one deficit and not the other, suggests that information about space, and about objects and their visual characteristics, may be stored separately. The presence of similarities between storage of serial order in visual and verbal memory suggests an analogous process, though not necessarily within a single system.

Central Executive

This is assumed to be an attentional control system of limited processing capacity that has the role of controlling action. Baddeley adopted a model proposed originally by Norman and Shallice which suggested that actions are controlled in two ways. Behavior that is routine and habitual is controlled automatically by a range of schemas, well-learned processes that allow us to respond appropriately to the environment. An experienced driver on a routine trip would be a good example of this, sometimes arriving at the destination with no memory of the journey. When such procedures are no longer adequate, for example finding the normal route blocked by an accident, a second system, the Supervisory Attentional System (SAS) comes into operation. This is capable of using long-term knowledge in order to set up possible solutions, and reflect on them before choosing the best. In the case of our interrupted journey, this might involve the central executive of working memory, probably in connection with LTM, the visuospatial sketchpad, and possibly the phonological loop. In its original version, the central executive was regarded as a general system capable of both processing and storage. In the interests of parsimony Baddeley and Logie proposed that it had a purely attentional capacity. Subsequent research has however, suggested the need to supplement the executive with a separate storage system, the episodic buffer.

Although the term 'central executive' might suggest a single monolithic controller, it seems more likely that it comprises an integrated alliance of executive control processes, probably including the capacity to focus attention, to divide attention between two or more tasks, and to control access to long-term memory, possibly based on one or more types of inhibition.

Executive functioning has been extensively investigated by Shallice, particularly in connection with its disruption following damage to the frontal lobes of the brain, a deficit referred to as the dysexecutive syndrome. This may result in major problems of attentional control, including sometimes repeatedly perseverating on a single action, while at others failing to maintain a goal against distraction. In the case of memory, this may result in confabulation where, in attempting to retrieve a memory, recall is captured by inappropriate associations, sometimes resulting in totally false memories.

Episodic Buffer

The initial three-component model of working memory ran into problems in accounting for the way in which the various subsystems could work together and in particular how they could interface with long-term memory. To tackle this problem, Baddeley proposed a fourth component, the episodic buffer. This was assumed to be a temporary store of limited capacity that was capable of combining a range of different storage dimensions, allowing it to collate information from perception, from the visuospatial and verbal subsystems and LTM. It was assumed to do so by representing them as multidimensional chunks or episodes, which were assumed to be available to consciousawareness. The capacity to bind a range of separate sensory channels into the perception of integrated objects is often regarded as an important function of consciousness. Our investigation of this binding function in recent years has caused us to modify the Baddeley model which predicts that disrupting the central executive will interfere with binding. This is not the case, suggesting that the episodic buffer should be regarded as a passive store, and that the processes of binding do not depend crucially on executive control. In this respect, the current model differs from the proposal by Baars that consciousness operates like a stage on which actors perform, replacing it with a concept more closely resembling that of a screen on which the results of binding processes operating elsewhere can be projected and utilised by the central executive.

An alternative view of working memory is provided by Cowan who, postulates an attentional system with a capacity of about four chunks as the central feature of working memory. Outside this central focus, short-term storage is assumed to depend on activated long-term memory. Cowan's model could be seen as one way of specifying the interaction between the central executive and the episodic buffer. Cowan's emphasis on working memory as activated long-term memory might seem to provide a clear contrast with the multicomponent model. The difference is however more apparent than real. Both assume that interaction with LTM plays an important role, with the multicomponent model assuming that such links operate at a number of different levels in ways that the simple concept of "activation" fails to capture.

Cowan's work has however, raised some important, and as yet unresolved issues, including:

1. Modularity: could the apparent separation of visuospatial and verbal working memory be accounted for on the basis of a more general principle of similarity-based interference in activated long-term memory?
2. Capacity: Do storage and processing draw on a single limited capacity, as proposed in the initial Baddeley and Hitch model, or are they separate, as in the episodic buffer version?

3. Decay or Interference: Is information lost through temporal decay of the memory trace, or is it displaced or over-written by other material?

These are not new questions, but have become issues of greatly renewed activity, largely as a result of Cowan's ideas and his extensive experimental program.

Individual Differences in Working Memory

Daneman and Carpenter were interested in the role of working memory in comprehension. They developed a task that involved simultaneously processing sentences and remembering the last word of each, which they called working memory span. They found a remarkably high correlation between performance on this task and measures of reading comprehension in their college student participants. This predictive capacity has been replicated many many times, and shown to generalise to a wide variety of tasks that combine temporary storage with processing. Some of these tasks are quite complex, for example remembering words that are sandwiched between arithmetical calculations, but even tasks involving quite simple operations may correlate with measures such as scholastic achievement, provided they involve combining memory and rapid processing. There is furthermore a very high correlation between tasks of this type and performance on conventional intelligence tests based on reasoning capacity. This has led a number of groups to search for the crucial capacity that allows these apparently simple tasks to predict such a wide range of cognitive skills.

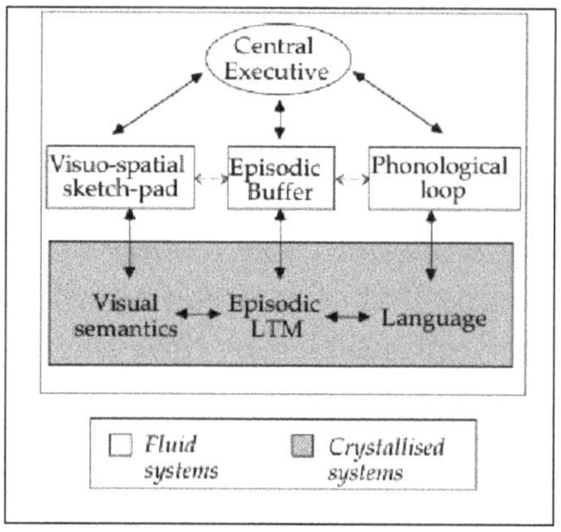

Model of working memory

Probably the most sustained attempt to solve the problem of why working memory span predicts so many cognitive tasks has come from Engle and his co-workers who have shown that the capacity to predict cognitive function is not limited to memory tasks, but can also be found in attentional control paradigms such as that involved in the antisaccade-task. This task involves participants moving their eyes from a fixation point to a target as rapidly as possible. Performance can be facilitated by a peripheral warning light occurring at the point where the target will appear, as there is a strong tendency for the eye to move automatically to a new stimulus. In a second condition however, rather than directly indicating the location of the target, the warning light signals participants to move their eyes to the opposite side. This information still proves helpful to high span but not low working memory span participants. Based on this and a range of other studies Engle and colleagues argue that the crucial feature of working memory is the capacity to maintain attention against distraction, whether this is perceptual or comes from other sources such as earlier memories.

However, while Engle makes a strong case for an association between working capacity and the ability to inhibit distracting stimuli, it is not clear that this is the only feature that characterises working memory capacity; it may indeed be just one example of a number of functions of a more general, multi-faceted attentional control system. Furthermore the concept of inhibition itself is open to a range of interpretations at both a psychological and physiological level.

The fact that we still do not fully understand how these complex working memory span tasks work does not, of course, mean that we can not use them profitably. Susan Gathercole and colleagues used the multicomponent working memory model to develop a working memory battery suitable for children of school age, using complex working memory span tasks as a measure of central executive capacity and other tasks to assess phonological and visuospatial subsystems. Factor analysis supported the multi-component model and showed that the structure of the working memory system remains remarkably stable as children develop. Although its capacity increases with age, there are nevertheless marked developmental changes in the way working memory is utilised. For example the developmental progression whereby the child masters increasingly complex intellectual operations has been linked to the growth of central executive capacity. There are also significant developmental changes in the subsystems of working memory, the best known being the expansion in the range of operation of the phonological loop, ranging from the development of the capacity for inner speech and rehearsal strategies in children to the involvement of a wider range of aspects of executive control in adults.

Gathercole's test battery is able to identify children who are at risk of encountering academic difficulties, with different patterns of working memory deficit associated with problems in different subject areas. Careful observation of children at school has showed that children with poor working memory skills tend to struggle because of a difficulty in following the sometimes surprisingly complex instructions provided by teachers. They also have trouble in coping with many of the techniques and strategies that are designed to help children cope, since these often require additional working memory capacity. Such children resemble those characterised as suffering from the attention deficit component of the ADHD syndrome. A programme that helps teachers identify such children and optimise teaching methods has been developed.

Neural Substrates of Working Memory

A good deal of research has been carried out on this topic, initially through the study of patients with localised lesions and subsequently using neuroimaging methods. Broadly speaking, the results fit the three-component model, with the phonological loop being represented in the left hemisphere where storage is associated with a region in the temporoparietal junction (Brodmann area), and rehearsal with the more anterior Brodmann area that is known to be associated with speech production. The visuospatial sketchpad appears to involve a number of predominantly right hemisphere areas, one visual, presumably reflecting the processing and retention of objects and their visual features, a second area is more parietal, presumably involving spatial aspects, while two frontal areas of activation have been associated with control functions. There is general acceptance that the frontal lobes play an important role in executive control, although opinions differ as to the extent to which different executive functions may be separately localisable. There is as yet little evidence as to the localisation of the episodic buffer, which seems likely to reflect a broadly distributed system which may possibly not give rise to activation in any one specific area.

Working Memory and the Brain

The blackboard of the mind, the brain's post-it note – these are just some of the monikers that have been awarded to your mental working memory. Defined as the active part of your mind, your working memory involves the simultaneous processing and storing of information.

What is your Working Memory?

Working memory is the mind's ability to keep information for a short span of time, as you utilize such facts for the tasks and activities you need to do. It makes use of two lobes: the frontal lobe, which is responsible for planning, reasoning, emotions, problem-solving, movement and speech; and the parietal lobe, which governs the perception of stimuli such as pain, pressure, touch and temperature.

Since working memory is naturally brief, it makes use of attention and memory, but only for a short span of time. It is considered the foundation of the mind's executive function, a group of mental processes that allows an individual to solve problems, plan ahead, pay attention and organize activities.

Kinds of Working Memory

There are two types of working memory used by all individuals from around the globe.

- Auditory/Verbal Working Memory:

  Makes use of the mind's phonological or sound system. A good example is repeatedly dictating a phone number while dialling it. While it cannot be retained while doing a certain a task, it is touted by many as a common learning disadvantage in most activities. Tasks that make use of verbal working memory include comprehension and language activities.

- Visual-Spatial Working Memory:

  Defined as the brain's ability to use an 'imaginary sketchpad,' it enables a person to visualize something – and keep it in his mind's eye. Individuals can use this type of working memory to remember images, sequences and patterns. It is also useful for computing mathematical equations in the mind.

When do we use Working Memory?

Working memory is used in most aspects of life. When you do the following activities, you utilize your mind's working memory:

- Remembering a phone number, plate number or web address while looking for a pen and paper to jot down the information.
- Following directions to a place you need to go without a map – just keeping in mind what the kind police officer has told you.
- Calculating in your mind the cost of all the items inside your grocery basket.
- Recalling the name of the person beside you so you can introduce him to another friend.
- Measuring an ingredient when you are at a different page of the recipe book.

Limitations of Working Memory

While working memory is an essential part of cognition, there are limitations that come with this sort of thinking. Here are some factors that can lead to the loss of information from your working memory:

- Distractions, such as a ringing phone, somebody talking to you, or suddenly remembering an unrelated thought.
- Keeping in mind too much information. As with any mind, working memory comes with limitations – especially when it comes to retaining numbers.
- Performing a difficult task. Activities such as multiplying and mental arithmetic can lead to information loss and an ineffective working memory.

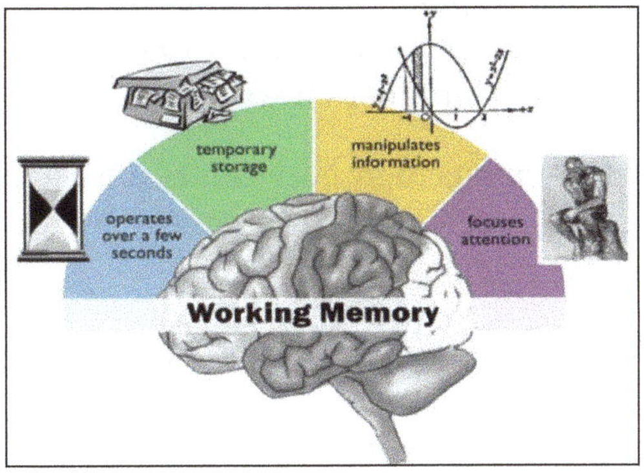

So we've talked about what it is and what it is not. But to sum it up, just remember these four aspects of working memory:

- Working memory operates in a very short timespan—in a matter of seconds.
- Working memory is used to temporarily store information for immediate usage, whereas long-term memory is used for permanent storage.
- Working memory is also use to manipulate information it stores.
- Working memory focuses your attention on one thing.

Short-term Memory

Short-term memory (STM) is the second stage of the multi-store memory model proposed by the Atkinson-Shiffrin. The duration of STM seems to be between 15 and 30 seconds, and the capacity about 7 items.

Short term memory has three key aspects:

- limited capacity (only about 7 items can be stored at a time).
- limited duration (storage is very fragile and information can be lost with distraction or passage of time).
- encoding (primarily acoustic, even translating visual information into sounds).

There are two ways in which capacity is tested, one being span, the other being recency effect.

The Magic number 7 (plus or minus two) provides evidence for the capacity of short term memory. Most adults can store between 5 and 9 items in their short-term memory. This idea was put forward by Miller (1956) and he called it the magic number 7. He though that short term memory could hold 7 (plus or minus 2 items) because it only had a certain number of "slots" in which items could be stored.

However, Miller didn't specify the amount of information that can be held in each slot. Indeed, if we can "chunk" information together we can store a lot more information in our short term memory.

Miller's theory is supported by evidence from various studies, such as Jacobs (1887). He used the digit span test with every letter in the alphabet and numbers apart from "w" and "7" because they had two syllables. He found out that people find it easier to recall numbers rather than letters. The average span for letters was 7.3 and for numbers it was 9.3.

The duration of short term memory seems to be between 15 and 30 seconds, according to Atkinson and Shiffrin (1971). Items can be kept in short term memory by repeating them verbally (acoustic encoding), a process known as rehearsal.

Using a technique called the Brown-Peterson technique which prevents the possibility of retrieval by having participants count backwards in 3s.

Peterson and Peterson (1959) showed that the longer the delay, the less information is recalled. The rapid loss of information from memory when rehearsal is prevented is taken as an indication of short term memory having a limited duration.

Baddeley and Hitch (1974) have developed an alternative model of short-term memory which they call working memory.

Long-term Memory

Long-term memory (LTM) is a hypothetical construct. Although you won't find a matching structure in the brain, it's a helpful mental model to think of long-term memory as a dynamic yet permanent store of information.

Rather than being a distinct structure, researchers have found regions in every lobe of the brain that store and retrieve memories of facts and events.

We are usually referring to long-term memory when we talk about remembering something.

Long-term memory encompasses three operations: encoding, storage and retrieval. These are all examined below.

Long-term memory is more than a knowledge archive. It provides the background information that we need to understand the world by bringing relevant knowledge into working memory as it's needed.

Types of Long-term Memory

1. Cognitive psychologists think of long-term memory as divided into two broad types. Explicit memory, also called declarative memory, consists of memories we are aware of or conscious memories. Implicit memory, also called nondeclarative memory, is unconscious. It consists of memories used without our conscious awareness.
2. Explicit memory (the conscious kind) consists of semantic memory—memory for facts and knowledge about the world—and episodic memory—memory for personal experiences.
3. There are several types of implicit memories (the unconscious kind). Most relevant to training is procedural memory. This is our memory for doing things that usually require action. When use a mouse on the computer or dial a phone number we are not consciously aware of the memories that enable us to perform these skills.

Capacity, Duration and Speed

1. It is unknown how long information in long-term memory can last. It could be stored indefinitely. Think of the older people you know who are experts in their field or who remember details of their childhood. Some information appears to last forever.
2. It is equally unknown how much information long-term memory can store. In practical terms, think of long-term memory as having an infinite capacity because it never gets used up.
3. The time it takes to access information in long-term memory is thought to be 200 milliseconds or .200 second.

Encoding

1. When information is transformed and "written" to long-term memory it is known as encoding. There are varied strategies that instructional designers and learners can use to improve encoding.
2. Information in long-term memory is most likely stored in network-type structures called schemas. Schemas are an efficient way to organize interrelated concepts in a meaningful way.
3. When we learn or experience something new and connect it with previously stored information, the process is known as assimilation.
4. Sometimes we learn something new or have experiences that don't fit in with existing schemas. We then alter existing schemas or create new ones in a process is known as accommodation.

Retrieval

1. Retrieval is the process of activating and using information from long-term memory. Retrieval is facilitated through retrieval cues, which is any stimulus that helps us recall information from long-term memory.

2. Some cognitive psychologists think that not being able to remember something is more a failure of not having the right cue than the fact that the information is not present in long-term memory.

3. Recognition memory is almost always better than recall. Recognition involves determining whether you've seen something before. With recall, you have to generate the remembered information.

4. Memories are more than a simple construction of recalled information. Rather, what we recall is influenced by attitudes, beliefs and previous experiences. So memories are reconstructed events.

Strategies to Enhance Encoding and Retrieval

1. The transfer of information into long-term memory is facilitated by elaboration or elaborative rehearsal. Some elaboration strategies include: thinking of related ideas or examples of the content, mentally tying the information together or creating a mental image of the information. Course designers and instructors can encourage this behavior.

2. Most likely, retrieval is improved when the type of elaboration used for encoding matches the type of task required for retrieval.

3. Making purposeful connections and associations with prior knowledge improves transfer to long-term memory. Many designers and instructors use this strategy and it is one of Gagne's Nine Events of Instruction.

4. Organizing information, such as categorizing it into subsets, can facilitate retrieval. Many people do this spontaneously and instructional designers spend a great deal of effort at organizing information into meaningful chunks.

5. Retention is improved through distributed practice across multiple study sessions rather than concentrating the same amount of practice into one session. This allows information to be consolidated into memory over time.

6. People can recall facts better when the facts are associated with a personal experience. Pairing semantic memories with episodic memories facilitates learning.

Comparing Long-term Memory and Short-term Memory

For the most part, memory and how it works has largely been a mystery to experts. However, what scientists do know is that memory is partitioned into several different parts—primarily short-term memory, long-term memory, and working memory.

Working memory, short-term memory, and long-term memory all play an important role in remembering, learning, and creating. It is safe to say that without memory, human progress would not exist.

Short-term memory differs from long-term memory in two fundamental ways, with only short-term memory demonstrating temporal decay and capacity limits. Long-term memory however, can store vast amounts of information and is permanent.

Short-term memory gives the ability for the human brain to keep information in the mind for a very short period of time, such as remembering a phone number long enough until you are able to dial it on our phones. The extent of short-term memory lasts within seconds to minutes then dissipates if effort is not made to retain the information for long-term use.

It is commonly believed that the capacity of short-term memory (and also working memory) is 7 +/- 2. That is, on average, humans are able to hold seven random and unrelated objects simultaneously in the short-term memory bank, give or take 2. In other words, short-term memory holds about 5-9 items at one time. This is also known as human memory span.

It is believed that short-term memory is a primary function of the prefrontal cortex. Once memory is consolidated (via long-term potentiation), it is carried over to the hippocampus wherein long-term memories are formed and stored permanently. This conversion from short-term to long-term memory requires concerted effort, the passage of time, and the absence of interference in memory consolidation.

Things learned on a daily basis dissipate unless consolidation takes place, in which it is transferred into the long-term memory bank. So how does consolidation take place? It takes place with repetition and review. The more something is repeated and used, the more neuronal connections the brain makes, wherein the neural pathways used for the specific information become stronger. In the process, the synapses become stronger between the two neurons as signals are more frequently passed between them.

In addition, sleeping has been said to be important in the consolidation of memory and learning. Studies of rats found that that more genes are expressed during sleep, and activities displayed during spatial learning are replayed in the hippocampus during sleep.

If short-term memory is consolidated and stored in the long-term memory, it becomes permanently ingrained, accessible for later use. If the memory does not consolidate, it will become available for later use and access. For instance, a phone number does not go through consolidation, it does not become a long-term memory and will not be remembered. In order for the number to be consolidated, one must make an effort to review the number or the number must be stored in the short-term memory bank multiple times to build neural connections.

Ultimately, the role of short-term memory is to file information for temporary usage. If it is not consolidated, it is discarded. This process of discarding is important to make room for learning and new memories. But once a memory is stored in the long-term memory bank, it is stored there forever. It may not feel like it is stored there forever. Sometimes, you may not be able to recall something that is stored in the long-term memory bank—nevertheless, it is there. Because once memory is stored, it is permanent.

Sometimes short-term memory and working memory are used interchangeably. Short-term memory definitely plays a function in working memory but it is not exactly the same thing. Both short-term memory and long-term memory hold information available for working memory usage. However, working memory is a theoretical framework of the structure of how memory manipulation works, in which short-term memory and long-term memory both serve extremely important functions.

The central executive region (located in the prefrontal cortex) seems to play a fundamental role in both short-term and working memory. The region serves as a temporary storage facility for short-term memory while at the same time making the memory available for recall and manipulation. The ability to manipulate information is essentially the theoretical difference between short-term memory and working memory. Short-term memory is used to describe the ability to store temporary information for immediate retrieval and discard, while working memory is used to describe the use of information for manipulation.

Encoding, Retrieval and Consolidation

Memory Encoding

When information comes into our memory system (from sensory input), it needs to be changed into a form that the system can cope with, so that it can be stored.

Think of this as similar to changing your money into a different currency when you travel from one country to another. For example, a word which is seen (in a book) may be stored if it is changed (encoded) into a sound or a meaning (i.e. semantic processing).

There are three main ways in which information can be encoded (changed):

1. Visual (picture)
2. Acoustic (sound)
3. Semantic (meaning)

For example, how do you remember a telephone number you have looked up in the phone book? If you can see it then you are using visual coding, but if you are repeating it to yourself you are using acoustic coding (by sound).

Evidence suggests that this is the principle coding system in short-term memory (STM) is acoustic coding. When a person is presented with a list of numbers and letters, they will try to hold them in STM by rehearsing them (verbally).

Rehearsal is a verbal process regardless of whether the list of items is presented acoustically (someone reads them out), or visually (on a sheet of paper).

The principle encoding system in long-term memory (LTM) appears to be semantic coding (by meaning). However, information in LTM can also be coded both visually and acoustically.

Memory Storage

This concerns the nature of memory stores, i.e., where the information is stored, how long the memory lasts for (duration), how much can be stored at any time (capacity) and what kind of information is held.

The way we store information affects the way we retrieve it. There has been a significant amount of research regarding the differences between Short Term Memory (STM) and Long Term Memory (LTM).

Most adults can store between 5 and 9 items in their short-term memory. Miller (1956) put this idea forward and he called it the magic number 7. He though that short-term memory capacity was 7 (plus or minus 2) items because it only had a certain number of "slots" in which items could be stored.

However, Miller didn't specify the amount of information that can be held in each slot. Indeed, if we can "chunk" information together we can store a lot more information in our short-term memory. In contrast, the capacity of LTM is thought to be unlimited.

Information can only be stored for a brief duration in STM (0-30 seconds), but LTM can last a lifetime.

Memory Retrieval

This refers to getting information out storage. If we can't remember something, it may be because we are unable to retrieve it. When we are asked to retrieve something from memory, the differences between STM and LTM become very clear.

STM is stored and retrieved sequentially. For example, if a group of participants are given a list of words to remember, and then asked to recall the fourth word on the list, participants go through the list in the order they heard it in order to retrieve the information.

LTM is stored and retrieved by association. This is why you can remember what you went upstairs for if you go back to the room where you first thought about it.

Organizing information can help aid retrieval. You can organize information in sequences (such as alphabetically, by size or by time). Imagine a patient being discharged from hospital whose treatment involved taking various pills at various times, changing their dressing and doing exercises.

If the doctor gives these instructions in the order which they must be carried out throughout the day (i.e., in the sequence of time), this will help the patient remember them.

Criticisms of Memory Experiments

A large part of the research on memory is based on experiments conducted in laboratories. Those who take part in the experiments - the participants - are asked to perform tasks such as recalling lists of words and numbers.

Both the setting - the laboratory - and the tasks are a long way from everyday life. In many cases, the setting is artificial and the tasks fairly meaningless. Does this matter?

Psychologists use the term ecological validity to refer to the extent to which the findings of research studies can be generalized to other settings. An experiment has high ecological validity if its findings can be generalized, that is applied or extended, to settings outside the laboratory.

It is often assumed that if an experiment is realistic or true-to-life, then there is a greater likelihood that its findings can be generalized. If it is not realistic (if the laboratory setting and the tasks are artificial) then there is less likelihood that the findings can be generalized. In this case, the experiment will have low ecological validity.

Many experiments designed to investigate memory have been criticized for having low ecological validity. First, the laboratory is an artificial situation. People are removed from their normal social settings and asked to take part in a psychological experiment.

They are directed by an 'experimenter' and may be placed in the company of complete strangers. For many people, this is a brand new experience, far removed from their everyday lives. Will this setting affect their actions, will they behave normally?

Often, the tasks participants are asked to perform can appear artificial and meaningless. Few, if any, people would attempt to memorize and recall a list of unconnected words in their daily lives. And it is not clear how tasks such as this relate to the use of memory in everyday life.

The artificiality of many experiments has led some researchers to question whether their findings can be generalized to real life. As a result, many memory experiments have been criticized for having low ecological validity.

Learning

Learning is perhaps the most important human capacity. Learning allows us to create effective lives by being able to respond to changes. We learn to avoid touching hot stoves, to find our way home from school, and to remember which people have helped us in the past and which people have been unkind. Without the ability to learn from our experiences, our lives would be remarkably dangerous and inefficient. The principles of learning can also be used to explain a wide variety of social interactions, including social dilemmas in which people make important, and often selfish, decisions about how to behave by calculating the costs and benefits of different outcomes.

The study of learning is closely associated with the behaviorist school of psychology, in which it was seen as an alternative scientific perspective to the failure of introspection. The behaviorists, including John B. Watson and B. F. Skinner, focused their research entirely on behavior, to the exclusion of any kinds of mental processes. For behaviorists, the fundamental aspect of learning is the process of conditioning—the ability to connect stimuli (the changes that occur in the environment) with responses (behaviors or other actions).

But conditioning is just one type of learning. We will also consider other types, including learning through insight, as well as observational learning (also known as modeling). In each case we will see not only what psychologists have learned about the topics but also the important influence that learning has on many aspects of our everyday lives.

Learning by Association: Classical Conditioning

Pavlov Demonstrates Conditioning in Dogs

In the early part of the 20th century, Russian physiologist Ivan Pavlov was studying the digestive system of dogs when he noticed an interesting behavioral phenomenon: The dogs began to salivate when the lab technicians who normally fed them entered the room, even though the dogs had not yet received any food. Pavlov realized that the dogs were salivating because they knew that they were about to be fed; the dogs had begun to associate the arrival of the technicians with the food that soon followed their appearance in the room.

With his team of researchers, Pavlov began studying this process in more detail. He conducted a series of experiments in which, over a number of trials, dogs were exposed to a sound immediately before receiving food. He systematically controlled the onset of the sound and the timing of the delivery of the food, and recorded the amount of the dogs' salivation. Initially the dogs salivated only when they saw or smelled the food, but after several pairings of the sound and the food, the dogs began to salivate as soon as they heard the sound. The animals had learned to associate the sound with the food that followed.

Pavlov had identified a fundamental associative learning process called classical conditioning. Classical conditioning refers to learning that occurs when a neutral stimulus (e.g., a tone) becomes associated with a stimulus (e.g., food) that naturally produces a behavior. After the association is learned, the previously neutral stimulus is sufficient to produce the behavior.

As you can see in figure Panel Image of Whistle and Dog", psychologists use specific terms to identify the stimuli and the responses in classical conditioning.

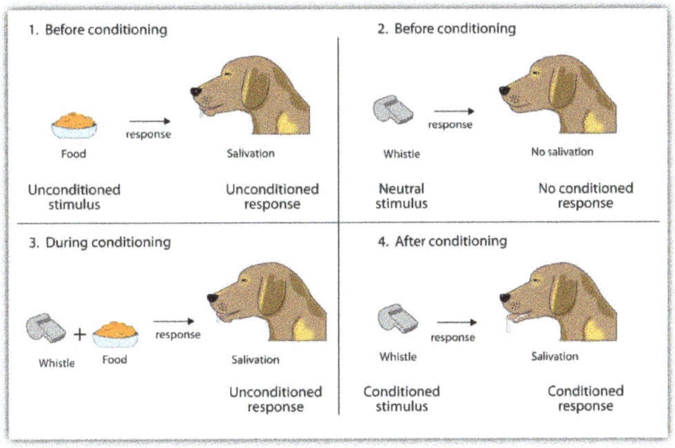

Figure: Panel Image of Whistle and Dog

The unconditioned stimulus (US) is something (such as food) that triggers a natural occurring response, and the unconditioned response (UR) is the naturally occurring response (such as salivation) that follows the unconditioned stimulus. The conditioned stimulus (CS) is a neutral stimulus that, after being repeatedly presented prior to the unconditioned stimulus, evokes a similar response as the unconditioned stimulus. In Pavlov's experiment, the sound of the tone served as the conditioned stimulus that, after learning, produced the conditioned response (CR), which is the acquired response to the formerly neutral stimulus. Note that the UR and the CR are the same behavior—in this case salivation—but they are given different names because they are produced by different stimuli (the US and the CS, respectively).

Top left: Before conditioning, the unconditioned stimulus (US) naturally produces the unconditioned response (UR). Top right: Before conditioning, the neutral stimulus (the whistle) does not produce the salivation response. Bottom left: The unconditioned stimulus (US), in this case the food, is repeatedly presented immediately after the neutral stimulus. Bottom right: After learning, the neutral stimulus (now known as the conditioned stimulus or CS), is sufficient to produce the conditioned responses (CR).

Conditioning is evolutionarily beneficial because it allows organisms to develop expectations that help them prepare for both good and bad events. Imagine, for instance, that an animal first smells a new food, eats it, and then gets sick. If the animal can learn to associate the smell (CS) with the food (US), then it will quickly learn that the food creates the negative outcome, and not eat it the next time.

The Persistence and Extinction of Conditioning

After he had demonstrated that learning could occur through association, Pavlov moved on to study the variables that influenced the strength and the persistence of conditioning. In some studies, after the conditioning had taken place, Pavlov presented the sound repeatedly but without presenting the food afterward. Figure "Acquisition, Extinction, and Spontaneous Recovery" shows what happened. As you can see, after the intial acquisition (learning) phase in which the conditioning occurred, when the CS was then presented alone, the behavior rapidly decreased—the dogs salivated less and less to the sound, and eventually the sound did not elicit salivation at all. Extinction refers to the reduction in responding that occurs when the conditioned stimulus is presented repeatedly without the unconditioned stimulus.

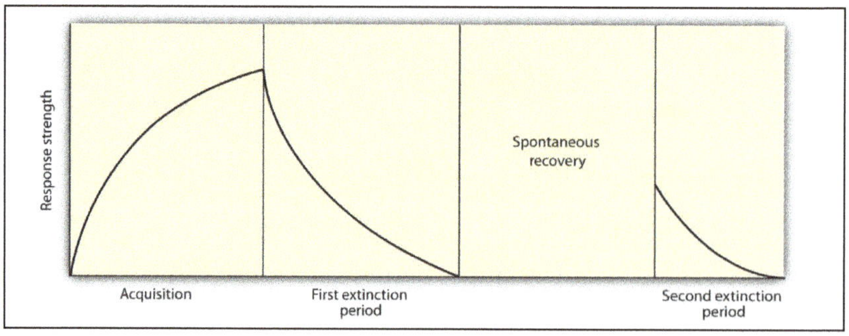

Acquisition, Extinction, and Spontaneous Recovery

Acquisition: The CS and the US are repeatedly paired together and behavior increases. Extinction: The CS is repeatedly presented alone, and the behavior slowly decreases. Spontaneous recovery: After a pause, when the CS is again presented alone, the behavior may again occur and then again show extinction.

Although at the end of the first extinction period the CS was no longer producing salivation, the effects of conditioning had not entirely disappeared. Pavlov found that, after a pause, sounding the tone again elicited salivation, although to a lesser extent than before extinction took place. The increase in responding to the CS following a pause after extinction is known as spontaneous recovery. When Pavlov again presented the CS alone, the behavior again showed extinction until it disappeared again.

Although the behavior has disappeared, extinction is never complete. If conditioning is again attempted, the animal will learn the new associations much faster than it did the first time.

Pavlov also experimented with presenting new stimuli that were similar, but not identical to, the original conditioned stimulus. For instance, if the dog had been conditioned to being scratched before the food arrived, the stimulus would be changed to being rubbed rather than scratched. He found that the dogs also salivated upon experiencing the similar stimulus, a process known as generalization. Generalization refers to the tendency to respond to stimuli that resemble the original conditioned stimulus. The ability to generalize has important evolutionary significance. If we eat some red berries and they make us sick, it would be a good idea to think twice before we eat some purple berries. Although the berries are not exactly the same, they nevertheless are similar and may have the same negative properties.

The flip side of generalization is discrimination—the tendency to respond differently to stimuli that are similar but not identical. Pavlov's dogs quickly learned, for example, to salivate when they heard the specific tone that had preceded food, but not upon hearing similar tones that had never been associated with food. Discrimination is also useful—if we do try the purple berries, and if they do not make us sick, we will be able to make the distinction in the future. And we can learn that although the two people in our class, Courtney and Sarah, may look a lot alike, they are nevertheless different people with different personalities.

In some cases, an existing conditioned stimulus can serve as an unconditioned stimulus for a pairing with a new conditioned stimulus—a process known as second-order conditioning. In one of Pavlov's studies, for instance, he first conditioned the dogs to salivate to a sound, and then repeatedly paired a new CS, a black square, with the sound. Eventually he found that the dogs would salivate at the sight of the black square alone, even though it had never been directly associated with the food. Secondary conditioners in everyday life include our attractions to things that stand for or remind us of something else, such as when we feel good on a Friday because it has become associated with the paycheck that we receive on that day, which itself is a conditioned stimulus for the pleasures that the paycheck buys us.

The Role of Nature in Classical Conditioning

Scientists associated with the behavioralist school argued that all learning is driven by experience, and that nature plays no role. Classical conditioning, which is based on learning through experience, represents an example of the importance of the environment. But classical conditioning cannot be understood entirely in terms of experience. Nature also plays a part, as our evolutionary history has made us better able to learn some associations than others.

Clinical psychologists make use of classical conditioning to explain the learning of a phobia—a strong and irrational fear of a specific object, activity, or situation. For example, driving a car is a neutral event that would not normally elicit a fear response in most people. But if a person were to experience a panic attack in which he suddenly experienced strong negative emotions while driving, he may learn to associate driving with the panic response. The driving has become the CS that now creates the fear response.

Psychologists have also discovered that people do not develop phobias to just anything. Although people may in some cases develop a driving phobia, they are more likely to develop phobias toward objects (such as snakes, spiders, heights, and open spaces) that have been dangerous to people in the past. In modern life, it is rare for humans to be bitten by spiders or snakes, to fall from trees or buildings, or to be attacked by a predator in an open area. Being injured while riding in a car or being cut by a knife are much more likely. But in our evolutionary past, the potential of being bitten by snakes or spiders, falling out of a tree, or being trapped in an open space were important evolutionary concerns, and therefore humans are still evolutionarily prepared to learn these associations over others.

Another evolutionarily important type of conditioning is conditioning related to food. In his important research on food conditioning, John Garcia and his colleagues attempted to condition rats by presenting either a taste, a sight, or a sound as a neutral stimulus before the rats were given drugs (the US) that made them nauseous. Garcia discovered that taste conditioning was extremely powerful— the rat learned to avoid the taste associated with illness, even if the illness occurred several hours later. But conditioning the behavioral response of nausea to a sight or a sound was much more difficult. These results contradicted the idea that conditioning occurs entirely as a result of environmental events, such that it would occur equally for any kind of unconditioned stimulus that followed any kind of conditioned stimulus. Rather, Garcia's research showed that genetics matters—organisms are evolutionarily prepared to learn some associations more easily than others. You can see that the ability to associate smells with illness is an important survival mechanism, allowing the organism to quickly learn to avoid foods that are poisonous.

1. Changing Behavior through Reinforcement and Punishment: Operant Conditioning.

In classical conditioning the organism learns to associate new stimuli with natural, biological responses such as salivation or fear. The organism does not learn something new but rather begins to perform in an existing behavior in the presence of a new signal. Operant conditioning, on the other hand, is learning that occurs based on the consequences of behavior and can involve the learning of new actions. Operant conditioning occurs when a dog rolls over on command because it has been praised for doing so in the past, when a schoolroom bully threatens his classmates because doing so allows him to get his way, and when a child gets good grades because her parents threaten to punish her if she doesn't. In operant conditioning the organism learns from the consequences of its own actions.

2. How Reinforcement and Punishment Influence Behavior: The Research of Thorndike and Skinner.

Psychologist Edward L. Thorndike was the first scientist to systematically study operant conditioning.

In his research Thorndike observed cats who had been placed in a "puzzle box" from which they tried to escape. At first the cats scratched, bit, and swatted haphazardly, without any idea of how to get out. But eventually, and accidentally, they pressed the lever that opened the door and exited to their prize, a scrap of fish. The next time the cat was constrained within the box it attempted fewer of the ineffective responses before carrying out the successful escape, and after several trials the cat learned to almost immediately make the correct response.

Observing these changes in the cats' behavior led Thorndike to develop his law of effect, the principle that responses that create a typically pleasant outcome in a particular situation are more likely to occur again in a similar situation, whereas responses that produce a typically unpleasant outcome are less likely to occur again in the situation. The essence of the law of effect is that successful responses, because they are pleasurable, are "stamped in" by experience and thus occur more frequently. Unsuccessful responses, which produce unpleasant experiences, are "stamped out" and subsequently occur less frequently.

When Thorndike placed his cats in a puzzle box, he found that they learned to engage in the important escape behavior faster after each trial. Thorndike described the learning that follows reinforcement in terms of the law of effect.

The influential behavioral psychologist B. F. Skinner expanded on Thorndike's ideas to develop a more complete set of principles to explain operant conditioning. Skinner created specially designed environments known as operant chambers (usually called Skinner boxes) to systemically study learning. A Skinner box (operant chamber) is a structure that is big enough to fit a rodent or bird and that contains a bar or key that the organism can press or peck to release food or water. It also contains a device to record the animal's responses.

The most basic of Skinner's experiments was quite similar to Thorndike's research with cats. A rat placed in the chamber reacted as one might expect, scurrying about the box and sniffing and clawing at the floor and walls. Eventually the rat chanced upon a lever, which it pressed to release pellets of food. The next time around, the rat took a little less time to press the lever, and on successive trials, the time it took to press the lever became shorter and shorter. Soon the rat was pressing the lever as fast as it could eat the food that appeared. As predicted by the law of effect, the rat had learned to repeat the action that brought about the food and cease the actions that did not.

Skinner studied, in detail, how animals changed their behavior through reinforcement and punishment, and he developed terms that explained the processes of operant learning (Table "How Positive and Negative Reinforcement and Punishment Influence Behavior"). Skinner used the term reinforcer to refer to any event that strengthens or increases the likelihood of a behavior and the term punisher to refer to any event that weakens or decreases the likelihood of a behavior. And he used the terms positive and negative to refer to whether a reinforcement was presented or removed, respectively. Thus positive reinforcement strengthens a response by presenting something pleasant after the response and negative reinforcement strengthens a response by reducing or removing something unpleasant. For example, giving a child praise for completing his homework represents positive reinforcement, whereas taking aspirin to reduced the pain of a headache represents negative reinforcement. In both cases, the reinforcement makes it more likely that behavior will occur again in the future.

Table: How Positive and Negative Reinforcement and Punishment Influence Behavior.

Operant conditioning term	Description	Outcome	Example
Positive reinforcement	Add or increase a pleasant stimulus	Behavior is strengthened	Giving a student a prize after he gets an A on a test.
Negative reinforcement	Reduce or remove an unpleasant stimulus	Behavior is strengthened	Taking painkillers that eliminate pain increases the likelihood that you will take painkillers again.
Positive punishment	Present or add an unpleasant stimulus	Behavior is weakened	Giving a student extra homework after she misbehaves in class.
Negative punishment	Reduce or remove a pleasant stimulus	Behavior is weakened	Taking away a teen's computer after he misses curfew.

Reinforcement, either positive or negative, works by increasing the likelihood of a behavior. Punishment, on the other hand, refers to any event that weakens or reduces the likelihood of a behavior. Positive punishment weakens a response by presenting something unpleasant after the response, whereas negative punishment weakens a response by reducing or removing something pleasant. A child who is grounded after fighting with a sibling (positive punishment) or who loses out on the opportunity to go to recess after getting a poor grade (negative punishment) is less likely to repeat these behaviors.

Although the distinction between reinforcement (which increases behavior) and punishment (which decreases it) is usually clear, in some cases it is difficult to determine whether a reinforcer is positive or negative. On a hot day a cool breeze could be seen as a positive reinforcer (because it brings in cool air) or a negative reinforcer (because it removes hot air). In other cases, reinforcement can be both positive and negative. One may smoke a cigarette both because it brings pleasure (positive reinforcement) and because it eliminates the craving for nicotine (negative reinforcement).

It is also important to note that reinforcement and punishment are not simply opposites. The use of positive reinforcement in changing behavior is almost always more effective than using punishment. This is because positive reinforcement makes the person or animal feel better, helping create a positive relationship with the person providing the reinforcement. Types of positive reinforcement that are effective in everyday life include verbal praise or approval, the awarding of status or prestige, and direct financial payment. Punishment, on the other hand, is more likely to create only temporary changes in behavior because it is based on coercion and typically creates a negative and adversarial relationship with the person providing the reinforcement. When the person who provides the punishment leaves the situation, the unwanted behavior is likely to return.

Creating Complex Behaviors through Operant Conditioning

Perhaps you remember watching a movie or being at a show in which an animal—maybe a dog, a horse, or a dolphin—did some pretty amazing things. The trainer gave a command and the dolphin swam to the bottom of the pool, picked up a ring on its nose, jumped out of the water through a hoop in the air, dived again to the bottom of the pool, picked up another ring, and then took both of the rings to the trainer at the edge of the pool. The animal was trained to do the trick, and the principles of operant conditioning were used to train it. But these complex behaviors are a far cry from the simple stimulus-response relationships that we have considered thus far. How can reinforcement be used to create complex behaviors such as these?

One way to expand the use of operant learning is to modify the schedule on which the reinforcement is applied. To this point we have only discussed a continuous reinforcement schedule, in which the desired response is reinforced every time it occurs; whenever the dog rolls over, for instance, it gets a biscuit. Continuous reinforcement results in relatively fast learning but also rapid extinction of the desired behavior once the reinforcer disappears. The problem is that because the organism is used to receiving the reinforcement after every behavior, the responder may give up quickly when it doesn't appear.

Most real-world reinforcers are not continuous; they occur on a partial (or intermittent) reinforcement schedule—a schedule in which the responses are sometimes reinforced, and sometimes not. In comparison to continuous reinforcement, partial reinforcement schedules lead to slower initial learning, but they also lead to greater resistance to extinction. Because the reinforcement does not appear after every behavior, it takes longer for the learner to determine that the reward is no longer coming, and thus extinction is slower. The four types of partial reinforcement schedules are summarized in Table "Reinforcement Schedules".

Reinforcement schedule	Explanation	Real-world example
Fixed-ratio	Behavior is reinforced after a specific number of responses.	Factory workers who are paid according to the number of products they produce.
Variable-ratio	Behavior is reinforced after an average, but unpredictable, number of responses.	Payoffs from slot machines and other games of chance.
Fixed-interval	Behavior is reinforced for the first response after a specific amount of time has passed.	People who earn a monthly salary.
Variable-interval	Behavior is reinforced for the first response after an average, but unpredictable, amount of time has passed.	Person who checks voice mail for messages.

Partial reinforcement schedules are determined by whether the reinforcement is presented on the basis of the time that elapses between reinforcement (interval) or on the basis of the number of responses that the organism engages in (ratio), and by whether the reinforcement occurs on a regular (fixed) or unpredictable (variable) schedule. In a fixed-interval schedule,reinforcement occurs for the first response made after a specific amount of time has passed. For instance, on a one-minute fixed-interval schedule the animal receives a reinforcement every minute, assuming it engages in the behavior at least once during the minute. As you can see in figure "Examples of Response Patterns by Animals Trained Under Different Partial Reinforcement Schedules", animals under fixed-interval schedules tend to slow down their responding immediately after the reinforcement but then increase the behavior again as the time of the next reinforcement gets closer. (Most students study for exams the same way.) In a variableinterval schedule,the reinforcers appear on an interval schedule, but the timing is varied around the average interval, making the actual appearance of the reinforcer unpredictable. An example might be checking your e-mail: You are reinforced by receiving messages that come, on average, say every 30 minutes, but the reinforcement occurs only at random times. Interval reinforcement schedules tend to produce slow and steady rates of responding.

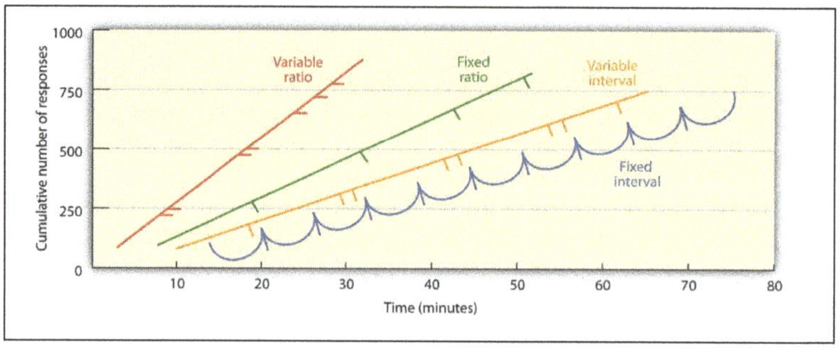

Examples of Response Patterns by Animals Trained Under Different Partial Reinforcement Schedules

Schedules based on the number of responses (ratio types) induce greater response rate than do schedules based on elapsed time (interval types). Also, unpredictable schedules (variable types) produce stronger responses than do predictable schedules (fixed types).

In a fixed-ratio schedule, a behavior is reinforced after a specific number of responses. For instance, a rat's behavior may be reinforced after it has pressed a key 20 times, or a salesperson may receive a bonus after she has sold 10 products. As you can see in Figure "Examples of Response Patterns by Animals Trained Under Different Partial Reinforcement Schedules", once the organism has learned to act in accordance with the fixed-reinforcement schedule, it will pause only briefly when reinforcement occurs before returning to a high level of responsiveness. A variable-ratio schedule provides reinforcers after a specific but average number of responses. Winning money from slot machines or on a lottery ticket are examples of reinforcement that occur on a variable-ratio schedule. For instance, a slot machine may be programmed to provide a win every 20 times the user pulls the handle, on average. As you can see in Figure "Slot Machine", ratio schedules tend to produce high rates of responding because reinforcement increases as the number of responses increase.

Complex behaviors are also created through shaping, the process of guiding an organism's behavior to the desired outcome through the use of successive approximation to a final desired behavior. Skinner made extensive use of this procedure in his boxes. For instance, he could train a rat to press a bar two times to receive food, by first providing food when the animal moved near the bar. Then when that behavior had been learned he would begin to provide food only when the rat touched the bar. Further shaping limited the reinforcement to only when the rat pressed the bar, to when it pressed the bar and touched it a second time, and finally, to only when it pressed the bar twice. Although it can take a long time, in this way operant conditioning can create chains of behaviors that are reinforced only when they are completed.

Reinforcing animals if they correctly discriminate between similar stimuli allows scientists to test the animals' ability to learn, and the discriminations that they can make are sometimes quite remarkable. Pigeons have been trained to distinguish between images of Charlie Brown and the other Peanuts characters, and between different styles of music and art.

Behaviors can also be trained through the use of secondary reinforcers. Whereas a primary reinforcer includes stimuli that are naturally preferred or enjoyed by the organism, such as food, water, and relief from pain, a secondary reinforcer (sometimes called conditioned reinforcer) is a neutral event that has become associated with a primary reinforcer through classical conditioning. An example of a secondary reinforcer would be the whistle given by an animal trainer, which has been associated over time with the primary reinforcer, food. An example of an everyday secondary reinforcer is money. We enjoy having money, not so much for the stimulus itself, but rather for the primary reinforcers (the things that money can buy) with which it is associated.

Learning by Insight and Observation

John B. Watson and B. F. Skinner were behaviorists who believed that all learning could be explained by the processes of conditioning—that is, that associations, and associations alone, influence learning. But some kinds of learning are very difficult to explain using only conditioning. Thus, although classical and operant conditioning play a key role in learning, they constitute only a part of the total picture.

One type of learning that is not determined only by conditioning occurs when we suddenly find the solution to a problem, as if the idea just popped into our head. This type of learning is known as insight, the sudden understanding of a solution to a problem. The German psychologist Wolfgang Köhler carefully observed what happened when he presented chimpanzees with a problem that was not easy for them to solve, such as placing food in an area that was too high in the cage to be reached. He found that the chimps first engaged in trial-and-error attempts at solving the problem, but when these failed they seemed to stop and contemplate for a while. Then, after this period of contemplation, they would suddenly seem to know how to solve the problem, for instance by using a stick to knock the food down or by standing on a chair to reach it. Köhler argued that it was this flash of insight, not the prior trial-and-error approaches, which were so important for conditioning theories, that allowed the animals to solve the problem.

Edward Tolman studied the behavior of three groups of rats that were learning to navigate through mazes. The first group always received a reward of food at the end of the maze. The second group never received any reward, and the third group received a reward, but only beginning on the 11th day of the experimental period. As you might expect when considering the principles of conditioning, the rats in the first group quickly learned to negotiate the maze, while the rats of the second group seemed to wander aimlessly through it. The rats in the third group, however, although they wandered aimlessly for the first 10 days, quickly learned to navigate to the end of the maze as soon as they received food on day 11. By the next day, the rats in the third group had caught up in their learning to the rats that had been rewarded from the beginning.

It was clear to Tolman that the rats that had been allowed to experience the maze, even without any reinforcement, had nevertheless learned something, and Tolman called this latent learning. Latent learning refers to learning that is not reinforced and not demonstrated until there is motivation to do so. Tolman argued that the rats had formed a "cognitive map" of the maze but did not demonstrate this knowledge until they received reinforcement.

Observational Learning: Learning by Watching

The idea of latent learning suggests that animals, and people, may learn simply by experiencing or watching. Observational learning (modeling) is learning by observing the behavior of others. To demonstrate the importance of observational learning in children, Bandura, Ross, and Ross showed children a live image of either a man or a woman interacting with a Bobo doll, a filmed version of the same events, or a cartoon version of the events. The Bobo doll is an inflatable balloon with a weight in the bottom that makes it bob back up when you knock it down. In all three conditions, the model violently punched the clown, kicked the doll, sat on it, and hit it with a hammer.

The researchers first let the children view one of the three types of modeling, and then let them play in a room in which there were some really fun toys. To create some frustration in the children, Bandura let the children play with the fun toys for only a couple of minutes before taking them away. Then Bandura gave the children a chance to play with the Bobo doll.

If you guessed that most of the children imitated the model, you would be correct. Regardless of which type of modeling the children had seen, and regardless of the sex of the model or the child, the children who had seen the model behaved aggressively—just as the model had done. They also punched, kicked, sat on the doll, and hit it with the hammer. Bandura and his colleagues had demonstrated that these children had learned new behaviors, simply by observing and imitating others.

Observational learning is useful for animals and for people because it allows us to learn without having to actually engage in what might be a risky behavior. Monkeys that see other monkeys respond with fear to the sight of a snake learn to fear the snake themselves, even if they have been raised in a laboratory and have never actually seen a snake.

The prospects for [human] survival would be slim indeed if one could learn only by suffering the consequences of trial and error. For this reason, one does not teach children to swim, adolescents to drive automobiles, and novice medical students to perform surgery by having them discover the appropriate behavior through the consequences of their successes and failures. The more costly and hazardous the possible mistakes, the heavier is the reliance on observational learning from competent learners.

Although modeling is normally adaptive, it can be problematic for children who grow up in violent families. These children are not only the victims of aggression, but they also see it happening to their parents and siblings. Because children learn how to be parents in large part by modeling the actions of their own parents, it is no surprise that there is a strong correlation between family violence in childhood and violence as an adult. Children who witness their parents being violent or who are themselves abused are more likely as adults to inflict abuse on intimate partners or their children, and to be victims of intimate violence. In turn, their children are more likely to interact violently with each other and to aggress against their parents.

State-dependent Memory

State-dependent memories are memories that are triggered or enhanced by a person's current mood because of the relationship to memories formed when you were in a similar state.

For instance, happy memories are more easily or intensely remembered when one is already feeling happy and the same goes for sadness or anger. Think about it, you're at a picnic with your family having a good time. It's really easy to flash back to other good times that you've had.

Likewise, if you're fighting with a partner you're more likely to bring up incidents or emotions that occurred in previous fights - the similar mood brings those memories to mind more readily.

This is related to state dependent learning in which an individual is more likely to recall information when they are in the same state of consciousness that they were when they learned the information.

References

- Memory: livescience.com, Retrieved 3 May, 2019
- Types-of-memory, psychology: lumenlearning.com, Retrieved 4 April, 2019
- Working_memory: scholarpedia.org, Retrieved 20 August, 2019
- What-is-working-memory-in-the-human-brain: examinedexistence.com, Retrieved 10 June, 2019
- Short-term-memory: simplypsychology.org, Retrieved 13 February, 2019
- Long-term-memory-and-learning: theelearningcoach.com, Retrieved 17 January, 2019
- Difference-between-short-term-long-term-and-working-memory: examinedexistence.com, Retrieved 7 March, 2019
- Memory: simplypsychology.org, Retrieved 29 July, 2019
- State-Dependent-Memories: alleydog.com, Retrieved 31 May, 2019

4

Cognitive Linguistics

The branch of linguistics which describes the manner in which language interacts with cognition and how language forms our thoughts is known as cognitive linguistics. Some of the aspects which are dealt with under this field are lexical semantics, language acquisition and non-verbal communication. All these diverse concepts of cognitive linguistics have been carefully analyzed in this chapter.

Cognitive linguistics is a cluster of overlapping approaches to the study of language as a mental phenomenon. Cognitive linguistics emerged as a school of linguistic thought in the 1970s.

In the introduction to Cognitive Linguistics: Basic Readings (2006), linguist Dirk Geeraerts makes a distinction between uncapitalized cognitive linguistics ("referring to all approaches in which natural language is studied as a mental phenomenon") and capitalized Cognitive Linguistics ("one form of cognitive linguistics").

- "Language offers a window into cognitive function, providing insights into the nature, structure and organization of thoughts and ideas. The most important way in which cognitive linguistics differs from other approaches to the study of language, then, is that language is assumed to reflect certain fundamental properties and design features of the human mind."
- "Cognitive Linguistics is the study of language in its cognitive function, where cognitive refers to the crucial role of intermediate informational structures with our encounters with the world. Cognitive Linguistics [assumes] that our interaction with the world is mediated through informational structures in the mind. It is more specific than cognitive psychology, however, by focusing on natural language as a means for organizing, processing, and conveying that information.
- "[W]hat holds together the diverse form of Cognitive Linguistics is the belief that linguistic knowledge involves not just knowledge of the language, but knowledge of our experience of the world as mediated by the language."

Cognitive Models and Cultural Models

- "Cognitive models, as the term suggests, represent a cognitive, basically psychological, view of the stored knowledge about a certain field. Since psychological states are always private and individual experiences, descriptions of such cognitive models necessarily involve a considerable degree of idealization. In other words, descriptions of cognitive models are based on the assumption that many people have roughly the same basic knowledge about things like sandcastles and beaches.

  "However, this is only part of the story. Cognitive models are of course not universal, but depend on the culture in which a person grows up and lives. The culture provides the background for all the situations that we have to experience in order to be able to form a cognitive model.

A Russian or German may not have formed a cognitive model of cricket simply because it is not part of the culture of his own country to play that game. So, cognitive models for particular domains ultimately depend on so-called cultural models. In reverse, cultural models can be seen as cognitive models that are shared by people belonging to a social group or subgroup. "Essentially, cognitive models and cultural models are thus just two sides of the same coin. While the term 'cognitive model' stresses the psychological nature of these cognitive entities and allows for inter-individual differences, the term 'cultural model' emphasizes the unifying aspect of its being collectively shared by many people. Although 'cognitive models' are related to cognitive linguistics and psycholinguistics while 'cultural models' belong to sociolinguistics and anthropological linguistics, researchers in all of these fields should be, and usually are, aware of both dimensions of their object of study."

Research in Cognitive Linguistics

- "One of the central assumptions underlying research in cognitive linguistics is that language use reflects conceptual structure, and that therefore the study of language can inform us of the mental structures on which language is based. One of the goals of the field is therefore to properly determine what sorts of mental representations are constructed by various sorts of linguistic utterances. Initial research in the field was conducted by way of theoretical discussions, which were based on the methods of introspection and rational reasoning. These methods were used to examine diverse topics such as the mental representation of presupposition, negation, counterfactuals and metaphor, to name a few".

  "Unfortunately, the observation of one's mental structures via introspection may be limited in its accuracy. As a result, investigators have come to realize that it is important to examine theoretical claims by using experimental methods".

Cognitive Psychologists vs. Cognitive Linguists

- "Cognitive psychologists, and others, criticize cognitive linguistic work because it is so heavily based on individual analysts' intuitions, and thus does not constitute the kind of objective, replicable data preferred by many scholars in the cognitive and natural sciences (e.g., data collected on large numbers of naive participants under controlled laboratory conditions."

Cognitive Semantics

Cognitive semantics is part of the cognitive linguistics movement. Semantics is the study of linguistic meaning. Cognitive semantics holds that language is part of a more general human cognitive ability, and can therefore only describe the world as people conceive of it. It is implicit that different linguistic communities conceive of simple things and processes in the world differently (different cultures), not necessarily some difference between a person's conceptual world and the real world (wrong beliefs).

The main tenets of cognitive semantics are:

- That grammar manifests a conception of the world held in a culture;
- That knowledge of language is acquired and contextual;

- That the ability to use language draws upon general cognitive resources and not a special language module.

As part of the field of cognitive linguistics, the cognitive semantics approach rejects the traditional separation of linguistics into phonology, morphology, syntax, pragmatics, etc. Instead, it divides semantics into meaning-construction and knowledge representation. Therefore, cognitive semantics studies much of the area traditionally devoted to pragmatics as well as semantics.

The techniques native to cognitive semantics are typically used in lexical studies such as those put forth by Leonard Talmy, George Lakoff, Dirk Geeraerts, and Bruce Wayne Hawkins. Some cognitive semantic frameworks, such as that developed by Talmy, take into account syntactic structures as well.

Points of Contrast

As a field, semantics is interested in three big questions: what does it mean for units of language, called lexemes, to have "meaning"? What does it mean for sentences to have meaning? Finally, how is it that meaningful units fit together to compose complete sentences? These are the main points of inquiry behind studies into lexical semantics, structural semantics, and theories of compositionality (respectively). In each category, traditional theories seem to be at odds with those accounts provided by cognitive semanticists.

Classic theories in semantics (in the tradition of Alfred Tarski and Donald Davidson) have tended to explain the meaning of parts in terms of necessary and sufficient conditions, sentences in terms of truth-conditions, and composition in terms of propositional functions. Each of these positions is tightly related to the others. According to these traditional theories, the meaning of a particular sentence may be understood as the conditions under which the proposition conveyed by the sentence hold true. For instance, the expression "snow is white" is true if and only if snow is, in fact, white. Lexical units can be understood as holding meaning either by virtue of set of things they may apply to (called the "extension" of the word), or in terms of the common properties that hold between these things (called its "intension"). The intension provides an interlocutor with the necessary and sufficient conditions that let a thing qualify as a member of some lexical unit's extension. Roughly, propositional functions are those abstract instructions that guide the interpreter in taking the free variables in an open sentence and filling them in, resulting in a correct understanding of the sentence as a whole.

Meanwhile, cognitive semantic theories are typically built on the argument that lexical meaning is conceptual. That is, meaning is not necessarily reference to the entity or relation in some real or possible world. Instead, meaning corresponds with a concept held in the mind based on personal understanding. As a result, semantic facts like "All bachelors are unmarried males" are not treated as special facts about our language practices; rather, these facts are not distinct from encyclopaedic knowledge. In treating linguistic knowledge as being a piece with everyday knowledge, the question is raised: how can cognitive semantics explain paradigmatically semantic phenomena, like category structure? Set to the challenge, researchers have drawn upon theories from related fields, like cognitive psychology and cognitive anthropology. One proposal is to treat in order to explain category structure in terms of nodes in a knowledge network. One example of a theory from cognitive science that has made its way into the cognitive semantic mainstream is the theory of prototypes, which cognitive semanticists generally argue is the cause of polysemy.

Cognitive semanticists argue that truth-conditional semantics is unduly limited in its account of full sentence meaning. While they are not on the whole hostile to truth-conditional semantics, they point out that it has limited explanatory power. That is to say, it is limited to indicative sentences, and does not seem to offer any straightforward or intuitive way of treating (say) commands or expressions. By contrast, cognitive semantics seeks to capture the full range of grammatical moods by also making use of the notions of framing and mental spaces.

Another trait of cognitive semantics is the recognition that meaning is not fixed but a matter of construal and conventionalization. The processes of linguistic construal, it is argued, are the same psychological processes involved in the processing of encyclopaedic knowledge and in perception. This view has implications for the problem of compositionality. An account in cognitive semantics called the dynamic construal theory makes the claim that words themselves are without meaning: they have, at best, "default construals," which are really just ways of using words. Along these lines, cognitive semantics argues that compositionality can only be intelligible if pragmatic elements like context and intention are taken into consideration.

The Structure of Concepts

Cognitive semantics has sought to challenge traditional theories in two ways: first, by providing an account of the meaning of sentences by going beyond truth-conditional accounts; and second, by attempting to go beyond accounts of word meaning that appeal to necessary and sufficient conditions. It accomplishes both by examining the structure of concepts.

Frame Semantics

Frame semantics, developed by Charles J. Fillmore, attempts to explain meaning in terms of their relation to general understanding, not just in the terms laid out by truth-conditional semantics. Fillmore explains meaning in general (including the meaning of lexemes) in terms of "frames". By "frame" is meant any concept that can only be understood if a larger system of concepts is also understood.

Fillmore: Framing

Many pieces of linguistic evidence motivate the frame-semantic project. First, it has been noted that word meaning is an extension of our bodily and cultural experiences. For example, the notion of restaurant is associated with a series of concepts, like food, service, waiters, tables, and eating. These rich-but-contingent associations cannot be captured by an analysis in terms of necessary and sufficient conditions, yet they still seem to be intimately related to our understanding of "restaurant".

Second, and more seriously, these conditions are not enough to account for asymmetries in the ways that words are used. According to a semantic feature analysis, there is nothing more to the meanings of "boy" and "girl" than:

1. BOY [+MALE], [+YOUNG]
2. GIRL [+FEMALE], [+YOUNG]

And there is surely some truth to this proposal. Indeed, cognitive semanticists understand the instances of the concept held by a given certain word may be said to exist in a schematic relation with the concept itself. And this is regarded as a legitimate approach to semantic analysis, so far as it goes.

However, linguists have found that language users regularly apply the terms "boy" and "girl" in ways that go beyond mere semantic features. That is, for instance, people tend to be more likely to consider a young female a "girl" (as opposed to "woman"), than they are to consider a borderline-young male a "boy" (as opposed to "man"). This fact suggests that there is a latent frame, made up of cultural attitudes, expectations, and background assumptions, which is part of word meaning. These background assumptions go up and beyond those necessary and sufficient conditions that correspond to a semantic feature account. Frame semantics, then, seeks to account for these puzzling features of lexical items in some systematic way.

Third, cognitive semanticists argue that truth-conditional semantics is incapable of dealing adequately with some aspects of the meanings at the level of the sentence.

You didn't Spare me a Day at the Seaside

In this case, the truth-conditions of the claim expressed by the antecedent in the sentence are not being denied by the proposition expressed after the clause. Instead, what is being denied is the way that the antecedent is framed.

Finally, with the frame-semantic paradigm's analytical tools, the linguist is able to explain a wider range of semantic phenomena than they would be able to with only necessary and sufficient conditions. Some words have the same definitions or intensions, and the same extensions, but have subtly different domains. For example, the lexemes land and ground are synonyms, yet they naturally contrast with different things -- sea and air, respectively.

As we have seen, the frame semantic account is by no means limited to the study of lexemes—with it, researchers may examine expressions at more complex levels, including the level of the sentence (or, more precisely, the utterance). The notion of framing is regarded as being of the same cast as the pragmatic notion of background assumptions. Philosopher of language John Searle explains the latter by asking readers to consider sentences like "The cat is on the mat". For such a sentence to make any sense, the interpreter makes a series of assumptions: i.e., that there is gravity, the cat is parallel to the mat, and the two touch. For the sentence to be intelligible, the speaker supposes that the interpreter has an idealized or default frame in mind.

Langacker: Profile and Base

An alternate strain of Fillmore's analysis can be found in the work of Ronald Langacker, who makes a distinction between the notions of profile and base. The profile is the concept symbolized by the word itself, while the base is the encyclopedic knowledge that the concept presupposes. For example, let the definition of "radius" be "a line segment that joins the center of a circle with any point on its circumference". If all we know of the concept radius is its profile, then we simply know that it is a line segment that is attached to something called the "circumference" in some greater whole called the "circle". That is to say, our understanding is fragmentary until the base concept of circle is firmly grasped.

When a single base supports a number of different profiles, then it can be called a "domain". For instance, the concept profiles of arc, center, and circumference are all in the domain of circle, because each uses the concept of circle as a base. We are then in a position to characterize the notion of a frame as being either the base of the concept profile, or (more generally) the domain that the profile is a part of.

Categorization and Cognition

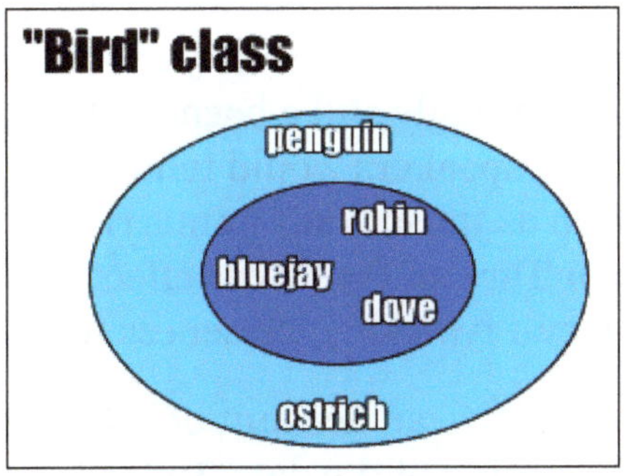

Membership of a graded class

A major divide in the approaches to cognitive semantics lies in the puzzle surrounding the nature of category structure. Semantic feature analyses fall short of accounting for the frames that categories may have. An alternative proposal would have to go beyond the minimalistic models given by classical accounts, and explain the richness of detail in meaning that language speakers attribute to categories.

Prototype theories, investigated by Eleanor Rosch, have given some reason to suppose that many natural lexical category structures are graded, i.e., they have prototypical members that are considered to be "better fit" the category than other examples. For instance, robins are generally viewed as better examples of the category "bird" than, say, penguins. If this view of category structure is the case, then categories can be understood to have central and peripheral members, and not just be evaluated in terms of members and non-members.

In a related vein, George Lakoff, following the later Ludwig Wittgenstein, noted that some categories are only connected to one another by way of family resemblances. While some classical categories may exist, i.e., which are structured by necessary and sufficient conditions, there are at least two other kinds: generative and radial.

Generative categories can be formed by taking central cases and applying certain principles to designate category membership. The principle of similarity is one example of a rule that might generate a broader category from given prototypes.

Radial categories are categories motivated by conventions, but not predictable from rules. The concept of "mother", for example, may be explained in terms of a variety of conditions that may or may not be sufficient. Those conditions may include: being married, has always been female, gave birth to the child, supplied half the child's genes, is a caregiver, is married to the genetic father, is one generation older than the child, and is the legal guardian. Any one of the above conditions might not be met: for instance, a "single mother" does not need to be married, and a "surrogate mother" does not necessarily provide nurturance. When these aspects collectively cluster together, they form a prototypical case of what it means to be a mother, but nevertheless they fail to outline the category crisply. Variations upon the central meaning are established by convention by the community of language users.

For Lakoff, prototype effects can be explained in large part due to the effects of idealized cognitive models. That is, domains are organized with an ideal notion of the world that may or may not fit reality. For example, the word "bachelor" is commonly defined as "unmarried adult male". However, this concept has been created with a particular ideal of what a bachelor is like: an adult, uncelibate, independent, socialized, and promiscuous. Reality might either strain the expectations of the concept, or create false positives. That is, people typically want to widen the meaning of "bachelor" to include exceptions like "a sexually active seventeen-year-old who lives alone and owns his own firm" (not technically an adult but seemingly still a bachelor), and this can be considered a kind of straining of the definition. Moreover, speakers would tend to want to exclude from the concept of bachelor certain false positives, such as those adult unmarried males that don't bear much resemblance to the ideal: i.e., the Pope, or Tarzan. Prototype effects may also be explained as a function of either basic-level categorization and typicality, closeness to an ideal, or stereotyping.

So viewed, prototype theory seems to give an account of category structure. However, there are a number of criticisms of this interpretation of the data. Indeed, Rosch and Lakoff, themselves chief advocates of prototype theory, have emphasized in their later works that the findings of prototype theory do not necessarily tell us anything about category structure. Some theorists in the cognitive semantics tradition have challenged both classical and prototype accounts of category structure by proposing the dynamic construal account, where category structure is always created "on-line"—and so, that categories have no structure outside of the context of use.

Mental Spaces

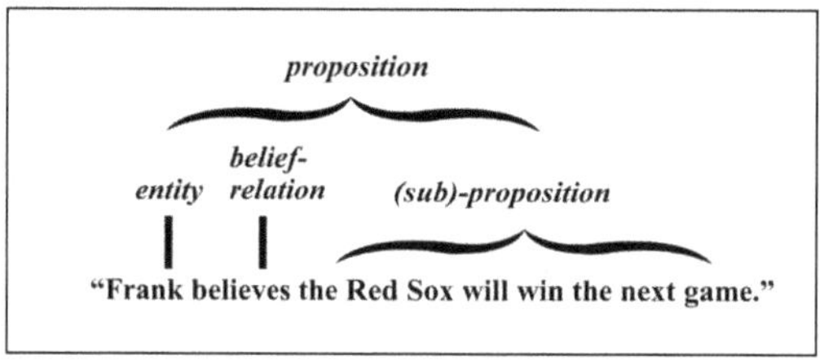

Propositional attitudes in Fodor's presentation of truth-conditional semantics

In traditional semantics, the meaning of a sentence is the situation it represents, and the situation can be described in terms of the possible world that it would be true of. Moreover, sentence meanings may be dependent upon propositional attitudes: those features that are relative to someone's beliefs, desires, and mental states. The role of propositional attitudes in truth-conditional semantics is controversial. However, by at least one line of argument, truth-conditional semantics seems to be able to capture the meaning of belief-sentences like "Frank believes that the Red Sox will win the next game" by appealing to propositional attitudes. The meaning of the overall proposition is described as a set of abstract conditions, wherein Frank holds a certain propositional attitude, and the attitude is itself a relationship between Frank and a particular proposition; and this proposition is the possible world where the Red Sox win the next game.

Still, many theorists have grown dissatisfied with the inelegance and dubious ontology behind possible-worlds semantics. An alternative can be found in the work of Gilles Fauconnier. For Fauconnier, the meaning of a sentence can be derived from "mental spaces". Mental spaces are cognitive structures entirely in the minds of interlocutors. In his account, there are two kinds of mental space. The base space is used to describe reality (as it is understood by both interlocutors). Space builders (or built space) are those mental spaces that go beyond reality by addressing possible worlds, along with temporal expressions, fictional constructs, games, and so on. Additionally, Fauconnier semantics distinguishes between roles and values. A semantic role is understood to be description of a category, while values are the instances that make up the category. (In this sense, the role-value distinction is a special case of the type-token distinction).

Fauconnier argues that curious semantic constructions can be explained handily by the above apparatus. Take the following sentence:

- In 1929, the Lady with White Hair was Blonde

The semanticist must construct an explanation for the obvious fact that the above sentence is not contradictory. Fauconnier constructs his analysis by observing that there are two mental spaces (the present-space and the 1929-space). His access principle supposes that "a value in one space can be described by the role its counterpart in another space has, even if that role is invalid for the value in the first space". So, to use the example above, the value in 1929-space is the blonde, while she is being described with the role of the lady with white hair in present-day space.

- Conceptualization and Construal

As we have seen, cognitive semantics gives a treatment of issues in the construction of meaning both at the level of the sentence and the level of the lexeme in terms of the structure of concepts. However, it is not entirely clear what cognitive processes are at work in these accounts. Moreover, it is not clear how we might go about explaining the ways that concepts are actively employed in conversation. It appears to be the case that, if our project is to look at how linguistic strings convey different semantic content, we must first catalogue what cognitive processes are being used to do it. Researchers can satisfy both requirements by attending to the construal operations involved in language processing—that is to say, by investigating the ways that people structure their experiences through language.

Language is full of conventions that allow for subtle and nuanced conveyances of experience. To use an example that is readily at hand, framing is all-pervasive, and it may extend across the full breadth of linguistic data, extending from the most complex utterances, to tone, to word choice, to expressions derived from the composition of morphemes. Another example is image-schemata, which are ways that we structure and understand the elements of our experience driven by any given sense.

According to linguists William Croft and D. Alan Cruse, there are four broad cognitive abilities that play an active part in the construction of construals. They are: attention/salience, judgment/comparison, situatedness, and constitution/gestalt. Each general category contains a number of subprocesses, each of which helps to explain the ways we encode experience into language in some unique way.

Lexical Semantics

Descriptive Scope of Lexical Semantics

The main phenomena studied by lexical semantics are organized along two dimensions. First, it makes a difference whether we look at semantic phenomena within individual words or whether we look at meaningful structures within the vocabulary as a whole. Terminologically, this difference of perspective can be expressed by referring to a 'semasiological' and an 'onomasiological' perspective. (Semasiology looks at the relationship between words and meaning with the word as starting point: it is basically interested in the polysemy of words. Onomasiology takes the converse perspective: given a concept to be expressed or a thing to be categorized, what options does a language offer, and how are the choices made?) Second, a distinction needs to be made between an approach that focuses on elements and relations only and one that takes into account the differences of structural weight between those elements and relations. Even though the terms are not perfect, we can use the terms 'qualitative approach' and 'quantitative approach' to refer to this second distinction. If we cross-classify the two distinctions, we get four groups of topics. 'Qualitative' semasiology deals with word senses and the semantic links among those senses, like metaphor and metonymy at the level of individual words. 'Qualitative' onomasiology deals with the semantic relations among lexical items, like lexical fields and lexical relations. 'Quantitative' semasiology deals with prototype effects: differences of salience and structural weight within an item or a meaning. 'Quantitative' onomasiology deals with salience effects in the lexicon at large, like basic-level phenomena.

Table: The Descriptive Scope of Lexical Semantics.

	Semasiology	onomasiology
'Qualitative' perspectives: elements and relations	• Polysemy • Semantic relations	• Lexical fields • Lexical relations • Distributional relations • Conceptual metaphor/metonymy • Frames
'Quantitative' perspectives: differences of salience	Prototype effects and radial sets	Basic levels and onomasiological salience

Polysemy and Vagueness

Establishing which meanings a word has is arguably the basic step in lexical semantic research. Polysemy is the common term for the situation in which a lexical item has more than one meaning, such as when late can mean 'after the usual, expected, or agreed time', 'advanced in day or night' (a late dinner), or 'no longer alive' (my late aunt Polly). Terminologically speaking, polysemy needs to be contrasted with homonymy and, more importantly, vagueness. When two (or more) words have the same shape, such as bank('slope, elevation in sea or river bed') and bank ('financial institution'), they are homonyms; whereas polysemy refers to multiplicity of meaning within a single word, the multiplicity is distributed over various words in the case of homonymy. As such, making a distinction between polysemy and homonymy comes down to determining whether we are dealing with one and the same word or with two different ones. The distinction between vagueness and polysemy involves the question of whether a particular piece of semantic information is part of the underlying semantic structure of the item or is the result of a contextual (and hence pragmatic) specification. For instance, neighbor is not polysemous between the readings 'male dweller next door' and 'female dweller next door,' in the sense that the utterance my neighbor is a civil servant will not be recognized as requiring disambiguation in the way that she is smart might (Do you mean 'bright' or 'stylish'?). The semantic information that is associated with the item neighbor in the lexicon does not, in other words, contain a specification regarding sex; neighbor is vague (or general, or unspecified) as to the dimension of gender.

To decide between polysemy and vagueness, a number of tests can be invoked. The three main ones are the following. First, from a truth-theoretical point of view, a lexical item is polysemous if it can simultaneously be clearly true and clearly false of the same referent. Considering the readings 'harbor' and 'fortified sweet wine from Portugal' of port, the polysemy of that item is established by sentences such as Sandeman is a port (in a bottle), but not a port (with ships). This criterion basically captures a semantic intuition: are two interpretations of a given expression intuitively sufficiently dissimilar so that one may be said to apply and the other not?

Second, linguistic tests involve syntactic rather than semantic intuitions. Specifically, they are based on acceptability judgments about sentences that contain two related occurrences of the item under consideration (one of which may be implicit). If the grammatical relationship between both occurrences requires their semantic identity, the resulting sentence may be an indication for the polysemy of the item. For instance, the so-called identity test involves 'identity-of-sense anaphora.' Thus, at midnight the ship passed the port, and so did the bartender is awkward if the two lexical meanings of port are at stake. Disregarding puns, it can only mean that the ship and the bartender alike passed the harbor, or conversely that both moved a particular kind of wine from one place to another. A mixed reading, in which the first occurrence of port refers to the harbor and the second to wine, is normally excluded. By contrast, the fact that the notions 'vintage sweet wine from Portugal' and 'blended sweet wine from Portugal' can be combined in Vintage Noval is a port, and so is blended Sandeman indicates that port is vague rather than polysemous with regard to the distinction between blended and vintage wines.

Third, the definitional criterion specifies that an item has more than one lexical meaning if there is no minimally specific definition covering the extension of the item as a whole, and that it has no more lexical meanings than there are maximally general definitions necessary to describe its extension. Definitions of lexical items should be maximally general in the sense that they should cover as large a subset of the extension of an item as possible. Thus, separate definitions for 'blended sweet fortified wine from Portugal' and 'vintage sweet fortified wine from Portugal' could not be considered definitions of lexical meanings, because they can be brought together under the definition 'sweet fortified wine from Portugal.' On the other hand, definitions should be minimally specific in the sense that they should be sufficient to distinguish the item from other nonsynonymous items. A maximally general definition covering both port 'harbor' and port 'kind of wine' under the definition 'thing, entity' is excluded because it does not capture the specificity of port as distinct from other words.

The distinction between polysemy and vagueness is not unproblematic, methodologically speaking. An examination of different basic criteria for distinguishing between polysemy and vagueness reveals, first, that those criteria may be in mutual conflict (in the sense that they need not lead to the same conclusion in the same circumstances) and, second, that each of them taken separately need not lead to a stable distinction between polysemy and vagueness (in the sense that what is a distinct meaning according to one of the tests in one context may be reduced to a case of vagueness according to the same test in another context). Without going into detail, let us illustrate the first type of problem. In the case of autohyponymous words, for instance, the definitional approach does not reveal an ambiguity, whereas the truth-theoretical criterion does. Dog is autohyponymous between the readings 'Canis familiaris,' contrasting with cat or wolf, and 'male Canis familiaris,' contrasting with bitch. A definition of dog as 'male Canis familiaris,' however, does not conform to the definitional criterion of maximal coverage, because it defines a proper subset of the 'Canis familiaris' reading. On the other hand, the sentence Lady is a dog, but not a dog, which exemplifies the logical criterion, cannot be ruled out as ungrammatical.

Semantic Relations

Once senses are identified (and assuming they can be identified with a reasonable degree of confidence), the type of relationship that exists between them needs to be established. The most common classification of semantic relations emerges from the tradition of historical semantics, that is, the vocabulary used to describe synchronic relations between word meanings is essentially the same as the vocabulary used to describe diachronic changes of meaning. In the simplest case, if sense a is synchronically related to sense b by metonymy, then a process of metonymy has acted diachronically to extend sense a to sense b: diachronic mechanisms of semasiological change reappear synchronically as semantic relations among word meanings.

The four basic types are specialization, generalization, metaphor, and metonymy. In the case of semantic specialization, the new meaning is a restriction of the old meaning: the new meaning is a subcase of the old. In the case of semantic generalization, the reverse holds: the old meaning is a subcase of the new. Classical examples of specialization are corn (originally a cover-term for all kinds of grain, now specialized to 'wheat' in England, to 'oats' in Scotland, and to 'maize' in the United States), starve (moving from 'to die' to 'to die of hunger'), and queen (originally 'wife, woman,' now restricted to 'king's wife, or female sovereign'). Examples of generalization are moon (primarily the earth's satellite, but extended to any planet's satellite), and French arriver (which originally meant 'to reach the river's shore, to embank,' but which now signifies 'to reach a destination' in general). There is a lot of terminological variation in connection with specialization and generalization. 'Restriction' and 'narrowing' of meaning equal 'specialization,' while 'extension,' 'schematization,' and 'broadening' of meaning equal 'generalization.' Also, the meanings involved can be said to entertain relations of taxonomical subordination or superordination: in a taxonomy (a tree-like hierarchical classification) of concepts, the specialized meaning is subordinate with regard to the original one, whereas the generalized meaning is superordinate with regard to the original.

Like specialization and generalization, it is convenient and customary to introduce metaphor and metonymy together, even though the relationship is not as close as with the former pair. Metaphor is then said to be based on a relationship of similarity between the old and the new reading, and metonymy on a relationship of contiguity. Current computer terminology yields examples of both types. The desktop of your computer screen, for instance, is not the same as the desktop of your office desk—except that in both cases, it is the space (a literal space in one case, a virtual one in the other) where you position a number of items that you regularly use or that urgently need attention. The computer desktop, in other words, is not literally a desktop in the original sense, but it has a functional similarity with the original: the computer reading is a metaphorical extension of the original office furniture reading. Functional similarities also underlie metaphorical expressions like bookmark, clipboard, file, folder, cut, and paste. Mouse, on the other hand, is also metaphorically motivated, but here, the metaphorical similarity involves shape rather than function. But now consider a statement to the effect that your desktop will keep you busy for the next two weeks, or that you ask aloud where your mouse has gone when you are trying to locate the pointer on the screen. In such cases, desktop and mouse are used metonymically. In the former case, it's not the virtual space as such that is relevant, but the items that are stored there. In the latter case, it's not the mouse as such (the thing that you hold in your hand) that you refer to, but the pointer on the screen that is operated by the mouse. The desktop and the stored items, or the mouse and the pointer, have a relationship of real-world connectedness that is usually captured by the notion of 'contiguity.' When, for instance, one drinks a whole bottle, it is not the bottle but merely its contents that are consumed: bottle can be used to refer to a certain type of container, and the (spatially contiguous) contents of that container. When lexical semanticians state that metonymical changes are based on contiguity, contiguity should not be understood in a narrow sense as referring to spatial proximity only, but more broadly as a general term for various associations in the spatial, temporal, or causal domain.

Lexical Fields and Componential Analysis

A lexical field is a set of semantically related lexical items whose meanings are mutually interdependent. The single most influential study in the history of lexical field theory is Trier's (1931) monograph, in which he presents a theoretical formulation of the field approach and investigates how the terminology for mental properties evolves from Old High German up to the beginning of the 13th century. Theoretically, Trier emphasizes that only a mutual demarcation of the words under consideration can provide a decisive answer regarding their exact value. Words should not be considered in isolation, but in their relationship to semantically related words: demarcation is always a demarcation relative to other words.

While different conceptions of the notion 'lexical field' were suggested after Trier's initial formulation, the most important development is the emergence of componential analysis as a technique for formalizing the semantic relationships between the items in a field: once a lexical field has been demarcated, the internal relations within the field will have to be described in more detail. It is not sufficient to say that the items in the field are in mutual opposition—these oppositions will have to be identified and defined. Componential analysis is a method for describing such oppositions that takes its inspiration from structuralist phonology: just like phonemes are described structurally by their position on a set of contrastive dimensions, words may be characterized on the basis of the dimensions that structure a lexical field. Componential analysis provides a descriptive model for semantic content, based on the assumption that meanings can be described on the basis of a restricted set of conceptual building blocks—the semantic 'components' or 'features.'

A brief illustration of the principles of componential analysis is given by Pottier (1964), who provides an example of a componential semantic analysis in his description of a field consisting of, among others, the terms siège, pouf, tabouret, chaise, fauteuil, and canapé (a subfield of the field of furniture terms in French). The word which acts as a superordinate to the field under consideration is siège, 'seating equipment with legs.' If we use the dimensions s1 'for seating,' s2 'for one person,' s3 'with legs,' s4 'with back,' s5 'with armrests,' s6 'of rigid material,' then chaise 'chair' can be componentially defined as [+ s1, + s2, + s3, + s4, – s5, + s6], and canapé 'sofa' as [+ s1, – s2, + s3, + s4, + s5, + s6], and so on.

While componential forms of description are common in formal types of semantic description, the most important theoretical development after the introduction of componential analysis is probably Wierzbicka's (1996) attempt to identify a restricted set of some 60 universally valid, innate components. The Natural Semantic Metalanguage aims at defining cross-linguistically transparent definitions by means of those allegedly universal building-blocks.

Lexical Relations

Like componential analysis, relational semantics, as introduced by Lyons (1963), develops the idea of describing the structural relations among related words. It, however, restricts the theoretical vocabulary to be used in such a description. In a componential analysis, the features are essentially of a 'real world' kind: as in Pottier's example, they name properties of the things referred to, rather than properties of the meanings as such. But if linguistics is interested in the structure of the language rather than the structure of the world, it may want to use a descriptive apparatus that is more purely linguistic. Relational semantics looks for such an apparatus in the form of sense relations like synonymy (identity of meaning) and antonymy (oppositeness of meaning): the fact that aunt and uncle refer to the same genealogical generation is a fact about the world, but the fact that black and white are opposites is a fact about words and language. Instead of deriving statements about the synonymy or antonymy of a word (and in general, statements about the meaning relations it entertains) from a separate and independent description of the word's meaning, the meaning of the word could be defined as the total set of meaning relations in which it participates. A traditional approach to synonymy would for instance describe the meaning of both quickly and speedily as 'in a fast way, not taking up much time,' and then conclude to the synonymy of both terms on the basis of their definitional identity. Lyons by contrast deliberately eschews such content descriptions, and equates the meaning of a word like quickly with the synonymy relation it has with speedily, plus any other relations of that kind.

In the actual practice of relational semantics, 'relations of that kind' specifically include—next to synonymy and antonymy—relations of hyponymy (or subordination) and hyperonymy (or superordination), which are both based on taxonomical inclusion. The major research line in relational semantics involves the refinement and extension of this initial set of relations. The most prominent contribution to this endeavor after Lyons is found in Cruse (1986). Murphy (2003) is a thoroughly documented critical overview of the relational research tradition.

Distributional Relations

Given a Saussurean distinction between paradigmatic and syntagmatic relations, lexical fields as originally conceived are based on paradigmatic relations of similarity. One extension of the field approach, then, consists of taking a syntagmatic point of view. Words may in fact have specific combinatorial features which it would be natural to include in a field analysis. A verb like to comb, for instance, selects direct objects that refer to hair, or hair-like things, or objects covered with hair. Describing that selectional preference should be part of the semantic description of to comb. For a considerable period, these syntagmatic affinities received less attention than the paradigmatic relations, but in the 1950s and 1960s, the idea surfaced under different names. Firth (1957) for instance introduced the (now widely used) term collocation.

The distributional approach can be more radical than the mere incorporation of lexical combinatorics into the description of words: if the environments in which a word occurs could be used to establish its meaning, lexical semantics could receive a firm methodological basis. The general approach of a distributionalist method is summarized by Firth's dictum: 'You shall know a word by the company it keeps,' that is, words that occur in the same contexts tend to have similar meanings. In the final decades of the 20th century, major advances in the distributional approach to semantics were achieved by applying a distributional way of meaning analysis to large text corpora. Sinclair, a pioneer of the approach, developed his ideas through his work on the Collins Cobuild English Language Dictionary, for which a 20-million-word corpus of contemporary English was compiled. In Sinclair's original conception, a collocational analysis is basically a heuristic device to support the lexicographer's manual work. A further step in the development of the distributional approach was taken through the application of statistics as a method for establishing the relevance of a collocation and, more broadly, for analyzing the distributional co-occurrence patterns of words.

Conceptual Metaphor and Metonymy

Metaphorical relations of the kind in topic ("Semantic Relations") do not only exist between the readings of a given word: several words may exhibit similar metaphorical patterns. Conceptual metaphor theory, the approach introduced by Lakoff and Johnson (1980), includes two basic ideas: first, the view that metaphor is a cognitive phenomenon, rather than a purely lexical one; second, the view that metaphor should be analyzed as a mapping between two domains. To illustrate the first point, metaphor comes in patterns that transcend the individual lexical item. A typical example is the following:

- Love is a journey.
- Look how far we've come.

We are at a crossroads. We'll just have to go our separate ways. We cannot turn back now. We are stuck. This relationship is a dead-end street. I don't think this relationship is going anywhere. It's been a long, bumpy road. We have gotten off the track.

The second pillar of conceptual metaphor theory is the analysis of the mappings inherent in metaphorical patterns. Metaphors conceptualize a target domain in terms of the source domain, and such a mapping takes the form of an alignment between aspects of the source and target. For love is a journey, for instance, the following correspondences hold.

Source	Target
The travelers	The lovers
The means of transport	The relationship itself
The journey	The development of the relationship
The obstacles encountered	The difficulties experienced
Decisions about which way to go	Choices about what to do
The destination of the journey	The goals of the relationship

Metonymies too can be systematic in the sense that they form patterns that apply to more than just an individual lexical item. Thus, the bottle example in topic ("Semantic Relations") exhibits the name of a container (source) being used for its contents (target), a pattern that can be abbreviated as container for contents. Making use of this abbreviated notation, other common types of metonymy are the following: a spatial location for what is located there (the whole theater was in tears);

a period of time for what happens in that period, for the people who live then, or for what is produced during that period (the 19th century had a nationalist approach to politics); a material for the product made from it (a cork); the origin for what originates from it (astrakhan, champagne, emmental); an activity or event for its consequences (when the blow you have received hurts, it is not the activity of your adversary that is painful, but the physical effects that it has on your body); an attribute for the entity that possesses the attribute' (majesty does not only refer to 'royal dignity or status,' but also to the sovereign himself); and of course part for whole (a hired hand). The relations can often work in the other direction as well. To fill up the car, for instance, illustrates a type whole for part: it's obviously only a part of the car that gets filled. For the current state of affairs in metonymy research from a cognitive semantic point of view.

Frames

Yet another approach to semantic structure in the lexicon focuses on the way our knowledge of the world is organized in larger 'chunks of knowledge' and how these interact with language. The most articulate model in this respect is Fillmore's frame theory. Frame theory is specifically interested in the way in which language may be used to perspectivize an underlying conceptualization of the world: it's not just that we see the world in terms of conceptual models, but those models may be verbalized in different ways. Each different way of bringing a conceptual model to expression so to speak adds another layer of meaning: the models themselves are meaningful ways of thinking about the world, but the way we express the models while talking adds perspective. This overall starting point of Fillmorean frame theory leads to a description on two levels. On the one hand, a description of the referential situation or event consists of an identification of the relevant elements and entities, and the conceptual role they play in the situation or event. On the other hand, the more purely linguistic part of the analysis indicates how certain expressions and grammatical patterns highlight aspects of that situation or event.

An illustration comes from the standard example of frame theory, the commercial transaction frame. The commercial transaction frame involves words like buy and sell. The commercial transaction frame can be characterized informally by a scenario in which one person gets control or possession of something from a second person, as a result of a mutual agreement through which the first person gives the second person a sum of money. Background knowledge involved in this scenario includes an understanding of ownership relations, a money economy, and commercial contracts. The categories that are needed for describing the lexical meanings of the verbs linked to the commercial transaction scene include Buyer, Seller, Goods, and Money as basic categories. Verbs like buy and sell then each encode a certain perspective on the commercial transaction scene by highlighting specific elements of the scene. In the case of buy, for instance, the buyer appears in the participant role of the agent, for instance as the subject of the (active) sentence. In active sentences, the goods then appear as the direct object; the seller and the money appear in prepositional phrases: Paloma bought a book from Teresa for 30. In the case of sell, on the other hand, it is the seller that appears in the participant role of the agent: Teresa sold a book to Paloma for 30.

Prototype Effects and Radial Sets

The prototype-based conception of categorization originated in the mid-1970s with Rosch's psycholinguistic research into the internal structure of categories. Rosch concluded that the tendency to define categories in a rigid way clashes with the actual psychological situation. Linguistic categories do not have sharply delimited borderlines. Instead of clear demarcations between equally important conceptual areas, one finds marginal areas between categories that are unambiguously defined only in their focal points. This observation was taken over and elaborated in linguistic lexical semantics. Specifically, it was applied not just to the internal structure of a single word meaning, but also to the structure of polysemous words, that is, to the relationship between the various meanings of a word. Four characteristics, then, are frequently in the linguistic literature as typical of prototypicality.

- Prototypical categories cannot be defined by means of a single set of criterial (necessary and sufficient) attributes.
- Prototypical categories exhibit a family-resemblance structure, i.e., one like the similarities that exist between relatives (some have the same typical hair color, some have the same typically shaped nose, some have the same typical eyes, but none have all and only the typical family traits); the different uses of a word have several features in common with one or more other uses, but no features are common to all uses. More generally, their semantic structure takes the form of a set of clustered and overlapping meanings (which may be related by similarity or by other associative links, such as metonymy). Because this clustered set is often built up round a central meaning, the term 'radial set' is often used for this kind of polysemic structure.
- Prototypical categories exhibit degrees of category membership; not every member is equally representative for a category.
- Prototypical categories are blurred at the edges.

By way of example, consider fruit as referring to a type of food. If you ask people to list kinds of fruit, some types come to mind more easily than others. For American and European subjects (there is clear cultural variation on this point), oranges, apples, and bananas are the most typical fruits, while pineapples, watermelons, and pomegranates receive low typicality ratings. This illustrates the third characteristic above. But now, consider coconuts and olives. Is a coconut or an olive a fruit in the ordinary everyday sense of that word? For many people, the answer is not immediately obvious, which illustrates the fourth characteristic: if we zoom in on the least typical exemplars of a category, membership in the category may become fuzzy. A category like fruit should be considered not only with regard to the exemplars that belong to it, but also with regard to the features that these category members share and that together define the category. Types of fruit do not, however, share a single set of definitional features that sufficiently distinguishes fruit from, say, vegetables and other natural foodstuffs. All are edible seed-bearing parts of plants, but most other features that we think of as typical for fruit are not general: while most are sweet, some are not, like lemons; while most are juicy, some are not, like bananas; while most grow on trees and tree-like plants, some grow on bushes, like strawberries; and so on. This absence of a neat definition illustrates the first characteristic. Instead of such a single definition, what seems to hold together the category are overlapping clusters of representative features. Whereas the most typical kinds of fruit are the sweet and juicy ones that grow on trees, other kinds may lack one or even more of these features.

The four characteristics are systematically related along two dimensions. On the one hand, the third and the fourth characteristics take into account the referential, extensional structure of a category. In particular, they consider the members of a category; they observe, respectively, that not all referents of a category are equal in representativeness for that category and that the denotational boundaries of a category are not always determinate. On the other hand, these two aspects (centrality and nonrigidity) recur on the intensional level, where the definitional rather than the referential structure of a category is envisaged. For one thing, nonrigidity shows up in the fact that there is no single necessary and sufficient definition for a prototypical concept. For another, family resemblances imply overlapping of the subsets of a category; consequently, meanings exhibiting a greater degree of overlapping will have more structural weight than meanings that cover only peripheral members of the category. As such, the clustering of meanings that is typical of family resemblances implies that not every meaning is structurally equally important (and a similar observation can be made with regard to the components into which those meanings may be analyzed).

The four characteristics are not coextensive; that is, they do not necessarily occur together. In that sense, some words may exhibit more prototypicality effects than others. In the practice of linguistics, the second feature in particular has attracted the attention, and the radial set model (which graphically represents the way in which less central meanings branch out from the prototypical, core reading) is a popular representational format in lexical semantics.

Basic Levels and Onomasiological Salience

Possibly the major innovation of the prototype model of categorization is to give salience a place in the description of semasiological structure: next to the qualitative relations among the elements in a semasiological structure (like metaphor and metonymy), a quantifiable center-periphery relationship is introduced as part of the architecture. But the concept of salience can also be applied to the onomasiological domain.

The initial step in the introduction of onomasiological salience is the basic-level hypothesis. The hypothesis is based on the ethnolinguistic observation that folk classifications of biological domains usually conform to a general organizational principle, in the sense that they consist of five or six taxonomical levels. The basic-level hypothesis embodies a notion of onomasiological salience, because it is a hypothesis about alternative categorizations of referents: if a particular referent (a particular piece of clothing) can be alternatively categorized as a garment, a skirt, or a wrap-around skirt, the choice will be preferentially made for the basic-level category 'skirt.' But differences of onomasiological preference also occur among categories on the same level in a taxonomical hierarchy. If a particular referent can be alternatively categorized as a wrap-around skirt or a miniskirt, there could just as well be a preferential choice: when you encounter something that is both a wrap-around skirt and a miniskirt, the most natural way of naming that referent in a neutral context would probably be 'miniskirt.' If, then, we have to reckon with intra-level differences of salience next to inter-level differences, the concept of onomasiological salience has to be generalized in such a way that it relates to individual categories at any level of the hierarchy.

This notion of generalized onomasiological salience was first introduced in Geeraerts, Grondelaers, and Bakema (1994). Using corpus materials, this study established that the choice for one lexical item rather than the other as the name for a given referent is determined by the semasiological salience of the referent (i.e., the degree of prototypicality of the referent with regard to the semasiological structure of the category), by the overall onomasiological salience of the category represented by the expression, and by contextual features of a classical sociolinguistic and geographical nature, involving the competition between different language varieties. By zooming in on the last type of factor, a further refinement of the notion of onomasiological salience is introduced, in the form the distinction between conceptual and formal onomasiological variation. Whereas conceptual onomasiological variation involves the choice of different conceptual categories for a referent (like the examples presented so far), formal onomasiological variation merely involves the use of different synonymous names for the same conceptual category. The names jeans and trousers for denim leisure-wear trousers constitute an instance of conceptual variation, for they represent categories at different taxonomical levels. Jeans and denims, however, represent no more than different (but synonymous) names for the same denotational category.

The Theoretical Evolution of Lexical Semantics

Four broadly defined theoretical traditions may be distinguished in the history of word-meaning research.

Prestucturalist Historical Semantics

The prestructuralist period (ranging from the middle of the 19th century up to the 1930s) was the heyday of historical semantics, in the sense that the study of meaning change reigned supreme within semantics. The main theoretical achievement of prestructuralist historical semantics consists of various classifications of types of semantic change, coupled with considerable attention to psychological processes as the explanatory background of changes: the general mechanisms of change included in the classifications were generally considered to be based on the associative patterns of thought of the human mind. Important figures (among many others) are Hermann Paul, Michel Bréal, and Gustaf Stern. With the shift toward a structuralist approach that occurred round 1930, lexical semantics switched from a preference for diachronic studies to a preference for synchronic studies. However, the poststructuralist cognitive approach provides a new impetus for historical lexical semantics.

Structuralist Semantics

Inspired by the Saussurean conception of language, structural semantics originated as a reaction against prestructural historical semantics. The origins of structural semantics are customarily attributed to Trier (1931), but while Trier's monograph may indeed be the first major descriptive work in structural semantics, the first theoretical and methodological definition of the new approach is to be found in Weisgerber (1927), a polemical article that criticized historical linguistics on three points. First and foremost, because the vocabulary of a language is not simply an unstructured set of separate items, and because the meaning of a linguistic sign is determined by its position in the linguistic structures in which it takes part, the proper subject matter of semantics is not the atomistic changes of word meanings that historical semantics had concentrated on, but the semantic structure of the language that demarcates the meanings of individual words with regard to each other. Second, because that structure is a linguistic rather than a psychological phenomenon, linguistic meanings should not be studied from a psychological perspective, but from a purely linguistic one. And third, because semantic change has to be redefined as change in semantic structures, synchronic semantics methodologically precedes diachronic semantics: the synchronic structures have to be studied before their changes can be considered. The realization of this attempt to develop a synchronic, nonpsychological, structural theory of semantics depends on the way in which the notion of semantic structure is conceived. In actual practice, there are mainly three distinct definitions of semantic structure that have been employed by structuralist semanticians. More particularly, three distinct kinds of structural relations among lexical items have been singled out as the proper methodological basis of lexical semantics. First, there is the relationship of semantic similarity that lies at the basis of semantic field analysis and componential analysis.

Neostructuralist Semantics

While componential analysis was developed in the second half of the 1950s and the beginning of the 1960s by European as well as American structural linguists, its major impact came from its incorporation into generative grammar: the publication of Katz and Fodor marked a theoretical migration of lexical semantics from a structuralist to a generativist framework. As a model for lexical semantics, Katzian semantics combined an essentially structuralist approach with two novel characteristics: the explicit inclusion of lexical description in a generative grammar and, accordingly (given that the grammar is a formal one), an interest in the formalization of lexical descriptions. Although Katzian semantics as such has long been abandoned, both features continue to play a role in this 'neostructuralist' tradition (the label is not an established one, but it will do for lack of a more conventional one). On the one hand, the integration of the lexicon into the grammar informs the continuing debate about the interface of lexicon and syntax. On the other hand, a number of models for the formalization of word meaning have been developed, the most prominent of which is Pustejovsky's 'generative lexicon' approach.

Cognitive Semantics

Compared to prestructuralist semantics, structuralism constitutes a move toward a more purely 'linguistic' type of lexical semantics, focusing on the linguistic system rather than the psychological background or the contextual flexibility of meaning. With the poststructuralist emergence of cognitive semantics, the pendulum swings back to a position in which the distinction between semantics and pragmatics is not a major issue, in which language is seen in the context of cognition at large, and in which language use is as much a focus of enquiry as the language system. Cognitive lexical semantics emerged in the 1980s as part of cognitive linguistics, a loosely structured theoretical movement that opposed the autonomy of grammar and the marginal position of semantics in the generativist theory of language. Important contributions to lexical semantics include prototype theory, conceptual metaphor theory, frame semantics, and the emergence of usage-based onomasiology.

From a theoretical perspective, the various traditions are to some extent at odds with each other (as may be expected). Specifically, structuralist (and to a large extent neostructuralist) theories tend to look at word meaning primarily as a property of the language, that is the linguistic system as an entity in its own right. Prestructuralist historical semantics and cognitive semantics, on the other hand, tend to emphasize the way in which word meanings are embedded in or interact with phenomena that lie outside language in a narrow sense, like general cognitive principles, or the cultural, social, historical experience of the language user. They then also take a more 'pragmatic' perspective: if the emphasis moves away from the linguistic system as a more or less stable, more or less autonomous repository of possibilities, there will be more attention to language use as the actualization of those possibilities.

Descriptively speaking, however, each of the major theoretical frameworks has contributed to the expansion of lexical semantics, that is they have drawn attention to specific phenomena and they have proposed terms, classifications, and representational formats for analyzing those phenomena. Focusing on the major topics, these contributions successively include the links between the various senses of words in prestructuralist historical semantics, the semantic relationships within the vocabulary in the structuralist era, and the importance of semasiological and onomasiological salience effects in cognitive semantics. Regardless of the theoretical oppositions, these phenomena all belong to the descriptive scope of current lexical semantics: the emergence of new points of attention has not made the older topics irrelevant.

Table: The contribution of the successive theoretical traditions.

	Semasiology	Onomasiology
'Qualitative' perspectives: elements and relations	Prestructuralist historical semantics	• Structuralist semantics • Cognitive semantics
'Quantitative' perspectives: differences of salience	Cognitive semantics	Cognitive semantics

A summary of the contribution of the major theoretical approaches is given in Table above. If one keeps in mind the chronology of the various theories, it will be clear that regardless of the theoretical differences, lexical semantics has witnessed an outspoken descriptive expansion, from a semasiological starting point to various forms of onomasiological structure, and from a focus on elements and structures alone to the relevance of salience effects on the semasiological and onomasiological architecture of meaning.

Language and Thought

We are all aware that language is not only essential to specialised disciplines such as linguistics and translation but is, in all its forms, at the core of human experience and civilisation. It is such an integral, natural part of our cultures and social lives that it may be worth stopping for a minute, not to smell the roses, but to consider what language really is, its implicatures and implications, and more importantly for this topic, how it is related to our thought process and interpretation of reality.

The correlation between language and thought has been the focus of many researchers in the past century and is still open for discussion nowadays. Many have indeed referred to the debate as a chicken-egg situation, to point to the famous impossibility of determining which one of the two processes shapes the other. How are language and thought related? Is language shaping our cognitive processes, are we talking about a mutual influence? Is there a universal language system, or is language completely relative?

From a communicative point of view, language possesses the duality of connecting people together when shared and creating barriers when inter comprehension fails. This duality is perfectly illustrated by the field of translation, whose purpose, as the etymology of the name itself suggests (lat. translatio, translationis originally meant carry across, convey), is to remove language barriers and allow people to communicate across them while still using non-universal target languages. When it comes to linguistic diversity, two schools of thought come to mind:

- Those who regard it as beneficial to human society and defend its preservation alongside ethnic, cultural and biodiversity, due not only to the traditions and knowledge that all languages encapsulate, but also to the multiplicity of thought patterns and interpretations of reality that they reflect. For instance, time can be perceived as linear, circular or cyclical, fixed or continuous, as moving from left to right, from front to back or back to front according to different cultures and languages; while Western cultures tend to compartmentalise time in smaller units and refer to it as a valuable entity that must not be wasted (think about expressions such as time is money, a waste of time), in cultures where time is seen as cyclical, the latter is not divided into small units such as minutes or hours, but is told, for instance in the Masai culture, by the cycle of rainfall. In that perspective, being multilingual would therefore allow us to have access not only to different cultures, but also to different perceptions of "reality".
- Those more concerned by practical questions, who may invoke the "survival of the fittest" argument to explain the natural extinction of hundreds of minority languages in the past centuries and centuries to come in favour of "globalised" languages, and put forward the obvious economic and communicative benefits (such as reduced translation costs) of a reduced number of spoken languages.

This debate could nevertheless be the subject of another, longer article. To come back to translation, both translators and non-translators are aware of some of the constraints that the exercise involves; the inability to convey certain ideas or expressions from the source language into the target language, and therefore to find linguistic, cultural and/or "psychological" equivalence, the necessity to resort to different strategies to alleviate meaning losses and respect the original message. As suggested by the words cultural and psychological, these constraints go well beyond language and bring an interesting question onto the table; should we indeed believe that individuals who speak different native languages perceive reality differently, which would imply that language itself influences our perception of reality?

Some linguists such as Sapir and Whorf, who gave their names to the Sapir-Whorf hypothesis, stated that certain thoughts in one language cannot be understood by other individuals who think in another language. The latter has gone as far as saying that reality is relative and subjective – in terms of physical objects or phenomena – because shaped by the different native languages through which individuals think. An example as famous as controversial used to illustrate linguistic relativity is the distinctive words in the Inuit language to refer to different types of snow; for instance, while "tlapripta" refers to a type of snow that burns your scalp and eyelids, "aqilokoq" refers to a "softly falling snow" and "piegnartoq" to a kind of snow good for driving sled.

Although these different words seem to suggest that Inuit speakers are able to perceive and name different "stages" of snow due to their repeated exposure to and experience of it, we could also argue, as Pullum did in "The great Eskimo vocabulary hoax", that it does not imply that the same ideas are expressed differently in other languages. Is the fact that these ideas are expressed through single words really relevant? These examples may indeed only illustrate the different natures of languages; as opposed to English, which tends to use separate words to convey a message,

Inuit conveys the same information with single words, which are created by combining – or *agglutinating*, to use the linguistic term – morphemes, the smallest units of meaning containing semantic information.

The different basic colour words that vary from one language to another have also been considered to determine whether they influence the colour perception of individuals. For instance, while English distinguishes green and blue, other languages, such as Tarahumara, only possess one word for both colours. Does it mean then that Tarahumara speakers do not perceive the difference between green and blue? Certainly not, but it may mean that their perception of colours is not discriminated by what is called a "naming strategy".

Some experiments have indeed been led to determine how much lexical categories for colours (e.g. blue versus green in English) affect our perception of them, and suggest that, although we cannot assume that all thought is constrained by language (otherwise, how could we explain prelinguistic thoughts of babies?), language may influence thought and our perception of reality. Many other researches, on the other hand, continue to point towards the existence of a universal language system, and notably to the existence of eleven basic colours that all languages are able to recognise, which continuously revive the old universalism-relativism debate.

The issue of linguistic relativism and the influence of language on our perception of reality is a vast field and leads to a questioning of many concepts that we may have taken for granted. The representation of gender – a very topical topic – in language and its influence on our perception of it may be one of them. Many feminists have turned to language to denounce it as the root of inequalities and sexism, and sensed the potential that changing what they perceive as a "man-made" language, resistant to change and subject to norms, could have on mentalities, since putting categories and labels on individuals affect the way that we perceive them.

This notably explains the attention that has been brought in those circles to the supposedly "gender neutral" use of masculine words in languages such as English (for instance, the use of the word "man" or "mankind" for human), Italian, Spanish or French (the masculine plural pronouns to refer to a group of people made up of at least one man), which, feminists argue, contribute further to the invisibility of women. The more and more common use of the word "gender" as a social construction opposed to sex (which refers to biological differences) and not as a grammatical category is evidence itself of the use of an alternative language to draw further attention to the social roles enforced on people through language, and demonstrates how intertwined language, culture and thought are.

Language Acquisition

Language is a cognition that truly makes us human. Whereas other species do communicate with an innate ability to produce a limited number of meaningful vocalizations (e.g. bonobos), or even with partially learned systems (e.g. bird songs), there is no other species known to date that can express infinite ideas (sentences) with a limited set of symbols (speech sounds and words).

This ability is remarkable in itself. What makes it even more remarkable is that researchers are finding evidence for mastery of this complex skill in increasingly younger children.

Infants as young as 12 months are reported to have sensitivity to the grammar needed to understand causative sentences.

After more than 60 years of research into child language development, the mechanism that enables children to segment syllables and words out of the strings of sounds they hear, and to acquire grammar to understand and produce language is still quite an enigma.

One of the earliest scientific explanations of language acquisition was provided by Skinner. As one of the pioneers of behaviorism, he accounted for language development by means of environmental influence.

Skinner argued that children learn language based on behaviorist reinforcement principles by associating words with meanings. Correct utterances are positively reinforced when the child realizes the communicative value of words and phrases.

For example, when the child says 'milk' and the mother will smile and give her some as a result, the child will find this outcome rewarding, enhancing the child's language development.

However, Skinner's account was soon heavily criticized by Noam Chomsky, the world's most famous linguist to date. In the spirit of cognitive revolution in the 1950's, Chomsky argued that children will never acquire the tools needed for processing an infinite number of sentences if the language acquisition mechanism was dependent on language input alone.

Consequently, he proposed the theory of Universal Grammar: an idea of innate, biological grammatical categories, such as a noun category and a verb category that facilitate the entire language development in children and overall language processing in adults.

Universal Grammar is considered to contain all the grammatical information needed to combine these categories, e.g. noun and verb, into phrases. The child's task is just to learn the words of her language.

For example, according to the Universal Grammar account, children instinctively know how to combine a noun (e.g. a boy) and a verb (to eat) into a meaningful, correct phrase (A boy eats).

This Chomskian (1965) approach to language acquisition has inspired hundreds of scholars to investigate the nature of these assumed grammatical categories and the research is still ongoing.

A decade or two later some psycho linguists began to question the existence of Universal Grammar. They argued that categories like noun and verb are biologically, evolutionarily and psychologically implausible and that the field called for an account that can explain for the acquisition process without innate categories.

Researchers started to suggest that instead of having a language-specific mechanism for language processing, children might utilise general cognitive and learning principles.

Whereas researchers approaching the language acquisition problem from the perspective of Universal Grammar argue for early full productivity, i.e. early adult-like knowledge of language, the opposing constructivist investigators argue for a more gradual developmental process. It is suggested that children are sensitive to patterns in language which enables the acquisition process.

An example of this gradual pattern learning is morphology acquisition. Morphemes are the smallest grammatical markers, or units, in language that alter words. In English, regular plurals are marked with an –s morpheme (e.g. dog+s).

Similarly, English third singular verb forms (she eat+s, a boy kick+s) are marked with the –s morpheme. Children are considered to acquire their first instances of third singular forms as entire phrasal chunks (Daddy kicks, a girl eats, a dog barks) without the ability of teasing the finest grammatical components apart.

When the child hears a sufficient number of instances of a linguistic construction (i.e. the third singular verb form), she will detect patterns across the utterances she has heard. In this case, the repeated pattern is the –s marker in this particular verb form.

As a result of many repetitions and examples of the –s marker in different verbs, the child will acquire sophisticated knowledge that, in English, verbs must be marked with an –s morpheme in the third singular form.

Approaching language acquisition from the perspective of general cognitive processing is an economical account of how children can learn their first language without an excessive biolinguistic mechanism.

Nonverbal Communication

Nonverbal communication is a very powerful medium of communication that entails sending and receiving messages through any of the human sense channels, without using language. Messages may occur on a conscious or unconscious level and may be intentional or not, and are usually, though are not limited to visual manifestations. Some forms of nonverbal communication include gestures, body language, facial expressions, eye contact, posture, in addition to body temperature, movement, time and personal space. It is said that nonverbal communication comprises approximately two-thirds of all communication among people and groups.

Functions of Nonverbal Communication

Whereas verbal language is used in communication of information about external events, nonverbal communication may serve the purpose of establishing and maintaining interpersonal relationships. Specifically, nonverbal behavior in human communication has been identified to serve the following functions:

1. To express emotions.
2. To present one's personality.
3. To convey attitudes.
4. To accompany and facilitate speech in managing interaction cues between individuals and groups.
5. To perpetuate rituals, such as greeting and taking leave.

Nonverbal Communication Examples

Haptics, an example of nonverbal communication, involves touch, kissing, high fives, shoulder pats, scratching, back slapping and a lot more manifestations that greatly differ in interpretation across cultures. In the United States, shaking hands is the most appropriate form of greeting when meeting someone for the first time. In Japan, however, touching an acquaintance and shaking his hand would be considered quite rude, therefore, encouraging them to bow to each other in greeting instead.

Chronemics, another example of nonverbal communication, involves the perception of time and how time is used to define identities. How people structure their time and react to time is a potent tool for communication. The speed at which a person speaks, the length of time that someone is willing to listen to somebody, the willingness to wait, and the timing of actions are examples of how time can be perceived differently by individuals and across cultures. Americans, for example, always seem to be in a hurry, rushing someplace to be on time while people from island countries are used to taking their time and are hardly ever in a hurry.

Kinesic communication or kinesics has to do with muscle or body movement such as head nods, facial expressions, hand gestures, and eye contact. These movements are very rich in message content. The body stance or posture of a person can be used to indicate level of interest or involvement as well as attitude toward another person. Gestures such as rolling one's eyes, hand waves, and shoulder shrugs are largely universal in interpretation while other gestures are very culture-specific. Eye contact and its various aspects such as duration, frequency, pupil dilation, and rate of blinking, are all cues that provide important emotional and social information.

Proxemics involves relationships of space, distance, territory, and duration in addition to how people perceive and use the physical space around them. Again, interpretations of these vary from culture to culture. Personal space for the American covers two feet around the person while for the Latin American, standing one foot away from another person is quite comfortable and touching or tapping strangers on the shoulder is quite common, something that Americans would find quite offensive and consider an intrusion.

Paralanguage, though a vocal means of communication, does not include words and is therefore still considered part of nonverbal communication. Included in paralanguage are murmurs, gasps, sighs, and even voice quality, pitch and intonation.

Other examples of nonverbal communication include artifacts, such as hairstyle, clothing, even architecture and environment where the communication takes place. Written texts also have nonverbal aspects such as spatial arrangement of words and handwriting style.

Nonverbal Communication in Different Genders

Gender differences are also observed in the use and interpretation of nonverbal communication. It has been documented that females are more adept than males at encoding and decoding nonverbal cues, when people are telling the truth. When people are telling a lie, however, men are more efficient at interpreting nonverbal cues and detecting the lie. A possible explanation for this gender difference is the division of labor that society has exercised on the two sexes.

Nonverbal Communication in Different Cultures

Just as verbal communication is learned in the context of one's society, so is nonverbal behavior. Patterns of nonverbal communication and behavior are culturally defined and are part of the arbitrary selection of symbols of the culture. Every culture has a distinct way of communicating nonverbally and these patterns of nonverbal behavior need to be learned as one enters a new culture.

Learning nonverbal cues, however, can be quite problematic, as the same symbol may mean different things in different cultures while opposing signals may in fact mean the same thing in varying cultures. Having different and sometimes even opposing meanings can be quite confusing and even frustrating for some people. As an example, an American businessman conducting meetings in an island country, would probably think it very rude of his hosts for not keeping appointments on the dot while it would not even occur to his hosts to be at the meeting place at the exact time set. Such cultural nuances could often lead to misunderstandings, strained relations and even hostility.

Needless to say, communication is a very complex process, the whole endeavor of which can only be carried out when the individual has a sufficient understanding of the verbal and nonverbal aspects of the culture.

Types of Nonverbal Communication

A substantial portion of our communication is nonverbal. Every day, we respond to thousands on nonverbal cues and behaviors including postures, facial expression, eye gaze, gestures, and tone of voice. From our handshakes to our hairstyles, nonverbal details reveal who we are and impact how we relate to other people.

Scientific research on nonverbal communication and behavior began with the 1872 publication of Charles Darwin's The Expression of the Emotions in Man and Animals. Since that time, abundant research on the types, effects, and expressions of unspoken communication and behavior. While these signals are often so subtle that we are not consciously aware of them, research has identified several different types of nonverbal communication.

In many cases, we communicate information in nonverbal ways using groups of behaviors. For example, we might combine a frown with crossed arms and unblinking eye gaze to indicate disapproval.

Facial Expressions

Facial expressions are responsible for a huge proportion of nonverbal communication.[1] Consider how much information can be conveyed with a smile or a frown. The look on a person's face is often the first thing we see, even before we hear what they have to say.

Gestures

While nonverbal communication and behavior can vary dramatically between cultures, the facial expressions for happiness, sadness, anger, and fear are similar throughout the world.

Deliberate movements and signals are an important way to communicate meaning without words.

Common gestures include waving, pointing, and using fingers to indicate numeric amounts. Other gestures are arbitrary and related to culture.

In courtroom settings, lawyers have been known to utilize different nonverbal signals to attempt to sway juror opinions. An attorney might glance at his watch to suggest that the opposing lawyer's argument is tedious or might even roll his eyes at the testimony offered by a witness in an attempt to undermine his or her credibility. These nonverbal signals are seen as being so powerful and influential that some judges even place limits on what type of nonverbal behaviors are allowed in the courtroom.

Paralinguistics

Paralinguistics refers to vocal communication that is separate from actual language.[3] This includes factors such as tone of voice, loudness, inflection, and pitch. Consider the powerful effect that tone of voice can have on the meaning of a sentence. When said in a strong tone of voice, listeners might interpret approval and enthusiasm. The same words said in a hesitant tone of voice might convey disapproval and a lack of interest.

Consider all the different ways that simply changing your tone of voice might change the meaning of a sentence. A friend might ask you how you are doing, and you might respond with the standard "I'm fine," but how you actually say those words might reveal a tremendous amount of how you are really feeling. A cold tone of voice might suggest that you are actually not fine, but you don't wish to discuss it. A bright, happy tone of voice will reveal that you are actually doing quite well. A somber, downcast tone would indicate that you are the opposite of fine and that perhaps your friend should inquire further.

Body Language and Posture

Posture and movement can also convey a great deal of information.[4] Research on body language has grown significantly since the 1970's, but popular media have focused on the over-interpretation of defensive postures, arm-crossing, and leg-crossing, especially after publishing Julius Fast's book Body Language.

Proxemics

People often refer to their need for "personal space," which is also an important type of nonverbal communication.[5] The amount of distance we need and the amount of space we perceive as belonging to us is influenced by a number of factors including social norms, cultural expectations, situational factors, personality characteristics, and level of familiarity. For example, the amount of personal space needed when having a casual conversation with another person usually varies between 18 inches to four feet. On the other hand, the personal distance needed when speaking to a crowd of people is around 10 to 12 feet.

Eye Gaze

The eyes play an important role in nonverbal communication and such things as looking, staring and blinking are important nonverbal behaviors. When people encounter people or things that they like, the rate of blinking increases and pupils dilate. Looking at another person can indicate a range of emotions including hostility, interest, and attraction.

People also utilize eye gaze as a means to determine if someone is being honest.[6] Normal, steady eye contact is often taken as a sign that a person is telling the truth and is trustworthy. Shifty eyes and an inability to maintain eye contact, on the other hand, is frequently seen as an indicator that someone is lying or being deceptive.

Haptics

Communicating through touch is another important nonverbal behavior. There has been a substantial amount of research on the importance of touch in infancy and early childhood. Harry Harlow's classic monkey studydemonstrated how deprived touch and contact impedes development. Baby monkeys raised by wire mothers experienced permanent deficits in behavior and social interaction. Touch can be used to communicate affection, familiarity, sympathy, and other emotions.

In her book Interpersonal Communication: Everyday Encounters, author Julia Wood writes that touch is also often used as a way to communicate both status and power.[7] Researchers have found that high-status individuals tend to invade other people's personal space with greater frequency and intensity than lower-status individuals. Sex differences also play a role in how people utilize touch to communicate meaning.

Women tend to use touch to convey care, concern, and nurturance. Men, on the other hand, are more likely to use touch to assert power or control over others.

Appearance

Our choice of color, clothing, hairstyles, and other factors affecting appearance are also considered a means of nonverbal communication. Research on color psychology has demonstrated that different colors can evoke different moods. Appearance can also alter physiological reactions, judgments, and interpretations. Just think of all the subtle judgments you quickly make about someone based on his or her appearance. These first impressions are important, which is why experts suggest that job seekers dress appropriately for interviews with potential employers.

Researchers have found that appearance can play a role in how people are perceived and even how much they earn. One 1996 study found that attorneys who were rated as more attractive than their peers earned nearly 15 percent more than those ranked as less attractive. Culture is an important influence on how appearances are judged. While thinness tends to be valued in Western cultures, some African cultures relate full-figured bodies to better health, wealth, and social status.

Artifacts

Objects and images are also tools that can be used to communicate nonverbally. On an online forum, for example, you might select an avatar to represent your identity online and to communicate information about who you are and the things you like. People often spend a great deal of time developing a particular image and surrounding themselves with objects designed to convey information about the things that are important to them. Uniforms, for example, can be used to transmit a tremendous amount of information about a person. A soldier will don fatigues, a police offers will wear a uniform, and a doctor will wear a white lab coat. At a mere glance, these outfits tell people what a person does for a living.

A Word from Verywell

Nonverbal communication plays an important role in how we convey meaning and information to others, as well as how we interpret the actions of those around us. The important thing to remember when looking at such nonverbal behaviors is to consider the actions in groups. What a person actually says along with his or her expressions, appearance, and tone of voice might tell you a great deal about what that person is really trying to say.

References

- What-is-cognitive-linguistics: thoughtco.com, Retrieved 2 February, 2019
- Relationship-language-thought: translit.ie, Retrieved 7 July, 2019
- Language: simplypsychology.org, Retrieved 11 May, 2019
- Nonverbalcommunication: psychologynoteshq.com, Retrieved 13 March, 2019
- Types-of-nonverbal-communication: verywellmind.com, Retrieved 28 January, 2019

5

Problem Solving and Reasoning

The usage of ad-hoc or generic methods for the purpose of finding solutions to problems is known as problem solving. The capacity of applying logic, understanding things and verifying facts is known as reasoning. The chapter closely examines the key concepts of problem solving and reasoning such as social cognition, decision-making strategies and deductive reasoning to provide an extensive understanding of the subject.

Problem Solving

People face problems every day—usually, multiple problems throughout the day. Sometimes these problems are straightforward: To double a recipe for pizza dough, for example, all that is required is that each ingredient in the recipe be doubled. Sometimes, however, the problems we encounter are more complex. For example, say you have a work deadline, and you must mail a printed copy of a report to your supervisor by the end of the business day. The report is time-sensitive and must be sent overnight. You finished the report last night, but your printer will not work today. What should you do? First, you need to identify the problem and then apply a strategy for solving the problem.

Problem-solving Strategies

When you are presented with a problem—whether it is a complex mathematical problem or a broken printer, how do you solve it? Before finding a solution to the problem, the problem must first be clearly identified. After that, one of many problem solving strategies can be applied, hopefully resulting in a solution.

A problem-solving strategy is a plan of action used to find a solution. Different strategies have different action plans associated with them. For example, a well-known strategy is trial and error. The old adage, "If at first you don't succeed, try, try again" describes trial and error. In terms of your broken printer, you could try checking the ink levels, and if that doesn't work, you could check to make sure the paper tray isn't jammed. Or maybe the printer isn't actually connected to your laptop. When using trial and error, you would continue to try different solutions until you solved your problem. Although trial and error is not typically one of the most time-efficient strategies, it is a commonly used one.

Method	Description	Example
Trial and error	Continue trying different solutions until problem is solved	Restarting phone, turning off WiFi, turning off bluetooth in order to determine why your phone is malfunctioning

Algorithm	Step-by-step problem-solving formula	Instruction manual for installing new software on your computer
Heuristic	General problem-solving framework	Working backwards; breaking a task into steps

Another type of strategy is an algorithm. An algorithm is a problem-solving formula that provides you with step-by-step instructions used to achieve a desired outcome. You can think of an algorithm as a recipe with highly detailed instructions that produce the same result every time they are performed. Algorithms are used frequently in our everyday lives, especially in computer science. When you run a search on the Internet, search engines like Google use algorithms to decide which entries will appear first in your list of results. Facebook also uses algorithms to decide which posts to display on your newsfeed. Can you identify other situations in which algorithms are used?

A heuristic is another type of problem solving strategy. While an algorithm must be followed exactly to produce a correct result, a heuristic is a general problem-solving framework. You can think of these as mental shortcuts that are used to solve problems. A "rule of thumb" is an example of a heuristic. Such a rule saves the person time and energy when making a decision, but despite its time-saving characteristics, it is not always the best method for making a rational decision. Different types of heuristics are used in different types of situations, but the impulse to use a heuristic occurs when one of five conditions is met:

- When one is faced with too much information.
- When the time to make a decision is limited.
- When the decision to be made is unimportant.
- When there is access to very little information to use in making the decision.
- When an appropriate heuristic happens to come to mind in the same moment.

Working backwards is a useful heuristic in which you begin solving the problem by focusing on the end result. Consider this example: You live in Washington, D.C. and have been invited to a wedding at 4 PM on Saturday in Philadelphia. Knowing that Interstate 95 tends to back up any day of the week, you need to plan your route and time your departure accordingly. If you want to be at the wedding service by 3:30 PM, and it takes 2.5 hours to get to Philadelphia without traffic, what time should you leave your house? You use the working backwards heuristic to plan the events of your day on a regular basis, probably without even thinking about it.

Another useful heuristic is the practice of accomplishing a large goal or task by breaking it into a series of smaller steps. Students often use this common method to complete a large research project or long essay for school. For example, students typically brainstorm, develop a thesis or main topic, research the chosen topic, organize their information into an outline, write a rough draft, revise and edit the rough draft, develop a final draft, organize the references list, and proofread their work before turning in the project. The large task becomes less overwhelming when it is broken down into a series of small steps.

Everyday Connections: Solving Puzzles

Problem-solving abilities can improve with practice. Many people challenge themselves every day with puzzles and other mental exercises to sharpen their problem-solving skills. Sudoku puzzles appear daily in most newspapers. Typically, a sudoku puzzle is a 9×9 grid. The simple sudoku below ([link]) is a 4×4 grid. To solve the puzzle, fill in the empty boxes with a single digit: 1, 2, 3, or 4. Here are the rules: The numbers must total 10 in each bolded box, each row, and each column; however, each digit can only appear once in a bolded box, row, and column. Time yourself as you solve this puzzle and compare your time with a classmate.

- How long did it take you to solve this sudoku puzzle?

3			2
	4	1	
	3	2	
4			1

Here is another popular type of puzzle, that challenges your spatial reasoning skills. Connect all nine dots with four connecting straight lines without lifting your pencil from the paper:

- Did you figure it out? Once you understand how to crack this puzzle, you won't forget.

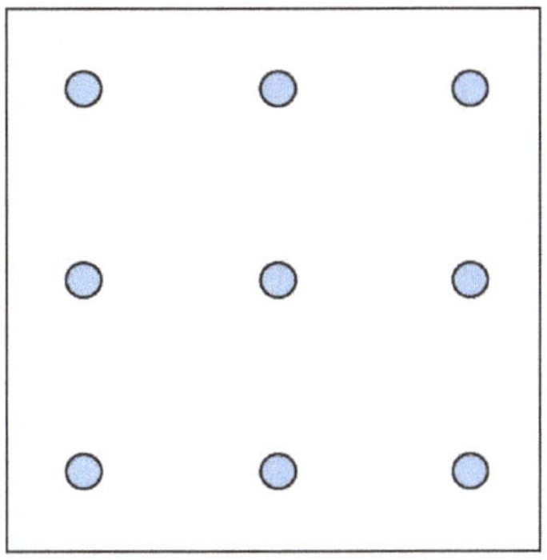

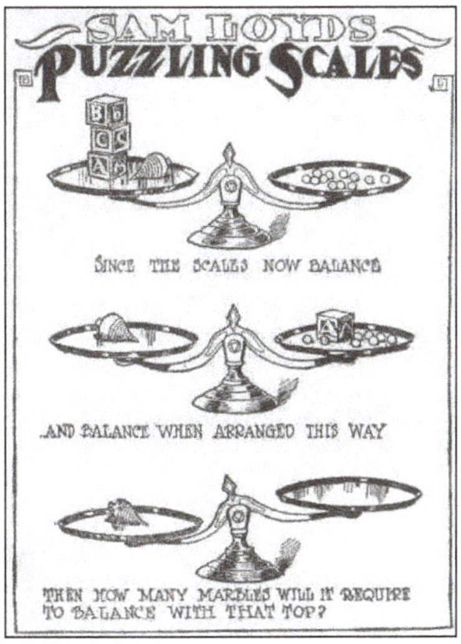

Pitfalls to Problem Solving

Not all problems are successfully solved, however. What challenges stop us from successfully solving a problem? Albert Einstein once said, "Insanity is doing the same thing over and over again and expecting a different result." Imagine a person in a room that has four doorways. One doorway that has always been open in the past is now locked. The person, accustomed to exiting the room by that particular doorway, keeps trying to get out through the same doorway even though the other three doorways are open. The person is stuck—but she just needs to go to another doorway, instead of trying to get out through the locked doorway. A mental set is where you persist in approaching a problem in a way that has worked in the past but is clearly not working now.

Functional fixedness is a type of mental set where you cannot perceive an object being used for something other than what it was designed for. During the Apollo 13mission to the moon, NASA engineers at Mission Control had to overcome functional fixedness to save the lives of the astronauts aboard the spacecraft. An explosion in a module of the spacecraft damaged multiple systems. The astronauts were in danger of being poisoned by rising levels of carbon dioxide because of problems with the carbon dioxide filters. The engineers found a way for the astronauts to use spare plastic bags, tape, and air hoses to create a makeshift air filter, which saved the lives of the astronauts.

Strategies and Obstacles

From organizing your movie collection to deciding to buy a house, problem-solving makes up a large part of daily life. Problems can range from small (solving a single math equation on your homework assignment) to very large (planning your future career).

In cognitive psychology, the term problem-solving refers to the mental process that people go through to discover, analyze, and solve problems. This involves all of the steps in the problem process, including the discovery of the problem, the decision to tackle the issue, understanding the problem, researching the available options and taking actions to achieve your goals. Before problem-solving can occur, it is important to first understand the exact nature of the problem itself. If your understanding of the issue is faulty, your attempts to resolve it will also be incorrect or flawed.

Mental Processes at Work during Problem-solving

There are a number of mental processes at work during problem-solving. These include:

- Perceptually recognizing a problem.
- Representing the problem in memory.
- Considering relevant information that applies to the current problem.
- Identify different aspects of the problem.
- Labeling and describing the problem.

Obstacles in Problem-solving

Of course, problem-solving is not a flawless process. There are a number of different obstacles that can interfere with our ability to solve a problem quickly and efficiently. Researchers have described a number of these mental obstacles, which include functional fixedness, irrelevant information, and assumptions:

- Functional Fixedness: This term refers to the tendency to view problems only in their customary manner. Functional fixedness prevents people from fully seeing all of the different options that might be available to find a solution.
- Irrelevant or Misleading Information: When you are trying to solve a problem, it is important to distinguish between information that is relevant to the issue and irrelevant data that can lead to faulty solutions. When a problem is very complex, the easier it becomes to focus on misleading or irrelevant information.
- Assumptions: When dealing with a problem, people often make assumptions about the constraints and obstacles that prevent certain solutions.
- Mental Set: Another common problem-solving obstacle is known as a mental set, which is the tendency people have to only use solutions that have worked in the past rather than looking for alternative ideas. A mental set can often work as a heuristic, making it a useful problem-solving tool. However, mental sets can also lead to inflexibility, making it more difficult to find effective solutions.

Newell and Simon Approach

Research on human problem solving has a venerable history that played a central role in the creation of cognitive science. Early studies of problem-solving behavior on puzzles and other novel tasks led to many insights about representation, performance, and learning that now underpin the field. Moreover, computational models developed from these studies remain some of the most detailed and precise accounts of human cognition.

However, the past decade has seen considerably less attention paid to this important topic, presumably because many researchers believe that it is sufficiently well understood. In contrast, we maintain that the standard theory of problem solving, although basically accurate, is still incomplete, and we need additional work, at the level of both theoretical principles and specific computational models, to extend our understanding of this complex cognitive activity.

The Standard Problem Solving Theory

The standard theory of problem solving, initially outlined by Newell, Shaw, and Simon, focuses on how humans respond when they are confronted with unfamiliar tasks. Early work focused on abstract problems like proving theorems in propositional logic and solving the Tower of Hanoi puzzle. Later research adapted the framework to explain cognition in semantically rich domains like solving word problems in physics and thermodynamics, as well as addressing the observed behavioral differences between domain experts and novices.

The theory makes a number of claims about human cognition. The most basic is that problem solving involves the mental inspection and manipulation of list structures. Newell and Simon later refined this into their physical symbol system hypothesis, which states that symbolic processing is a necessary and sufficient condition for intelligent behavior. Another central claim, termed the problem space hypothesis, is that problem solving involves search through a space of candidate states generated by operators.

A more detailed aspect of the theory is that, in many cases, problem solvers utilize means-ends analysis. This class of search methods involves a combination of selecting differences between the desired and current states, selecting operators that will reduce the chosen differences, and either applying the operators or creating subproblems to transform the current states into ones in which they can apply. This requires one to chain backward from aspects of the goal state to find relevant operators and determine useful subgoals. However, with experience this novice strategy is replaced in experts with forward chaining that leads directly to the goal.

Nevertheless, closer analyses of human behavior on novel tasks have suggested that this story is incomplete and that the actual situation is more complicated. Here we make some additional observations that are not addressed by the standard theory.

- Problem solving occurs in a physical context. Puzzles like the Tower of Hanoi are typically presented in some physical form, with solutions relying on manual actions and tests for legal moves requiring visual inspection. This physical setting simplifies the task by providing an external memory, but it also introduces irrelevant features.
- Problem solving abstracts away from physical details, yet must return to them to implement the solution. For instance, when solving the Tower of Hanoi, humans appear to search through an abstract problem space that describes states in terms of disk-peg configurations and operators as transitions between them. They ignore the details of grasping and moving required to demonstrate the solution, but they can execute these actions when necessary.
- Problem solving is seldom a purely mental activity, but rather interleaves reasoning with execution. In the Tower of Hanoi, the problem solver may reason backward to select an intended move, but typically makes that move as soon as it is legal, without waiting to make sure that he can solve the remainder of the problem from that point.
- Eager execution of partial plans can lead the problem solver into physical dead ends that require restarting the task. For the Tower of Hanoi, initially moving the smallest disk to the goal peg on an even-disk problem means one cannot solve the puzzle without later retracting this objective. However, once the problem solver has made such an execution error, he is unlikely to repeat it on later attempts.
- Learning from successful solutions transforms backward chaining search into informed skill execution. When a person first solves the Tower of Hanoi, he resorts to means-ends analysis, but sufficient experience on the task replaces this with an automatized execution procedure that involves no search.

Naturally, because these facets of human problem solving have not received attention as interesting phenomena, computational models have also tended to ignore them.

An Extended Problem Solving Theory

We are now ready to present an extended theory of human problem solving that moves beyond the abstract framework provided by the standard version. This forms a key part of Icarus, an account of the human cognitive architecture.

Physical Setting of Problem Solving

First, Icarus is an architecture for physical, embodied agents. Although the framework incorporates many ideas from traditional work on cognitive modeling, it maintains that cognition is closely tied to perception and action, and one cannot build an Icarus model that is not linked to some environment external to the agent. For the Tower of Hanoi, we have developed a simulated world that contains disks, pegs, and a hand. Each object has attributes that describe its height, width, and position, and the hand also has a status of open or closed.

Like other cognitive architectures, Icarus operates in cycles, but processing involves more than cognitive activity. On each cycle, the agent perceives objects in its immediate environment and their descriptions are deposited into a short-lived perceptual buffer. The system may also carry out actions associated with primitive skills; for the Tower of Hanoi, these correspond to grasping and ungrasping a disk, as well as moving the hand up, down, left, or right. Naturally, we could model both perception and action at a finer granularity, but this level is sufficient to make our point about the embodied nature of problem solving.

Of course, the situated cognition movement has also argued that human behavior occurs in a physical setting, with Zhang and Norman even reanalyzing behavior on the classic Tower of Hanoi puzzle in these terms. Newell and Simon were quite aware that much of their subjects' behavior occurred in this context; they simply chose not to distinguish between internal and external states in their models. However, we have developed a cognitive architecture that treats the physical side of problem solving as a central tenet, as contrasted with frameworks like Soar and ACT-R, which view embodiment as peripheral to cognitive processing.

Abstraction from Physical Details

As noted, although humans have the perceptual-motor abilities necessary to execute solutions to tasks like the Tower of Hanoi, their mental problem solving occurs at a more abstract level. Icarus models this capability in two ways. One involves a long-term conceptual memory that, on each cycle, recognizes instances of generic situations and adds them to a short-term memory that contains current beliefs about the agent's environment. For instance, our model for the Tower of Hanoi includes concepts for noting when a peg is empty and when a disk is the smallest on a peg.

The other involves a long-term skill memory that describes higher-level skills, like moving a disk, in terms of subskills like grasping a disk, lifting it off a peg, carrying it from one peg to another, lowering the disk onto a peg, and ungrasping it. On each cycle, the architecture selects for execution a path through the skill hierarchy with application conditions that match. These skills are durative, in that they may take many cycles to complete; for example, this holds for carrying a disk from one peg to another in our Hanoi environment. We assume the execution of such complex skills occurs in an automatized way that demands very few attentional resources.

Thus, Icarus' sensory-motor control cycle provides both abstract descriptions of the environment and ways to execute abstract operators. This lets much of problem solving occur at an abstract level, which verbal protocols consistently suggest is how humans deal with such tasks. However, our framework is more constraining than the physical symbol system hypothesis, in that problem states are always grounded in real or imagined physical states, and problem-space operators always expand to primitive skills with executable actions. We believe a more accurate claim is that cognition relies on a symbolic physical system, which comes closer to JohnsonLaird's (1989) views on thinking with mental models.

Interleaved Cognition and Execution

In addition to modules for conceptual inference and skill execution, Icarus includes a module for means-ends analysis. As in traditional accounts, we assume the problem solver begins with a declarative goal that describes aspects of the desired state. This must be stated as an instance of some known concept, so that the agent cannot even formulate a problem unless it has a long-term structure that can recognize its solution. This assumption is novel, but not a difference we will focus on here.

Skills contain not only application conditions and subskills, but also descriptions of their expected effects. If the agent has a skill in long-term memory that would achieve the goal, it checks to see whether that skill can be applied in the current setting. If so, then the agent simply executes the stored solution in the environment. But if it lacks such a skill, as it would for an unfamiliar task, it resorts to means-ends problem solving.

In this case, two situations can arise. The agent may know a skill that would achieve the goal concept, but it cannot yet be applied. Here the module adds the instantiated precondition of the skill, which is stated as a single concept, to a goal stack, then repeats the process by looking for skills that will achieve this subgoal. Alternatively, the agent may have no skill that achieves the goal concept, in which case it examines the concept definition and adds one of its unsatisfied sub concepts to the goal stack, making it the focus of problem solving.

This process follows the standard theory fairly closely, but it diverges when the agent retrieves a skill that can be applied in the current state. Unlike traditional models, Icarus does not apply the skill mentally and continue reasoning from the new internal state. Instead, it executes the skill physically in the environment, interrupting cognitive activity for as many cycles as needed, then resumes internal problem solving in the context of the new situation. This may lead to more execution, if the precondition of the next skill on the stack is met, or to more subgoaling, if more remains to be achieved.

As a result, Icarus never retains in goal memory a complete plan about how it will solve the problem, but only a single path backward through its concept and skill definitions that would lead toward its initial goal. The advantage of this scheme is that it places a much lighter memory load on the problem solver by using the environment as an external store.2 Again, this account does not conflict with Newell and Simon, who never claimed that problem solving took place entirely in the human mind, but it does contrast with most follow-on efforts.

Problem Restarts

Of course, the disadvantage of this mixed strategy is that the problem solver may make an incorrect choice, such as which subgoal it should achieve first. Heuristics can reduce the chances of this happening, but they can seldom eliminate it entirely. Traditional systems, including the General Problem Solver, responded by backtracking in the problem space. This produces a systematic strategy of depth-first search that does not match the details of human problem solving.

Icarus engages in a limited form of depth-first search, but only if it can accomplish this by pushing subgoals onto, or popping them from, the current goal stack. Once it has made a physical move, the system will not consider retracing this step as part of a systematic search. Moreover, the goal stack retains information about subgoals the system has accomplished in pursuit of higher-level goals, and it does not consider skills that would undo them. Thus, the agent may find itself in situations where it has achieved some subgoals necessary for a solution but where it has no actions available.

In such cases, the problem solver gives up on its current attempt and starts the problem again. Anzai and Simon note two instances of this strategy in their protocols, and many readers will recall taking such steps on complex or tricky tasks. Restarting on a problem requires physically moving it to the initial configuration, which can be viewed as a form of backtracking, but it is certainly not the systematic version usually discussed in the literature. Icarus assumes that this restarting process plays a key role in human problem solving.

We should note one earlier model, reported by Jones and Langley, combined restarts with means-ends analysis. However, their Eureka system carried out purely mental problem solving and had limited access to memories of previous solution attempts, which meant it could make the same errors in choice repeatedly. Humans may retrace some errorful steps, but they also try to avoid these choices on later attempts. To model this tendency, Icarus stores the goal stack associated with a move later judged to be mistaken and uses it to eliminate the move from consideration on successive trials. One might view this as systematic search across problem attempts, but it still differs from most models of problem solving and, we hold, comes closer to human strategies.

Learning from Problem Solutions

Icarus' storage of long-term structures about what moves to avoid constitutes a simple form of learning, but the traces are highly specific and meant only to avoid previous errors. However, people can also acquire more general knowledge about how to solve a class of problems, and the architecture incorporates a mechanism with this capability. This learning method is interleaved with performance, it operates in an incremental manner, and it is cumulative in that it builds on knowledge acquired earlier, all characteristics of human behavior.

The learning process is driven by impasses that occur during execution and problem solving, which in turn lead to pushing entries onto the goal stack. Because Icarus aims to avoid such impasses in the future, the architecture creates a new skill whenever it pops the stack upon achieving its current goal. However, recall that the means-ends module creates two distinct types of subgoal that require slightly different forms of learning.

One type occurs when the agent selects a skill instance S2 to achieve a goal G, but, upon finding its start condition unsatisfied, selects another skill instance S1 so as to achieve it. When the agent has executed both skills successfully and reached the goal, Icarus constructs a new skill that has the same name and arguments as the goal concept G, the two skills S1 and S2 as ordered subskills, and a start condition that is the same as that for S1. In addition, arguments and other peceived objects are replaced by variables in a consistent manner.

The other form of learning occurs when the agent finds no skill to achieve a goal G, and thus creates subgoals for the unsatisfied conditions of G's concept definition. If the agent achieves each subgoal in turn, the architecture constructs a new skill that has the same name and arguments as the goal concept G, the subgoals that are achieved as ordered subskills, and a start condition based on the subconcepts of G that held initially. Both mechanisms name new skills after the goals they achieve, which leads naturally to disjunctive and recursive definitions.

After learning, when the agent encounters a problem that is isomorphic to one it has solved before, it avoids an impasse by accessing the stored skill. The architecture instantiates this skill and executes it, continuing until achieving the goal that led to its retrieval. Similar events transpire if the system encounters any subproblem it has solved previously, which can produce transfer to new tasks with familiar subtasks. Note that the agent transitions from the backward-chaining search of meansends analysis to forward execution. This is consistent with observations of novice-expert shifts, but clarifies that the "forward chaining" occurs in the environment, rather than in the agent's mind.

A Model for the Tower of Hanoi

To illustrate these ideas further, we will consider an Icarus model for the Tower of Hanoi puzzle. The system begins with some 14 concepts that describe configurations of disks and pegs, organized in a hierarchy that has five levels. We also provide the system with five primitive skills for manipulating disks, along with four higher-level skills that correspond to problem-space operators,4 some of which appear in Table. In addition, we embed the system in a simulated environment with three disks and three pegs, which it perceives on each cycle and can alter using the actions in its primitive skills.

The agent begins by perceiving three disks stacked on the leftmost peg, along with two other empty pegs, and inferring a number of higher-level concepts from these percepts.

```
(pickup-putdown (?disk ?from ?to)
 :start    ((pickup-putdownable ?disk ?from ?to))
 :ordered  ((grasp-disk ?disk)
            (lift-disk ?disk)
            (carry-disk ?disk ?from ?to)
            (lower-disk ?disk ?to)
            (ungrasp-disk ?disk))
 :effects  ((no-disk-on ?from)
            (on-peg ?disk ?to)
            (only-disk-on ?disk ?to)))
(unstack-putdown (?d1 ?d2 ?from ?to)
 :start    ((unstack-putdownable ?d1 ?d2 ?from ?to))
 :ordered  ((grasp-disk ?d1)
            (lift-disk ?d1)
            (carry-disk ?d1 ?from ?to)
            (lower-disk ?d1 ?to)
            (ungrasp-disk ?d1))
 :effects  ((on-peg ?d1 ?to)
            (top-disk-on ?d2 ?from)
            (only-disk-on ?d1 ?to)))
(lift-disk (?disk)
 :start    ((on-peg ?disk ?from)
            (no-smaller-disk-on ?disk ?from)
            (grasped ?disk))
 :actions  ((*vertical-move ?disk 1))
 :effects  ((above-peg ?disk ?from)))
(carry-disk (?disk ?from ?to)
 :percepts ((peg ?from xpos ?fxpos)
            (peg ?to xpos ?txpos))
 :start    ((above-peg ?disk ?from)
            (grasped ?disk))
 :actions  ((*horizontal-move ?disk ?fxpos ?txpos))
 :effects  ((above-peg ?disk ?to)))
(lower-disk (?disk ?to)
 :start    ((above-peg ?disk ?to)
            (no-disk-on ?to)
            (grasped ?disk))
 :actions  ((*vertical-move ?disk -1))
 :effects  ((on-base ?disk ?to)))
(lower-disk (?disk1 ?to)
 :start    ((above-peg ?disk1 ?to)
            (on-peg ?disk2 ?to)
            (no-smaller-disk-on ?disk1 ?to)
            (no-smaller-disk-on ?disk2 ?to)
            (grasped ?disk1))
 :actions  ((*vertical-move ?disk1 -1))
 :effects  ((on-disk ?disk1 ?disk2)))
```

These do not satisfy its goal of having a tower composed of the same disks on the rightmost peg, so it attempts to retrieve a skill that will transform its current state into the desired one. Failing to retrieve such a skill, it decomposes the tower goal into three subgoals, each of which involves getting a separate disk on the rightmost peg, and selects among them.

Because the model knows it can move the smallest disk to the goal immediately, it selects this alternative, although the choice causes problems later. The agent selects a skill that will achieve this subgoal and, since its conditions are satisfied, executes it in the environment. This skill invokes subskills for grasping, lifting, carrying, lowering, and ungrasping the disk, most of which take multiple cycles to complete. When it has finished the move, it pops the subgoal from the goal stack.

The system next selects the subgoal of getting the second smallest disk on the goal peg, along with the skill instance that would move it there. However, the start condition for this skill is not matched, so the model pushes a subgoal onto the stack to achieve it. But it cannot find any skill that would accomplish it and not undo the subgoal regarding the smallest disk it has already achieved. As a result, it pops the goal stack and marks the proposed skill as failed, then selects another that it hopes will move the second smallest disk to the rightmost peg. However, it finds that this skill leads to the same problem and abandons it as well. Thus, the system pops the subgoal for the second smallest disk and replaces it with the subgoal of moving the largest disk to the goal peg. But this encounters the same problems as before, which eventually causes it to abandon this subgoal.

Lacking any further options, the model realizes its first subgoal was an error, so it stores the context in which it made this selection in order to avoid the subgoal in future attempts. The agent then resets the environment to the initial configuration and tries the puzzle again. This time it avoids the previous mistake but instead attempts to get the second smallest disk onto the goal peg, which leads to similar problems. After some effort, it decides to abandon this attempt and restart the problem again.

The model continues in this fashion, chaining backward to select subgoals and skills and executing the latter whenever they are applicable. On its eighth attempt, the agent selects the subgoal involving the largest disk first, followed by the second largest disk, which together let it solve the problem successfully. Along the way, the system creates a new skill whenever it achieves a subgoal that requires executing two or more component skills.

For the three-disk puzzle, the model acquires 13 skills that build on initial hierarchy. When given the same problem, the agent retrieves the relevant learned skill and executes it without invoking means-ends analysis. There are two ways to instantiate this skill, one that moves disks to the goal peg and another that moves them to the other peg. The model makes the right choice half the time, in which case it makes the correct sequence of moves in a reactive manner. When it makes the wrong choice, the model fails and restarts, either to repeat its error or make the right one on the next round. Humans often make similar errors even after practice on the task.

We have included this example to illustrate the ways in which Icarus' behavior is qualitatively consistent with the phenomena discussed earlier. Other researchers have presented models of behavior on the Tower of Hanoi, including some that match closely the timing observed on the task. Such detailed modeling has benefits, but it should not be expected in the early stages of developing a unified theory that covers new phenomena, when qualitative evaluation is appropriate.

Related Theoretical Extensions

We are hardly the first to propose extensions to the standard theory of problem solving. For example, Icarus' learning mechanisms are closely related to the chunking process in Soar and to knowledge compilation in ACT-R. All three create new structures that reduce an agent's efforts on future tasks. A key difference is that the older architectures determine conditions on learned rules by analyzing dependencies in reasoning traces, whereas Icarus simply stores generalized elements from its goal stack. Moreover, their learning mechanisms eliminate intermediate structures to reduce internal processing, whereas Icarus' mechanisms operate in a cumulative manner that leads to the creation of hierarchical structures.

We have also mentioned Jones and Langley's Eureka, which incorporated a modified means-ends problem solver that combined search down a single path with restarts upon failure. Their model did not learn either generalized chunks or hierarchical skills, but it did include a form of analogical search control based on problem-solving traces accessed through spreading activation. Icarus stores instances of specific failures, but uses them in a more limited way to keep from repeating mistakes. Eureka also utilized a flexible version of means-ends analysis which preferred operators that reduced more differences and fell back on forward-chaining search when no other choices were available. We intend to incorporate this idea into future versions of Icarus.

Jones and Langley also used their model to account for insight in problem solving, a topic which Ohlsson has discussed at more length. In his treatment, problem solving sometimes leads to impasses that cannot be overcome in the initial problem space. Insight occurs when the problem solver restructures the space in some manner that makes a solution possible. Ohlsson suggested three distinct restructuring mechanisms that can produce this effect. In some ways, his proposal constitutes a more radical extension to the standard theory than our own, but it also expands on Newell et al.'s original analysis without rejecting its basic contributions.

Other researchers have extended the standard framework to explain the benefits of diagrams in problem solving. For example, Larkin and Simon have argued that, besides serving as external memories, diagrams reduce search by grouping elements that are used together, utilize location to group information about a given element, and support perceptual inferences that are easy for humans. This extension seems closely related to our concern with the embodied context of problem solving, although diagrams have a somewhat different character from the physical structures in many puzzles and games.

Heuristic Affects Decision Making

Which job is more dangerous—being a police officer or a logger? While high profile police shootings might lead to you think that cops have the most dangerous job, statistics actually show that loggers are more likely to die on the job than cops. When it comes to making this type of judgment about relative risk or danger, our brains rely on a number of different strategies to make quick decisions. This illustrates what is known as the availability heuristic, a mental shortcut that helps you make fast, but sometimes incorrect, assessments.

There are all kinds of mental shortcuts, but one common one involves relying on information that comes to mind quickly. This is known as the availability. If you can quickly think of multiple examples of something happening—such as police shootings—you will believe that it is more common.

How the Availability Heuristic Works

When you are trying to make a decision, a number of related events or situations might immediately spring to the forefront of your thoughts. As a result, you might judge that those events are more frequent or probably than others. You give greater credence to this information and tend to overestimate the probability and likelihood of similar things happening in the future.

For example, after seeing several news reports about car thefts, you might make a judgment that vehicle theft is much more common than it really is in your area. This type of availability heuristic can be helpful and important in decision-making. When faced with a choice, we often lack the time or resources to investigate in greater depth.

Faced with the need for an immediate decision, the availability heuristic allows people to quickly arrive at a conclusion. This can be helpful when you are trying to make a decision or judgment about the world around you.

For example, would you say that there are more words in the English language that begin with the letter t or with the letter k? You might try to answer this question by thinking of as many words as you can that begin with each letter. Since you can think of more words that begin with t, you might then believe that more words begin with this letter than with k. In this instance, the availability heuristic has let you to a correct answer.

In another example, researchers have found that people who are more easily able to recall seeing antidepressant advertising were also more likely to give high estimates about the prevalence of depression.

Why the Availability Heuristic Sometimes Leads to Incorrect Decisions

Like other heuristics, the availability heuristic can be useful at times. However, it can lead to problems and errors. Reports of child abductions, airplane accidents, and train derailments often lead people to believe that such events are much more typical than they truly are.

The term was first coined in 1973 by Nobel-prize winning psychologists Amos Tversky and Daniel Kahneman. They suggested that the availability heuristic occurs unconsciously and operates under the principle that "if you can think of it, it must be important." Things that come to mind more easily are believed to be far more common and more accurate reflections of the real world.

As Tversky and Kahneman explained, one of the most obvious examples of the availability heuristic in action is the impact of readily available examples. For example, after you see a movie about a nuclear disaster, you might become convinced that a nuclear war or accident is highly likely. After seeing a car overturned on the side of the road, you might believe that your own likelihood of getting in an accident is very high. And the longer you stay preoccupied with the event, the more available it will be in your mind and the more probable you will believe it to be.

The problem is that certain events tend to stand out in our minds more than others. Excessive media coverage can cause this to happen, but sometimes the novelty or drama surrounding an event can cause it to become more available in your memory. Because the event is so unusual, it takes on greater significance, which leads you to incorrectly assume that the event is much more common than it really is.

Examples of the Availability Heuristic

- After seeing news reports about people losing their jobs, you might start to believe that you are in danger of being laid-off. You start lying awake in bed each night worrying that you are about to be fired.
- After seeing several television programs on shark attacks, you start to think that such incidences are relatively common. When you go on vacation, you refuse to swim in the ocean because you believe the probability of a shark attack is high.
- After reading an article about lottery winners, you start to overestimate your own likelihood of winning the jackpot. You start spending more money than you should each week on lottery tickets.
- After seeing news stories about high-profile child abductions, you begin to believe that such tragedies are quite common. You refuse to let your child play outside by herself and never let her leave your sight.

Heuristics play an important role in how we make decisions and act upon information in the world around us. The availability heuristic can be a helpful tool, but it is also important to remember that it can sometimes lead to incorrect assessments.

Just because something looms large in your memory does not necessarily mean that it is more common, so it can be helpful to rely on numerous tools and decision-making strategies when you are trying to make a choice.

Deductive Reasoning vs. Inductive Reasoning

During the scientific process, deductive reasoning is used to reach a logical true conclusion. Another type of reasoning, inductive, is also used. Often, people confuse deductive reasoning with inductive reasoning, and vice versa. It is important to learn the meaning of each type of reasoning so that proper logic can be identified.

Deductive Reasoning

Deductive reasoning is a basic form of valid reasoning. Deductive reasoning, or deduction, starts out with a general statement, or hypothesis, and examines the possibilities to reach a specific, logical conclusion. The scientific method uses deduction to test hypotheses and theories. "In deductive inference, we hold a theory and based on it we make a prediction of its consequences. That is, we predict what the observations should be if the theory were correct. We go from the general — the theory — to the specific — the observations," said Dr. Sylvia Wassertheil-Smoller, a researcher and professor emerita at Albert Einstein College of Medicine.

Deductive reasoning usually follows steps. First, there is a premise, then a second premise, and finally an inference. A common form of deductive reasoning is the syllogism, in which two statements — a major premise and a minor premise — reach a logical conclusion. For example, the premise "Every A is B" could be followed by another premise, "This C is A." Those statements would lead to the conclusion "This C is B." Syllogisms are considered a good way to test deductive reasoning to make sure the argument is valid.

For example, "All men are mortal. Harold is a man. Therefore, Harold is mortal." For deductive reasoning to be sound, the hypothesis must be correct. It is assumed that the premises, "All men are mortal" and "Harold is a man" are true. Therefore, the conclusion is logical and true. In deductive reasoning, if something is true of a class of things in general, it is also true for all members of that class.

According to California State University, deductive inference conclusions are certain provided the premises are true. It's possible to come to a logical conclusion even if the generalization is not true. If the generalization is wrong, the conclusion may be logical, but it may also be untrue. For example, the argument, "All bald men are grandfathers. Harold is bald. Therefore, Harold is a grandfather," is valid logically but it is untrue because the original statement is false.

Inductive Reasoning

Inductive reasoning is the opposite of deductive reasoning. Inductive reasoning makes broad generalizations from specific observations. Basically, there is data, then conclusions are drawn from the data. This is called inductive logic, according to Utah State University.

"In inductive inference, we go from the specific to the general. We make many observations, discern a pattern, make a generalization, and infer an explanation or a theory," Wassertheil-Smoller told Live Science. "In science, there is a constant interplay between inductive inference (based on observations) and deductive inference (based on theory), until we get closer and closer to the 'truth,' which we can only approach but not ascertain with complete certainty."

An example of inductive logic is, "The coin you pulled from the bag is a penny. That coin is a penny. A third coin from the bag is a penny. Therefore, all the coins in the bag are pennies."

Even if all of the premises are true in a statement, inductive reasoning allows for the conclusion to be false. Here's an example: "Harold is a grandfather. Harold is bald. Therefore, all grandfathers are bald." The conclusion does not follow logically from the statements.

Inductive reasoning has its place in the scientific method. Scientists use it to form hypotheses and theories. Deductive reasoning allows them to apply the theories to specific situations.

Abductive Reasoning

Another form of scientific reasoning that doesn't fit in with inductive or deductive reasoning is abductive. Abductive reasoning usually starts with an incomplete set of observations and proceeds to the likeliest possible explanation for the group of observations. It is based on making and testing hypotheses using the best information available. It often entails making an educated guess after observing a phenomenon for which there is no clear explanation.

For example, a person walks into their living room and finds torn up papers all over the floor. The person's dog has been alone in the room all day. The person concludes that the dog tore up the papers because it is the most likely scenario. Now, the person's sister may have brought by his niece and she may have torn up the papers, or it may have been done by the landlord, but the dog theory is the more likely conclusion.

Abductive reasoning is useful for forming hypotheses to be tested. Abductive reasoning is often used by doctors who make a diagnosis based on test results and by jurors who make decisions based on the evidence presented to them.

Social Cognition

Social psychology is based on the ABCs of affect, behavior, and cognition. In order to effectively maintain and enhance our own lives through successful interaction with others, we rely on these three basic and interrelated human capacities:

1. Affect (feelings)
2. Behavior (interactions)
3. Cognition (thought)

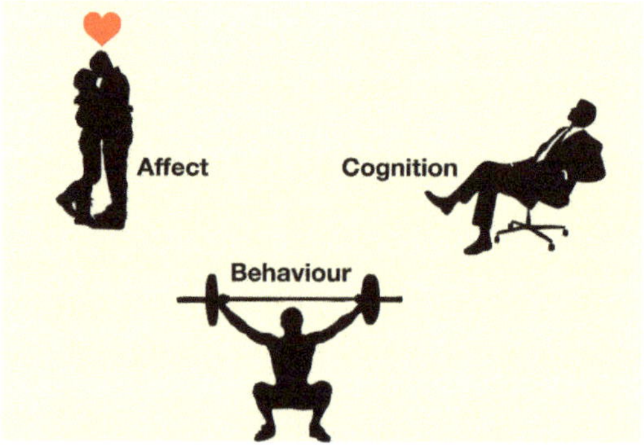

Figure: Human beings rely on the three capacities of affect, behavior, and cognition, which work together to help them create successful social interactions.

You can see that these three aspects directly reflect the idea in our definition of social psychology—the study of the feelings, behaviors, and thoughts of individuals in the social situation. Although we will frequently discuss each of the capacities separately, keep in mind that all three work together to produce human experience. Now let's consider separately the roles of cognition, affect, and behavior.

Social Cognition: Thinking and Learning about others

The human brain contains about 86 billion neurons, each of which can make contact with tens of thousands of other neurons. The distinguishing brain feature in mammals, including humans, is the more recently evolved cerebral cortex—the part of the brain that is involved in thinking. Humans are highly intelligent, and they use cognition in every part of their social lives. Psychologists refer to cognition as the mental activity of processing information and using that information in judgment. Social cognition is cognition that relates to social activities and that helps us understand and predict the behavior of ourselves and others.

Figure: The cerebral cortex is the part of the brain that is involved in thinking. A big part of its job is social cognition—thinking about and understanding other people.

Over time, people develop a set of social knowledge that contains information about the self, other people, social relationships, and social groups. Two types of knowledge are particularly important in social psychology: schemas and *attitudes.* A schema is *a knowledge representation that includes information about a person or group* (e.g., our knowledge that Joe is a friendly guy or that Italians are romantic). An attitude is a knowledge representation that includes primarily our liking or disliking of a person, thing, or group ("I really like Julie"; "I dislike my new apartment"). Once we have formed them, both schemas and attitudes allow us to judge quickly and without much thought whether someone or something we encounter is good or bad, helpful or hurtful, to be sought out or avoided. Thus schemas and attitudes have an important influence on our social information processing and social behavior.

Social cognition involves the active interpretation of events. As a result, different people may draw different conclusions about the same events. When Indira smiles at Robert, he might think that she is romantically attracted to him, whereas she might think that she's just being friendly. When Mike tells a joke about Polish people, he might think it's funny, but Wanda might think he is being prejudiced. The 12 members of a jury who are deliberating about the outcome in a trial have all heard the same evidence, but each juror's own schemas and attitudes may lead him or her to interpret the evidence differently. The fact that different people interpret the same events differently makes life interesting, but it can sometimes lead to disagreement and conflict. Social psychologists study how people interpret and understand their worlds and, particularly, how they make judgments about the causes of other people's behavior.

Social Affect: Feelings about Ourselves and Others

Affect refers to the feelings we experience as part of our everyday lives. As our day progresses, we may find ourselves feeling happy or sad, jealous or grateful, proud or embarrassed. Although affect can be harmful if it is unregulated or unchecked, our affective experiences normally help us to function efficiently and in a way that increases our chances of survival. Affect signals us that things are going all right (e.g., because we are in a good mood or are experiencing joy or serenity) or that things are not going so well (we are in a bad mood, anxious, upset, or angry). Affect can also lead us to engage in behaviors that are appropriate to our perceptions of a given situation. When we are happy, we may seek out and socialize with others; when we are angry, we may attack; when we are fearful, we may run away.

We experience affect in the form of mood and emotions. Mood refers to the positive or negative feelings that are in the background of our everyday experiences. Most of the time, we are in a relatively good mood, and positive mood has some positive consequences—it encourages us to do what needs to be done and to make the most of the situations we are in. When we are in a good mood, our thought processes open up and we are more likely to approach others. We are more friendly and helpful to others when we are in a good mood than when we are in a bad mood, and we may think more creatively. On the other hand, when we are in a bad mood, we are more likely to prefer to remain by ourselves rather than interact with others, and our creativity suffers.

Emotions are brief, but often intense, mental and physiological feeling states. In comparison with moods, emotions are shorter lived, stronger, and more specific forms of affect. Emotions are caused by specific events (things that make us, for instance, jealous or angry), and they are accompanied by high levels of arousal. Whereas we experience moods in normal, everyday situations, we experience emotions only when things are out of the ordinary or unusual. Emotions serve an adaptive role in helping us guide our social behaviors. Just as we run from a snake because the snake elicits fear, we may try to make amends with other people when we feel guilty.

Social Behavior: Interacting with Others

Because we interact with and influence each other every day, we have developed the ability to make these interactions proceed efficiently and effectively. We cooperate with other people to gain outcomes that we could not obtain on our own, and we exchange goods, services, and other benefits with other people. These behaviors are essential for survival in any society.

The sharing of goods, services, emotions, and other social outcomes is known as social exchange. Social rewards (the positive outcomes that we give and receive when we interact with others) include such benefits as attention, praise, affection, love, and financial support. Social costs (the negative outcomes that we give and receive when we interact with others), on the other hand, include, for instance, the frustrations that accrue when disagreements with others develop, the guilt that results if we perceive that we have acted inappropriately, and the effort involved in developing and maintaining harmonious interpersonal relationships.

Imagine a first-year student at college or university who is trying to decide whether or not to join a student club. Joining the club has costs, in terms of the dues that have to be paid, the need to make friends with each of the other club members and to attend club meetings, and so forth. On the other hand, there are the potential benefits of group membership, including having a group of friends with similar interests and a social network to help find activities to participate in. To determine whether or not to join, the student has to weigh both the social and the material costs and benefits before coming to a conclusion.

People generally prefer to maximize their own outcomes by attempting to gain as many social rewards as possible and by attempting to minimize their social costs. Such behavior is consistent with the goal of protecting and enhancing the self. But although people do behave according to the goals of self-concern, these goals are tempered by other-concern: the goals of respecting, accepting, and cooperating with others. As a result, social exchange is generally fair and equitable, at least in the long run. Imagine, for example, that someone asks you to do a favor for them, and you do it. If they were only concerned about their own self-enhancement, they might simply accept the favor without any thought of paying you back. Yet both you and they would realize that you would most certainly expect them to be willing to do the same type of favor for you, should you ask them at some later time.

One of the outcomes of humans living together in small groups over thousands of years is that people have learned to cooperate by giving benefits to those who are in need, with the expectation of a return of benefits at a future time. This mutual, and generally equitable, exchange of benefits is known as reciprocal altruism. An individual who is temporarily sick or injured will benefit from the help that he or she might get from others during this time. And according to the principle of reciprocal altruism, other group members will be willing to give that help to the needy individual because they expect that similar help will be given to them should they need it. However, in order for reciprocal altruism to work, people have to keep track of how benefits are exchanged, to be sure that everyone plays by the rules. If one person starts to take benefits without paying them back, this violates the principle of reciprocity and should not be allowed to continue for very long. In fact, research has shown that people seem to be particularly good at detecting "cheaters"—those who do not live up to their obligations in reciprocal altruism—and that these individuals are judged extremely negatively.

How Emotions Impact Cognition

Two information-processing systems determine the human emotional response: the affective and cognitive processing systems. The affective system operates outside of conscious thought and is reactive, in that a series of psychophysiological events are initiated automatically following the receipt of sensory information. In contrast, the cognitive processing system is conscious and involves analysis of sensory information to influence and even counteract the affective system. Affects (i.e. things that induce some change to the affective system) are divided into positive and negative groups. Positive affect has the potential to improve creative thinking, while negative affect narrows thinking and has the potential to adversely affect performance on simple tasks. Emotions are the product of changes in the affective system brought about by sensory information stimulation. positive emotions—such as happiness, comfort, contentedness, and pleasure—help us make decisions, allow us to consider a larger set of options, decide quicker, and develop more creative problem-solving strategies. These findings suggest attractive things really do work better, even if this is only the case because they make us feel better when we are using them.

Much of the work into how users and customers behave focuses on the emotional responses elicited by a product. However, emotions are the product of complex processing systems, which essentially convert sensory information into the psychophysiological and behavioral changes that we refer to as emotional responses. According to Don Norman, cognition and affect are in charge of these emotional responses. Cognition and affect are information-processing systems, which help us convert information from our environment into accurate representations of the world and make value judgments that determine how we respond and behave.

Norman distinguishes the cognitive and affective systems, and defines emotion, thusly: "The cognitive system interprets and makes sense of the world. Affect is the general term for the judgemental system, whether conscious or subconscious. Emotion is the conscious experience of affect, complete with attribution of its cause and identification of its object". The affective and cognitive systems are thought to work independently, but they influence one another, with the former operating unconsciously while the latter operates at the conscious level. For example, imagine you are about to make a speech in front of a room full of people; the affective system is immediately called into action, with chemicals released in your body in response to the situation automatically and without your ability to control this physiological response. However, you may then try to rationalize the situation and focus on your lines, what you want to say, the points you want to get across and the techniques you might have covered beforehand. All of these mental operations are under the control of the cognitive system, which, on this occasion, is working in opposition to the affective system to help us perform to the best of our ability.

For this public speaker, the affective and cognitive systems seem to be in sync. For other public speakers, the rational system must work in opposition to the affective system.

The Affective System: Helping us Distinguish between the 'Good', the 'Bad' and the 'Ugly'

While the example above gives the impression that the affective system is our enemy – making us feel nervous and stressed, threatening our performance levels as result – it performs an essential function: helping us distinguish 'good' from 'bad'. The affective system is responsible for the 'fight-or-flight' response, which refers to the human instinct to either combat a particular situation or flee instead, as a means of self-preservation. When sensory information signals a significant threat, brain regions responsible for physical activation are stimulated, resulting in the release of various chemicals and hormones. These physiological changes are a double-edged sword; they ensure we are prepared to fight or flee, but they also give rise to negative emotions which affect how well we can perform under pressure. Even in the speech example, the affective system is trying to help us out, telling us to avoid this potentially humiliating or embarrassing experience by flooding our body with adrenaline and cortisol, but unfortunately this also elicits negative emotions such as fear and anxiety.

Negative and Positive Affect

Negative emotions are examples of affective states: "affect changes how well we do cognitive tasks". The classification of an affect as positive or negative is dependent upon the state of psychophysiological arousal we experience. Negative affect refers to any situation or thing which brings about some unpleasant emotional state, such as sadness or tension. In contrast, positive affect refers to any stimulus which elicits a pleasant or advantageous emotional state, such as happiness, awe and optimism. Negative affect has the potential to make simple tasks more difficult or complicated, while positive affect can help reduce the difficulty of complex tasks. For example, if you are trying to write down a telephone number from an answer phone message, but it is being read quickly, you might feel uptight and frustrated, which then affects how fast you can write. In contrast, if you are calm and happy or there is something to make you feel at ease, writing the number down would probably seem less difficult.

Negative and positive affect have different implications for cognition; negative affect limits thinking, but focuses our attention, while positive affect allows us to think more broadly, which enables creativity and supports problem-solving. Therefore, when you want people to concentrate intently, but there is no call for creative thinking, you might induce some negative affect by using warnings or alerts, for example, or using different types of audio. However, if you want your users to tackle complex problems, develop new strategies or simply think creatively, you might use design features which induce positive affect. Some computer games use this knowledge to good effect for designing the user experience, by setting the background music to something dramatic and ominous when the player enters an area where enemies are present (thus, creating anxiety and helping the player to focus on the bad guys), and by using calming and gentle music when the player enters an area where they need to solve a puzzle (thus, supporting their creative thinking).

Negative affect focuses our attention e.g. when we perceive a threat, allowing us to react quickly to get out of harms way.

Affect and Decision-making

"Without emotions, your decision-making ability would be impaired. Emotion is always passing judgments, presenting you with immediate information about the world: here is potential danger, there is potential comfort; this is nice, that bad. One of the ways by which emotions work is through neurochemicals that bathe particular brain centers and modify perception, decision making, and behavior. These neurochemicals change the parameters of thought." in "Emotional Design: Why we love (or hate) everyday things

As the cognitive and affective systems are in charge of our emotional responses, we must consider how we can influence these systems in a positive way to increase the likelihood customers will not only enjoy our products but, first of all, consider buying them. We are still in the early stages of applying our understanding of cognition and affect to user and customer decision-making, but from the research conducted so far, there are some compelling findings. Alice M. Isen, a researcher at Cornell University carried out a number of studies investigating how positive affect can influence decision-making. She found the effect of positive affect varied according to the importance or meaningfulness attached to a task.

In one such study, Alice M. Isen and Barbara Means, researchers at the time in the University of Maryland, asked consumers to make an informed choice between six hypothetical cars. They found consumers in whom positive affects had been induced prior to the decision-making process were noticeably more efficient in their task processing. Superior performance was judged on the basis of the speed decisions were made, the efficiency of the search process, and the number of dimensions that positive affect consumers eliminated due to their low importance to the final decision. The researchers concluded the car-choice findings indicate people are less confused by large numbers of possible options following positive affect, which allows them to gather the necessary information to direct their final decision with greater speed.

Affect and Behavior

A number of studies have shown increased levels of generosity and helpfulness following some form of positive affect. Furthermore, research has shown facilitation of creativity, cognitive flexibility, innovative responding and openness to information following positive affect. Lisa Aspinwall and Richard Tedeschi, researchers at the University of Utah and North Carolina, among other researchers, found positive affect can facilitate coping processes and health-promoting behavior. Positive affect is thought to change cognitive processing through greater elaboration and by promoting the consideration of more options. Elaboration serves to improve cognitive organization and increases cognitive capacity, which allows a more active approach to problem-solving. Furthermore, positive affect can greatly influence consumer behavior as the increased, or broader, thinking associated with pleasurable experiences has been found to lead customers to consider a wider range of products from the same brand. Research also suggests positive affect has the potential to influence our value judgments, encouraging us to view products in a better light when they make us feel some positive emotion.

These findings have significant implications for design: positive affect has the capacity to influence:

- The breadth of options considered,
- The speed a final decision is made,
- The emotional responses induced in potential customers.

Simple changes to your product can have significant results. Each type of product will present specific challenges when attempting to influence the affective system in some positive way, but there are some things to consider regardless of your product:

- At the visceral level of design (i.e. the aesthetics) simple, minimalistic designs are generally more pleasant on the eye, certain colors are associated with positive emotional experiences, and smooth shapes are appealing.
- At the behavioral level (i.e. the user experience) there are various possibilities, but first and foremost the product must be easy to use.
- At the reflective level, designing for positive affect at the reflective level (i.e. the conscious consideration of the product) is difficult, but if you are dealing with an existing brand, familiarity may be a positive quality, so use aspects of previous products to promote reflective processing.

These are just some of the basic considerations when aiming for positive emotional responses, but you must also identify the potential ways your product, in particular, can influence the affective system.

Two information-processing systems determine the human emotional response: the affective and cognitive processing systems. The affective system operates outside of conscious thought and is reactive, in that a series of psychophysiological events are initiated automatically following the receipt of sensory information. In contrast, the cognitive processing system is conscious and involves analysis of sensory information to influence and even counteract the affective system. Affects (i.e. things that induce some change to the affective system) are divided into positive and negative groups. Positive affect has the potential to improve creative thinking, while negative affect narrows thinking and has the potential to adversely affect performance on simple tasks. Emotions are the product of changes in the affective system brought about by sensory information stimulation. Positive emotions, such as happiness, comfort, contentedness, and pleasure, help us make decisions, allow us to consider a larger set of options, decide quicker, and develop more creative problem-solving strategies. These findings suggest attractive things really do work better, even if this is only the case because they make us feel better when we are using them.

Syllogisms: Deductive Reasoning

There is a difference between asserting that a premise is untrue, and asserting that the logic of the argument is faulty. "All dogs can fly. Fido is a dog. Fido can fly." That is a perfectly valid argument in terms of logic, but this flawless logic is based on an untrue premise. If a person accepts the major and minor premises of an argument, the conclusion follows undeniably by the sheer force of reason. If in an argument, the logic reaches a conclusion that seems absurd, it behooves you to analyze each sentence separately (to see if each premise is true without exception) and then to analyze the structure of the argument (to see if the reasoning of the argument itself is valid). Also be on the lookout for "equivocation," the use of two different meanings of one word during the process of an argument.

Directions: Decide whether the following syllogisms are valid in format (as opposed to using true premises). If one is invalid, either explain why, or illustrate using circles.

Invalid example: All snakes are cold-blooded. Valid example: All humans are selfish. All snails are cold-blooded. Confucius is a human. All snails are snakes.	Valid example: All humans are selfish. Confucius is a human. Confucius is selfish.
Invalid: Snakes and snails could overlap as categories, but they both could also be in the largest circle without overlapping.	Valid. We might not agree that the individual premises are true, but if we accept these premises, the conclusion does logically follow.

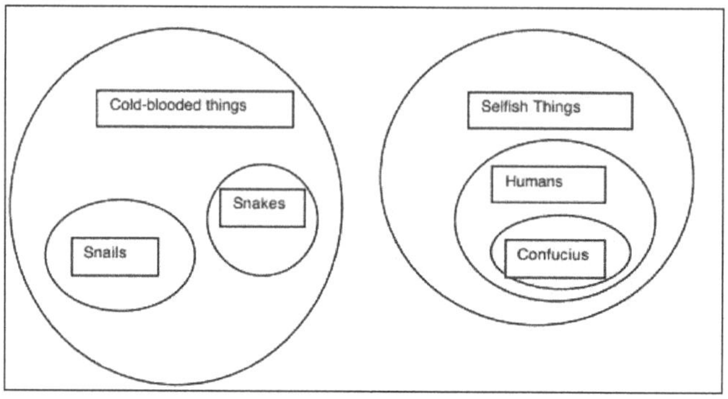

1. All human societies are doomed to deteriorate over time. America is a human society. America is doomed to deteriorate over time.
2. No philosophers are evil. All Greeks are philosophers. No Greeks are evil.
3. All women are potential mothers. Betty is a potential mother. Betty is a woman.
4. All students are eligible for student government. No teachers are eligible for student government. No teachers are students.
5. All barbiturates are drugs. Marijuana is not a barbiturate. Marijuana is not a drug.
6. Pizza is a substance made of cardboard. All substances made of cardboard are good to eat. Pizza is a substance that is good to eat.
7. All rational people believe in rule by law. Some rational people are college professors. Some college people are believers in rule by law.
8. All purple items are green. All yellow items are green. All purple items are yellow.
9. Violent television influences some children in negative ways. Some children are violent. Some children are influenced by violent television.
10. All red items are blue. All pink items are red. All pink items are blue.
11. Since all robins have two legs and since all birds are two-legged, it follows that all robins are birds.
12. Laughter is a meretricious act. All meretricious acts are melancholic in nature. Laughter is melancholic in nature.

13. All environmentalists are activists. Some activists are uninformed. Some environmentalists are uninformed.
14. As Emerson said, "All the world loves a lover." Now that I think about it, Susan is a part of the world. I am a lover, now that I think about it. Susan must love me! The logic is irresistible.
15. Nothing is better than God. Having a lobster is better than having nothing. Lobsters are better than God.
16. God is love. Love is blind. Ray Charles is blind. Ray Charles is God.
17. If he has leukemia, he will die. He will die. Thus, he must have leukemia.

Reasoning

It is one of the best forms of controlled thinking consciously towards the solution of a problem. It is realistic in the sense that the solution is sought always in reference to the reality of the situation. We can solve many problems in our day-dreams, dreams and imaginations but they are unrealistic solutions.

As Sherman defined, "reasoning is a process of thinking during which the individual is aware of a problem identifies, evaluates, and decides upon a solution".

Reasoning is used not only when we want to solve an immediate problem but also when we anticipate future problems.

Reasoning plays a significant role in one's adjustment to the environment. It not only determines one's cognitive activities but also influences the behaviour and personality.

Types of Reasoning

Reasoning may be classified into two types:

1. Inductive reasoning:

   It is a specialized thinking aimed at the discovery or construction of a generalized principle by making use of particular cases, special examples and identifying of elements or relations.

   For example, Mohan is mortal, Radha is mortal, Karim is mortal; therefore, all human beings are mortal.

2. Deductive reasoning:

   It is the ability to draw some logical conclusions from known statement or evidences. Here one starts with already known or established generalized statement or principle and applies it to specific cases. For example, all human beings are mortal you are a human being, therefore, you are mortal.

Henry has categorized three types of deductive reasoning:

1. Conditioned reasoning:

   It is the reasoning tied down by some specific condition such as the following.

   For example, if there is a solar eclipse, the street will be dork. There is a solar eclipse

   ∴ The streets are dark.

2. Categorical reasoning:

   This type of reasoning is based on some categorical statements.

   For example, all Robins are birds.

   All birds lay eggs.

   ∴ All Robins lay eggs.

3. Linear reasoning:

   This type of reasoning involves straight forward relationships among elements.

   For example, If Ram is taller than Mohan and Mohan is taller than Sohan, Ram is the tallest.

Decision-making Strategies

The Single-feature Model

This approach involves hinging your decision solely on a single feature. For example, imagine that you are buying soap. Faced with a wide variety of options at your local superstore, you decide to base your decision on price and buy the cheapest type of soap available. In this case, you ignored other variables (such as scent, brand, reputation, and effectiveness) and focused on just a single feature.

The single-feature approach can be effective in situations where the decision is relatively simple and you are pressed for time. However, it is generally not the best strategy when dealing with more complex decisions.

The Additive Feature Model

This method involves taking into account all the important features of the possible choices and then systematically evaluating each option. This approach tends to be a better method when making more complex decisions.

For example, imagine that you are interested in buying a new camera. You create a list of important features that you want the camera to have, then you rate each possible option on a scale of -5 to +5. Cameras that have important advantages might get a +5 rating for that factor, while those that have major drawbacks might get a -5 rating for that factor. Once you have looked at each option, you can then tally up the results to determine which option has the highest rating.

The additive feature model can be a great way to determine the best option for a variety of choices. As you can imagine, however, it can be quite time-consuming and is probably not the best decision-making strategy to use if you are pressed for time.

The Elimination by Aspects Model

The elimination by aspects model was first proposed by psychologist Amos Tversky in 1972. In this approach, you evaluate each option one characteristic at a time beginning with whatever feature you believe is the most important. When an item fails to meet the criteria you have established, you cross the item off your list of options. Your list of possible choices gets smaller and smaller as you cross items off the list until you eventually arrive at just one alternative.

The additive feature model can be a great way to determine the best option for a variety of choices. As you can imagine, however, it can be quite time-consuming and is probably not the best decision-making strategy to use if you are pressed for time.

Making Decisions in the Face of Uncertainty

The previous three processes are often used in cases where decisions are pretty straightforward, but what happens when there is a certain amount of risk, ambiguity, or uncertainty involved? For example, imagine that you are running late for your psychology class. Should you drive above the speed limit in order to get there on time, but risk getting a speeding ticket? Or should you drive the speed limit, risk being late, and possibly get docked points for missing a scheduled pop quiz? In this case, you have to weigh the possibility that you might be late for your appointment against the probability that you will get a speeding ticket.

When making a decision in such a situation, people tend to employ two different decision-making strategies: the availability heuristic and the representativeness heuristic. Remember, a heuristic is a rule-of-thumb mental short-cut that allows people to make decisions and judgments quickly.

- The Availability Heuristic: When we are trying to determine how likely something is, we often base such estimates on how easily we can remember similar events happening in the past. For example, if you are trying to determine if you should drive over the speed limit and risk getting a ticket, you might think of how many times you have seen people getting pulled over by a police officer on a particular stretch of highway. If you cannot immediately think of any examples, you might decide to go ahead and take a chance, since the availability heuristic has led to you judge that few people get pulled over for speeding on your particular route. If you can think of numerous examples of people getting pulled over, you might decide to just play it safe and drive the suggested speed limit.
- The Representativeness Heuristic: This mental shortcut involves comparing our current situation to our prototype of a particular event or behavior. For example, when trying to determine whether you should speed to get to your class on time, you might compare yourself to your image a person who is most likely to get a speeding ticket. If your prototype is

that of a careless teen that drives a hot-rod car and you are a young businesswoman who drives a sedan, you might estimate that the probability of getting a speeding ticket is quite low.

The decision-making process can be both simple (such as randomly picking out of our available options) or complex (such as systematically rating different aspects of the existing choices). The strategy we use depends on various factors, including how much time we have to make the decision, the overall complexity of the decision, and the amount of ambiguity that is involved.

References

- Problem-solving: lumenlearning.com, Retrieved 4 April, 2019
- Problem-solving: verywellmind.com, Retrieved 11 February, 2019
- ExtendedTheory: ingenieriasimple.com, Retrieved 8 July, 2019
- Availability-heuristic: verywellmind.com, Retrieved 6 June, 2019
- Deduction-vs-induction: livescience.com, Retrieved 25 April, 2019
- Affect-behavior-and-cognition: opentextbc.ca, Retrieved 5 January, 2019
- How-emotions-impact-cognition: interaction-design.org, Retrieved 7 August, 2019
- Reasoning-meaning-definition-and-types, thinking: psychologydiscussion.net, Retrieved 10 May, 2019
- Decision-making-strategies: verywellmind.com, Retrieved 20 March, 2019

6

General Intelligence

The capacity to perceive and retain information as well as applying it for adaptive behaviors is known as intelligence. This chapter closely examines the key concepts of general intelligence such as the theories of intelligence and models of intelligence in order to provide an extensive understanding of the subject.

Theories of Intelligence

Intelligence is a complex thing to define. But it can be broadly thought of as the measure of a person's ability to master a specific cognitive function, such as problem-solving, logical reasoning, and self-awareness.

We're going to explore three competing theories of intelligenceto help you understand the different cognitive strengths you may possess:

- Spearman's Two-factor theory of intelligence.
- Sternberg's Triarchic Theory of Intelligence.
- Gardner's Theory Of Multiple Intelligence.

Spearman's Theory of Intelligence

Charles Spearman, an English psychologist, noticed that students who did well in one subject area tended to do well in corresponding subjects.

He concluded that human beings possess a generalized form of intelligence, known as a g-factor,which can lead to other specialized forms of intelligence, measured by *s-factor*.

G-factor is a sum of s-factor scores that measure a person's abilities in one particular area. Generally excepted s-factors of intelligence include memory, attention, verbal comprehension, spatial skills, and abstract reasoning.

The g-factor and the s-factor are two parts of Spearman's Two-factor theory of intelligence. IQ tests, which measure general cognitive ability, are derived from his theory of general intelligence.

Triarchic Theory of Intelligence

American psychologist, Robert Sternberg, made his name by proposing the triarchic theory of intelligence. This theory asserts that human intelligence can be divided into three types: analytical, creative, and practical intelligence:

- Analytical intelligence refers to a person's ability to assess information and use deductive reasoning to arrive at plausible solutions.
- Creative intelligence draws on a person's ability to create something from nothing or to do something in a unique and novel way.
- Practical intelligence is the intelligence of common sense reasoning, commonly referred to as "street smarts".

Sternberg believed that a balanced measure of all three forms of intelligence would result in the greatest life success.

Gardner's Theory of Multiple Intelligence

In contrast to the two theories of intelligence we've just examined, Gardner's theory proposes nine different types of intelligence.

Howard Gardner is an American psychologist who first proposed his theory in the 1980s. He counters the standard psychological view of generalized intelligence by suggesting nine unique forms of intelligence:

Naturalistic Intelligence

Naturalistic intelligence is the intelligence of the natural world. People who possess naturalistic intelligence to have keen outdoor sensibilities, are born wayfinders, and have a strong connection with Mother Nature.

Musical Intelligence

People who are musically intelligent have a natural draw to all things acoustic and musical. They have a talent for identifying sound, pitch, rhythm, and timbre.

Logical-mathematical Intelligence

We're all familiar with this form of intelligence. If you are logically intelligent, you're able to use deductive analysis, logical reasoning, and executive planningto your advantage. Those with this form of intelligence work well with numbers and are skilled problem solvers.

Existential Intelligence

Those with existential intelligence have a knack for tackling the big questions of life. What is life? Where does it come from? Who am I? What should I do with my life? If you possess existential intelligence, you have a philosophical mind and have no trouble grappling with abstract concept and theory.

Interpersonal Intelligence

If you possess great interpersonal abilities, you possess emotional intelligence. People with this intelligence have a natural ability to understand the thoughts, actions, and motives of others.

Bodily-kinesthetic Intelligence

This type of intelligence is displayed by those with great control over their physical bodies. Many dancers, athletes, and physical therapists possess kinesthetic intelligence. These people have mastered control over the physical form and are effective physical communicators.

Linguistic Intelligence

People with linguistic intelligence are skilled wordsmiths. They're able to use words to convey different feelings, ideas, and theories with ease. They also have a predisposition for visual learning, so they can quickly master new languages.

Intrapersonal Intelligence

Intrapersonal intelligence is the intelligence of the self. True self-awareness is rare in today's world, and those with intrapersonal intelligence know themselves more intimately than any other. This is the intelligence of introspection and self-knowing.

Visual-spatial Intelligence

Those with visual-spatial intelligence relate well to the world around them. They are natural born navigators and possess a keen understanding of the visual world. They often pick up on fine details others are unaware of and can manipulate three-dimensional images in their mind's eye.

Fluid Intelligence vs. Crystallized Intelligence

The theory of fluid and crystallized intelligence proposes that there are two distinct kinds of intelligence. Fluid intelligence refers to the ability to reason and solve problems in unique and novel situations, while crystallized intelligence refers to the ability to use knowledge acquired through past learning or experience.

The theory was first proposed by psychologist Raymond B. Cattell and developed further with John Horn.

The theory of fluid intelligence challenges the idea of generalized intelligence factor (known as g), which contends that intelligence is a single construct. Instead, Cattell contended that there are two independent intelligence factors: "fluid" or g_f intelligence, and "crystallized" or g_c intelligence.

As he explained in his 1987 book Intelligence: Its Structure, Growth, and Action, Cattell referred to the ability to reason as fluid intelligence because it "has the 'fluid' quality of being directable to almost any problem." He referred to knowledge acquisition as crystalized intelligence because it "is invested in the particular areas of crystallized skills which can be upset individually without affecting the others."

Fluid Intelligence

Fluid intelligence refers to the ability to reason, analyze, and solve problems. When we use fluid intelligence, we aren't relying on any pre-existing knowledge. Instead, we are using logic, pattern recognition, and abstract thinking to solve new problems.

We use fluid intelligence when we encounter novel, often nonverbal tasks, such as math problems and puzzles. Fluid intelligence also plays a role in the creative process, as when someone picks up a paintbrush or starts plucking on a piano with no prior training.

Fluid intelligence is rooted in physiological functioning. As a result, these abilities start to decline as people age, sometimes starting as early as their 20s.

Crystallized Intelligence

Crystallized intelligence refers to the knowledge you acquire through experience and education. When you use crystallized intelligence, you reference your pre-existing knowledge: facts, skills, and information you learned in school or from past experience.

You utilize crystallized intelligence when you encounter tasks that require the use of previously acquired knowledge, including verbal tests in subjects like reading comprehension or grammar. Given its reliance on the accumulation of knowledge, crystallized intelligence is typically maintained or even increased throughout one's lifetime.

How the Intelligence Types Work Together

Although fluid and crystallized intelligence represent two distinct sets of abilities, they can and often do work together. For example, when cooking a meal, you use crystallized intelligence to understand and follow the instructions in a recipe, and use fluid intelligence when modifying spices and other ingredients to suit your tastes or dietary requirements. Similarly, when taking a math test, the formulas and math knowledge (like the meaning of a plus sign) comes from crystallized intelligence. The ability to develop a strategy to complete a complicated problem, on the other hand, is the product of fluid intelligence.

Fluid intelligence is often used when learning new things. When you encounter a new subject, you use your fluid intelligence to understand the material through logical and analysis. Once you understand the material, the information will be incorporated into your long-term memory, where it can develop into crystallized knowledge.

Can Fluid Intelligence be Improved?

While crystalized intelligence improves or remains stable with age, fluid intelligence is known to decline fairly rapidly after adolescence. Several studies have investigated whether it is possible to improve fluid intelligence.

In 2008, psychologist Susanne M. Jaeggi and her colleagues conducted experiments in which four groups of young, healthy participants performed a highly demanding working memory (short-term memory) task every day. The groups performed the task for 8, 12, 17, or 19 days respectively. The researchers found that participants' fluid intelligence improved following the training, and that the more training participants underwent, the more their fluid intelligence improved. Their study concluded that fluid intelligence can, in fact, improve through training.

Fluid vs. Crystallized Intelligence

- The theory contends that there are two distinct types of intelligence. It challenges, and extends, the concept of g, or generalized intelligence factor.
- Fluid intelligence is the ability to use logic and solve problems in new or novel situations without reference to pre-existing knowledge.
- Crystallized intelligence is the ability to use knowledge that was previously acquired through education and experience.
- Fluid intelligence declines with age, while crystallized intelligence is maintained or improved.

Emotional Intelligence

The ability to express and control our emotions is essential, but so is our ability to understand, interpret, and respond to the emotions of others. Imagine a world in which you could not understand when a friend was feeling sad or when a co-worker was angry. Psychologists refer to this ability as emotional intelligence, and some experts even suggest that it can be more important than IQ in your overall success in life.

Emotional intelligence (EI) refers to the ability to perceive, control, and evaluate emotions. Some researchers suggest that emotional intelligence can be learned and strengthened, while others claim it's an inborn characteristic.

Since 1990, Peter Salovey and John D. Mayer have been the leading researchers on emotional intelligence. In their influential article "Emotional Intelligence," they defined emotional intelligence as "the ability to monitor one's own and others' feelings and emotions, to discriminate among them and to use this information to guide one's thinking and actions."

Emotional intelligence as a term didn't come into our vernacular until around 1990. Despite being a relatively young term, interest in the concept has grown tremendously over the last 20 years.

Early Growth

As early as the 1930s, however, the psychologist Edward Thorndike described the concept of "social intelligence" as the ability to get along with other people. During the 1940s, psychologist David Wechsler proposed that different effective components of intelligencecould play an important role in how successful people are in life.

Later Developments

The 1950s saw the rise of the school of thought known as humanistic psychology, and thinkers such as Abraham Maslow focused greater attention on the different ways that people could build emotional strength. Another important concept to emerge in the development of emotional intelligence was the notion of multiple intelligences. This concept was put forth in the mid-1970s by Howard Gardner, introducing the idea that intelligence was more than just a single, general ability.

The Emergence of Emotional Intelligence

It was not until 1985 that the term "emotional intelligence" was first used by in a doctoral dissertation by Wayne Payne. In 1987, an article published in Mensa Magazine, Keith Beasley uses the term "emotional quotient." Some suggest that this is the first published use of the phrase, although Reuven Bar-On claims to have used the term in an unpublished version of his graduate thesis. In 1990, psychologists Peter Salovey and John Mayer publish their landmark article, "Emotional Intelligence," in the journal Imagination, Cognition, and Personality.

In 1995, the concept of emotional intelligence is popularized after the publication of psychologist and New York Times science writer Daniel Goleman's book Emotional Intelligence: Why It Can Matter More Than IQ. The topic of emotional intelligence has continued to capture the public interest since, and has become important in fields outside of psychology including education and business.

Components

Salovey and Mayer proposed a model that identified four different levels of emotional intelligence, including emotional perception, the ability to reason using emotions, the ability to understand emotion, and the ability to manage emotions:

1. Perceiving emotions: The first step in understanding emotions is to perceive them accurately. In many cases, this might involve understanding nonverbal signals such as body language and facial expressions.
2. Reasoning with emotions: The next step involves using emotions to promote thinking and cognitive activity. Emotions help prioritize what we pay attention and react to; we respond emotionally to things that garner our attention.
3. Understanding emotions: The emotions that we perceive can carry a wide variety of meanings. If someone is expressing angry emotions, the observer must interpret the cause of the person's anger and what it could mean. For example, if your boss is acting angry, it might mean that he is dissatisfied with your work, or it could be because he got a speeding ticket on his way to work that morning or that he's been fighting with his wife.
4. Managing emotions: The ability to manage emotions effectively is a crucial part of emotional intelligence and the highest level. Regulating emotions, responding appropriately, and responding to the emotions of others are all important aspect of emotional management.

According to Salovey and Mayer, the four branches of their model are "arranged from more basic psychological processes to higher, more psychologically integrated processes. For example, the lowest level branch concerns the (relatively) simple abilities of perceiving and expressing emotion. In contrast, the highest level branch concerns the conscious, reflective regulation of emotion."

Examples:

There are many examples of how emotional intelligence can play a role in daily life.

Being able to put yourself in someone else's shoes: A large part of emotional intelligence is being able to think about and empathize with how other people are feeling. This often involves considering how you would respond if you were in the same situation. People who have strong emotional intelligence are able to consider the perspectives, experiences, and emotions of other people and use this information to explain why people behave the way that they do.

Considering a situation before reacting: Emotionally intelligent people know that emotions can be powerful, but also temporary. When a highly charged emotional event happens, such as becoming angry with a co-worker over some type of conflict, the emotionally intelligent response would be to take some time before responding. This allows everyone to calm their emotions and think more rationally about all the factors surrounding the argument.

Being aware of one's own emotions: Emotionally intelligent people are not only good at thinking about how other people might feel; they are also adept at understanding their own feelings. Self-awareness allows people to consider the many different factors that contribute to their emotions.

Testing

A number of different assessments have emerged to measure levels of emotional intelligence. Such tests generally fall into one of two types: self-report tests and ability tests.

Self-report tests are the most common because they are the easiest to administer and score. On such tests, respondents respond to questions or statements by rating their own behaviors. For example, on a statement such as "I often feel that I understand how others are feeling," a test-taker might describe the statement as disagree, somewhat disagree, agree, or strongly agree.

Ability tests involve having people respond to situations and then assessing their skills. Such tests often require people to demonstrate their abilities, which are then rated by a third party.

If you are taking an emotional intelligence administered by a mental health professional, here are some of the measures that might be used:

- Bar-On's Emotional Quotient Inventory (EQ-i): A self-report test designed to measure competencies including self-perception, decision making, stress management, self-expression, and interpersonal relationships. The test is available to professionals who are qualified to use the assessment.
- Mayer-Salovey-Caruso Emotional Intelligence Test (MSCEIT): An ability-based test that measures the four branches of Mayer and Salovey's EI model. Test-takers perform tasks designed to assess their ability to perceive, identify, understand, and manage emotions.
- Emotional and Social Competence Inventory (ESCI): Based on an older instrument known as the Self-Assessment Questionnaire, the ESCI involves having people who know the individual offer ratings of that person's abilities in several different emotional competencies. The test is designed to evaluate the social and emotional abilities that help distinguish people as strong leaders.

There are also plenty of more informal online resources, many of them free, to investigate your emotional intelligence. For example, this EQ test is a fun way to learn more about some of your emotional strengths and weaknesses.

Improving

Interest in teaching and learning social and emotional intelligence has grown in recent years. Social and emotional learning (SEL) programs have become a standard part of the curriculum for many schools. The goal of these initiatives is not only to improve health and well-being but also to help students succeed academically and prevent bullying.

Clearly, being emotionally intelligent is important, but what steps can you take to improve your own social and emotional skills? Here are some tips.

- Listen: If you want to understand what other people are feeling, the first step is to pay attention. Take the time to listen to what people are trying to tell you, both verbally and non-verbally. Body language can carry a great deal of meaning. When you sense that someone is feeling a certain way, consider the different factors that might be contributing to that emotion.
- Empathize: Picking up on emotions is critical, but you also need to be able to put yourself into someone else's shoes in order to truly understand their point of view. Practice empathizing with other people. Imagine how you would feel in their situation. Such activities can help

you build an emotional understanding of a specific situation as well as develop stronger emotional skills in the long-term.

- Reflect: The ability to reason with emotions is an important part of emotional intelligence. Consider how your own emotions influence your decisions and behaviors. When you are thinking about how other people respond, assess the role that their emotions play. Why is this person feeling this way? Are there any unseen factors that might be contributing to these feelings? How to your emotions differ from theirs? As you explore such questions, you may find that it becomes easier to understand the role that emotions play in how people think and behave.

Emotional intelligence is essential for good interpersonal communication. Some experts believe that this ability is more important in determining life success than IQ alone. Fortunately, there are things that you can do to strengthen your own social and emotional intelligence. Understanding emotions can be the key to better relationships, improved well-being, and stronger communication skills.

Models of Intelligence

One of the greatest challenges in intelligence research is the identification of cognitive processes underlying cognitive abilities and the measurement of process parameters giving rise to individual differences in general intelligence. Traditional as well as current theories of general intelligence either assume that intelligent behavior is the result of individual differences in various independent cognitive abilities, or that there is a hierarchical structure of cognitive abilities with a domain general and broad factor of general intelligence g that determines individual differences in cognitive abilities. Theoretically and empirically the most discussed process parameters related to individual differences in general intelligence are the speed of information processing e.g., the capacity of short-term memory e.g., working memory e.g., or secondary memory e.g., and the efficiency of executive functions e.g. with respect to these theoretical and empirical considerations, there are three main goals to this process-oriented approach to intelligence research: First, understanding whether one or several cognitive processes give rise to individual differences in general intelligence will help to decide whether g should be conceived of as a single cognitive process, as suggested by Spearman's two-factor theory, or as an emerging phenomenon due to several independent or interacting cognitive processes, as suggested by sampling theories. Second, a process-oriented approach aims to identify the mechanisms limiting or facilitating performance in certain cognitive processes by developing formal theories of the mechanisms constituting these processes. Third, such a process-oriented approach may ultimately lead to the development of formal theories of general intelligence by combining psychometric approaches and previous insights into the mechanisms of cognitive processes strongly related to general intelligence.

In empirical research, individual differences in these cognitive processes are usually measured by behavioral indicators such as response times and accuracies in tasks supposedly engaging one specific cognitive process. The behavioral performance in these tasks is then used to quantify the relationship of these cognitive processes to overall performance in intelligence tests. This approach presumes that a specific task provides a process-pure measure of a single cognitive process—an assumption that is often violated as most cognitive tasks do not measure one specific cognitive process, but rather a combination of several cognitive processes. For example, tasks measuring the efficiency of inhibitory processes such as the Stroop or Flanker task usually use reaction times as performance measures. These reaction times arguably reflect not only the efficiency of inhibitory processes, but also basic information-processing speed. Another example is complex cognitive tasks such as complex span tasks measuring working memory capacity that not only require the storage of information in the face of processing, but may also rely on attentional control processes and speed of information processing. In sum, typical measures for a specific cognitive process thus require additional cognitive processes beyond the cognitive process aimed to be measured.

Two approaches are typically pursued to overcome this problem. First, variance decomposition methods may be used to isolate the variance of one latent cognitive process parameter from the influence of other variables e.g. This method is feasible as long as there are "pure" measurements of the confounding cognitive processes available that can be controlled for. However, this approach may be resource- and time-consuming, as participants have to complete large test batteries including both measures of interest and of possible confounds.

A second approach to this measurement problem is to design experimental tasks that contain a baseline condition requiring the engagement of all confounding processes and an experimental condition that is equal to the baseline condition except for the insertion of one additional processing requirement of interest. Subtracting performance in the baseline condition from performance from the experimental condition is supposed to isolate the efficiency or speed of the added process. However, it is questionable if the resulting difference scores only contain variance that can be attributed to the inserted process or if the insertion of additional processing demands may affect or interact with other task demands that are also reflected in the difference scores. Moreover, the low between-subject variability and low reliability of difference scores in typical cognitive tasks renders the isolation of individual differences in experimental effects by means of difference scores virtually impossible.

Advantages of Cognitive Modeling in Intelligence Research

Statistical Models

Although often not explicitly in mind, each measurement of a cognitive process and more generally any property of a person is based on a model. Most often we use statistical models, such as classical test theory or latent variable models for this measurement procedure. These models typically assume that the measured and observed behavior is the compound of some true or latent property of a person and of an error of measurement. Across repeated measurements of the same property, this results in a distribution of observations of which the average or expected value given a person (i.e., the arithmetic mean) is conceptualized as the best estimate of the true person property, while deviations from this value (i.e., the standard deviation) correspond to the amount of error or uncertainty in the measurement. Taken together, statistical models describe statistical properties of observed variables such as their mean and reliability (according to classical test theory), or the covariances among different variables (according to latent variable models).

Even though statistical models have proven to be very useful in the context of measurement, such models bear serious conceptual problems and the selection of an adequate statistical model for measurement is anything but trivial. Apart from these general philosophical and epistemological problems of measurement with statistical models such as the ontological status of true-scores or latent variables and the adoption of a realist or constructionist perspective on science and measurement, all of these models have another serious shortcoming: Statistical models do not specify any psychological or cognitive processes underlying the true part of the measurement, but rather focus on separating true properties of a person from the error of measurement.

In response to this problem, it has been recommended to use more elaborate statistical models such as ex-Gaussian- or Wald- distributions for reaction times, and Binomial-distributions for accuracies or mental test scores. Although these distributions correspond more closely to the empirical shape of the distributions of observed variables, the parameters of these distributions do not consistently resemble indicators of distinct cognitive processes. More importantly, these models still only describe statistical characteristics of the observed variables and do not provide a theoretical account of the cognitive processes underlying the observed behavior. In sum, statistical models may be useful to quantify the amount of variance in a measurement attributable to the true personality trait (i.e., the reliability), however they do not allow any theoretically founded statements about the cognitive processes underlying the observed behavior or the latent personality trait.

Cognitive Models

Conversely, cognitive models may provide a mathematically-guided quantification of specific cognitive processes. Specifically, cognitive models translate explicit verbal theories of cognitive processes in specific tasks into mathematical formulations of these theories. In this, the behavioral measures within a task are described as the result of different interacting processes or parameters of the model. The detailed interplay and interaction of these processes is specified within the formal architecture of the model and represents the assumptions the model makes with respect to a specific cognitive process. Thus, a cognitive model represents a formalized theory of a cognitive process that objectively states which parameters of the cognitive process affect differences in observed behavior across conditions or individuals. The adequacy and validity of this formalization can be evaluated by parameter recovery studies and by testing the selective effects of theoretically-guided experimental manipulations on model parameters.

Taken together, cognitive models provide several advantages over statistical models: (1) They provide falsifiable descriptions of the cognitive process underlying behavioral responses in a specific task; (2) Model parameters can be interpreted in an objective and formally described manner; and (3) Model parameters can be used to quantify individual differences in specific cognitive processes based on the underlying model architecture.

Selecting Cognitive Models Suitable for Intelligence Research

Usually, cognitive models are used with two different aims: (1) A cognitive model aims to formally describe the cognitive processes underlying the observed behavior in a specific task and explain specific experimental effects observed within this task; (2) The parameters of a cognitive model estimated from the observed behavior in a task are used as measures for differences across individuals or experimental conditions. These measures quantify how far people or conditions differ with respect to a specific process of the cognitive model. Within the field of cognitive modeling, cognitive models serving the first aim are often described as explanatory cognitive models or cognitive process models, while cognitive models used with the second aim are often called cognitive measurement models. Accordingly, any cognitive model can be considered both an explanatory cognitive model and a cognitive measurement model depending on the circumstances of its use. Nevertheless, cognitive models that are used to explain the observed behavior within a specific task (i.e., explanatory cognitive models) often differ from cognitive models that are used to quantify differences in their parameters across individuals or conditions (i.e., cognitive measurement models).

In detail, explanatory cognitive models aim to provide formal explanations for variations across experimental conditions in specific paradigms in terms of cognitive processes. These models formally describe the architecture of a cognitive process and focus on the interplay of different mechanisms that lead to specific experimental results. In contrast, cognitive measurement models typically decompose the observed behavior of a person into meaningful parameters of a latent cognitive process. Thus, instead of explaining differences across individuals or experimental conditions, cognitive measurement models are highly flexible tools that reflect these differences in variations of their estimated parameters (for a comparison of these two model types). Often cognitive measurement models rely on a more elaborated explanatory cognitive model. However, there are many cognitive measurement models that have been developed independently of any explanatory cognitive model.

With respect to their application, cognitive models used to explain observed behavior, such as the SOB-CS, the slot-averaging model, or the interference model of visual working memory, often resemble highly elaborated model architectures that specify detailed formal models for a cognitive process. These models are often very complex and require high computing power to calculate predictions for a given set of parameters. In contrast, cognitive models used to measure differences of parameters across individuals or conditions, such as signal-detection theory, the two-high threshold model for recognition, or the drift-diffusion model, are mostly simplified descriptions of a cognitive process that can be generalized to a broad set of paradigms and observed variables. Beyond that, such cognitive measurement models are easy to use and parameters of cognitive measurement models can either be readily calculated from observed variables or estimated with adequate fitting procedures.

In intelligence research, the use of cognitive measurement models is far more widespread than the use of explanatory cognitive models. Although explanatory cognitive models provide a powerful tool for comparing different theories with respect to their predictions for experimental paradigms and manipulations; their complexity and especially the lack of estimable parameters renders their application in intelligence research difficult. Still, results from explanatory cognitive models may provide the theoretical foundation for deciding for or against a specific cognitive measurement model.

Furthermore, there have been efforts to formulate explanatory models of intelligence test performance such as the Carpenter et al. model for performance in the Raven matrices. In this model, Carpenter et al. described different cognitive processes that are used while solving the Raven matrices. Some of these processes such as incremental encoding processes and rule induction for each matrix were used by all participants, while other processes such as the induction of abstract relations of the dynamic management of different goals in memory were specific to participants with above-average performance. Although this model provides a strong theoretical explanation for individual differences in Raven performance, its application remains limited.

Cognitive measurement models may instead provide person- and condition-specific parameters for distinct cognitive processes. These person-specific parameters can be easily used as measures of individual differences in specific aspects of cognitive processes, which can then be related to performance in intelligence tests. For instance, parameters of the drift-diffusion model, that will be introduced later, have been associated with performance in intelligence test or memory tasks. In this, parameters from cognitive measurement models may thus provide insights on which cognitive processes are actually linked to intelligence.

While all cognitive models are deliberate simplifications of the cognitive processes within a task and rely on often critically discussed assumptions, there is actually no alternative to the use of a measurement model, may it be statistical or cognitive. While most research does not explicitly decide for a specific measurement model, by calculating the mean performance for a person in a task (as often done) they implicitly adopt a statistical measurement model that makes no explicit statements about the underlying cognitive processes of the measurement. It may even be argued that not explicitly deciding for a specific measurement model is practically similar to implicitly using the most simple cognitive model at hand: A model assuming that the observed variable directly represents the cognitive processes of interest. As already mentioned earlier, this assumption is almost always false. Therefore, we would argue that using explicit measurement models is always superior to equating observed variables with the cognitive process of interest.

To convey an idea of the benefits of the application of cognitive modeling in intelligence research, we will discuss three examples of cognitive models in the following topics. We selected different models describing cognitive processes of particular interest to intelligence research, such as decision making, working memory, and cognitive control, and demonstrate how they may be used to quantify individual differences in the respective cognitive processes. Please note that the three models described below differ in their breadth of application and in their former use as explanatory or measurement model. Following these examples, we then provide guidelines for choosing the appropriate model for a particular research question.

Different Cognitive Models of Interest for Intelligence Research

The Drift Diffusion Model of Binary Decision Making

The drift diffusion model (DDM) describes performance in two-alternative forced choice decisions tasks. The model assumes that evidence is accumulated in a random walk process until one of two decision thresholds is reached, the decision process is terminated, and a motor response (usually a key press) is initiated. This evidence accumulation process can be described by a Wiener diffusion process that consists of a systematic component, the drift rate v, and normally distributed random noise with a mean of 0 and a variance of s 2 (this so-called diffusion constant s is usually fixed to a standardized value such as 0.1 or 1 for reasons of identifiability). The drift rate can be considered as a performance measure that directly quantifies the velocity of information uptake. In addition, the DDM quantifies the distance between decision thresholds as a measure of speed-accuracy trade-offs and decision cautiousness in the boundary separation as the parameter a, the starting point of evidence accumulation as the parameter z, and the time of non-decisional processes such as encoding and response preparation and execution as the parameter ter or t0. Beyond these basic parameters, intra-individual variability parameters have been added to the DDM (i.e., st0, sv, and sz) to account for inter-trial variability within a person.

The validity of DDM parameters has been demonstrated both by parameter recovery studies and by experimental validation studies. Moreover, model parameters have been showing satisfying reliabilities estimated with test-retest correlations given sufficiently large trial numbers and at least drift rates have been shown to exhibit trait-like properties. Specifically, Schubert et al. used latent-state trait models with additional method factors to separate different variance sources across three different tasks and two measurement occasions. The results showed that the variance consistent across tasks and measurement occasions was largest for drift rates (on average 44%), while this variance was considerably lower for boundary separations and non-decision times (between 32 to 36%). Although drift rates captured this amount of variance that was consistent across tasks and measurement occasions best, single task estimates of drift rates were only moderately reliable (Rel = 0.38 – 0.69) and still contained considerable method specific variance (9 to 17%). Therefore, individual differences in drift rates should always be measured across different tasks if one is interested in individual differences in the underlying latent trait.

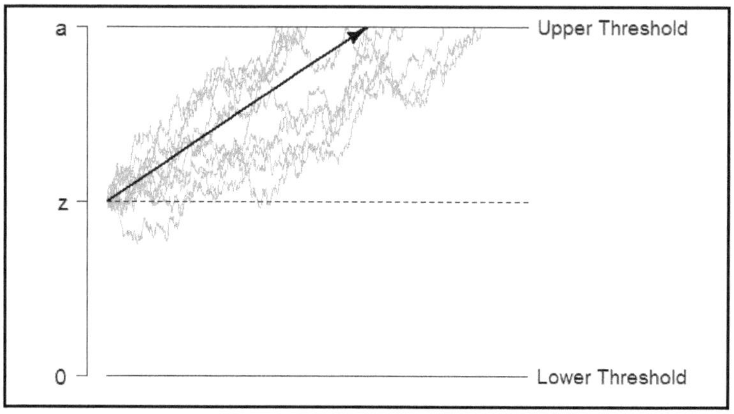

Graphical illustration of the drift-diffusion model.

The decision process starts at the starting point z, and information is accumulated until the boundary a is reached. The systematic part of the accumulation process, the drift rate v, is illustrated with the black arrow. The non-decision time t0 is not included in this figure.

Altogether, it is not surprising that the DDM is the most frequently used cognitive model in intelligence research. By mathematically identifying parameters quantifying the speed of information uptake (v), the decision cautiousness (a), and encoding and movement times (ter), it renders complicated experimental setups that have been used to dissociate these elements of the decision process with little success unnecessary. Several studies have reported positive associations between cognitive abilities and drift rates e.g., whereas the other model parameters have been shown to be largely unrelated to fluid intelligence. The application of the DDM to data sets is made fairly easy by user-friendly software such as EZ and fast-dm.

The DDM is part of a larger family of evidence accumulation models that provide a general description of decision processes. Another member of this model family is the linear ballistic accumulator model (LBA;), which presumes that a number of independent accumulators race towards a common response threshold. Hence, where the DDM can only be applied to data from two-choice reaction times tasks, the LBA can be applied to data from both two- and multiple-choice reaction time tasks. Another member of this model family is the leaky, competing accumulator model (LCA;), which entails a number of stochastic accumulators that compete against each other via mutual inhibition to reach a decision threshold. Both models have not been applied in intelligence research yet, probably because they do not provide a single performance measure such as the drift rate of the DDM, as one drift parameter for each of the accumulators is estimated in LBA and LCA models, resulting in several drift rates.

The Time-based Resource-sharing Model of Working Memory

The time-based resource sharing (TBRS) model of working memory started out as a verbal theory explaining the performance in complex span tasks measuring working memory capacity, but has been extended to verbal and visual WM in general. The TBRS model claims that processing and the maintenance of stored information rely on the same attentional resource in working memory. Because of this attentional bottleneck, only one of these two processes can be performed at a given time. In detail, the model assumes that information stored in working memory decays over time, unless this decay is counteracted by an attentional refreshing process or verbal rehearsal. Moreover, additional processing demands as imposed in complex span tasks shift attention towards these secondary processing tasks, resulting in the decay of items stored in working memory. Altogether, working memory as conceptualized in the TBRS model continuously shares attentional resources between maintenance and processing in order to counteract decay of memory items and efficiently process information.

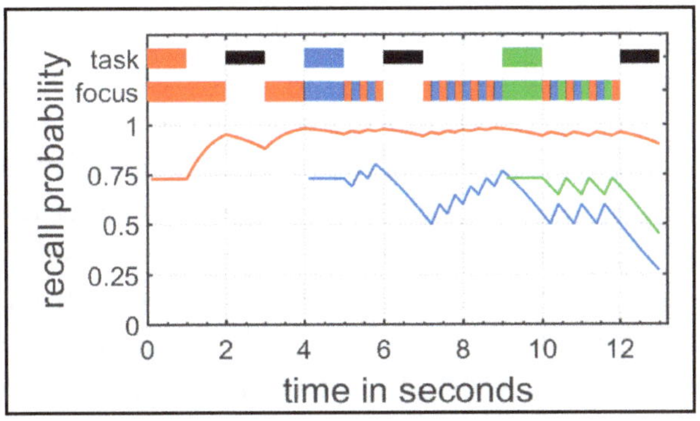

Visualization of the time-based resource sharing (TBRS) theory as implemented in the TBRS2 model by Gauvrit and Mathy. At the top, the current task is displayed.

A colored box represents a to- be-encoded memory item, a black box represents a distractor task, and a white box represents free time. Below, the focus of attention is shown. During free time, participants engage in refreshing of the already encoded memory item; during distractor tasks or encoding of other items, the already encoded memory items decay over time.

In recent years there have been formalizations of the TBRS model as an explanatory model and as a simplified measurement model. Such models may be of great interest for the field of intelligence research, not only because intelligence is strongly related to working memory, but because the field is still in debate about which specific cognitive processes within working memory, storage or executive processing, underlie its strong relationship with intelligence. While the explanatory TBRS* model by Oberauer and Lewandowsky is fairly complex and foremost an in-depth test for the experimental predictions of the TBRS theory, the TBRS2 implementation by Gauvrit and Mathy provides a simplified version of the TBRS model and allows to estimate parameters that are directly linked to specific processes within the TBRS model. Such a model may provide person specific estimates of different processes in working memory, such as the encoding strength when an item is presented (i.e., the baseline β) or the speed of attentional refreshing (i.e., the refreshing rate r). These parameters may provide further information on which specific processes within working memory give rise to the strong relationship between working memory and intelligence.

As the mathematical implementations of the TBRS model have been developed only recently, there have not been any independent, systematic validation studies for the parameters of the model. Moreover, the psychometric properties of the model estimates (i.e., their reliability and validity) have not yet been assessed. Additionally, there is still a controversial debate in cognitive psychology whether decay actually is the core process limiting working memory capacity. Although there are competing explanatory models of working memory questioning the role of decay as a limiting factor for working memory capacity, these models have not yet been translated into simple measurement models that allow estimating person-specific parameters of cognitive processes within working memory. Until then, the TBRS2 model may provide a first step for including cognitive measurement models of working memory in intelligence research.

The Shrinking Spotlight Model of Selective Attention

The shrinking spotlight model of selective attention describes processing in the Eriksen flanker task, in which participants have to respond according to the orientation of a centrally presented target arrow while ignoring irrelevant arrows flanking the target stimulus. The shrinking spotlight model is an extension of the drift diffusion model of sequential processing: It assumes that both target and flanker arrows provide perceptual evidence p for a particular response weighted by the amount of attention a allocated to each of these stimuli. The drift rate consists of the sum of weighted perceptual evidence across all stimuli at a given time. Over time, attention is assumed to zoom in on the central arrow, reflecting a narrowing of the focus of selective attention on the target stimulus. Thus, the target stimulus is weighted more strongly in comparison to the flanker stimuli and therefore affects the drift rate more strongly over time. The initial width of attentional distribution is estimated in the attentional spotlight parameter sda, which reflects the standard deviation of a Gaussian distribution centered on the target stimulus, whereas the rate of attentional distribution reduction is estimated in the parameter rd. In addition, the model also allows estimating the encoding and movement times in the ter parameter, and the distance of symmetrical response thresholds from the starting point of evidence accumulation in the parameters A and B = –A.

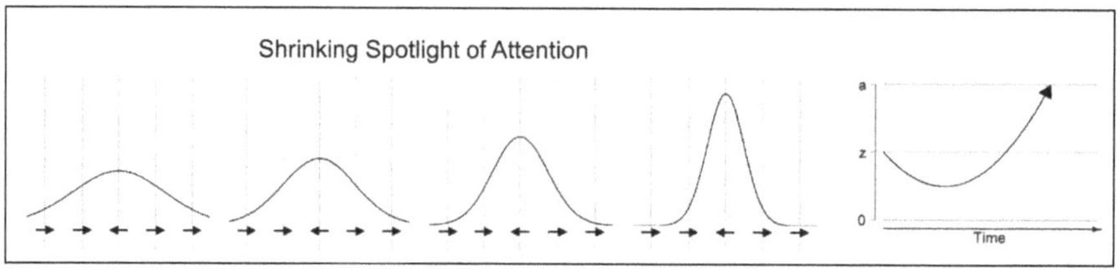

Illustration of the Shrinking Spotlight model for selective attention.

The attentional focus narrows to the central arrow over time (left part). This results in a stronger weight of the critical information (i.e., the central stimulus) in the drift-rate of an associated diffusion process (right part).

The model has been shown to be able to account for data from a standard flanker task and experimental manipulations of task properties have been shown to specifically affect single model parameters. Moreover, parameter recovery studies have shown that model parameters can be accurately recovered with as few as only 50 experimental trials. However, simulation results have also shown that the model is not able to recover the attentional spotlight and the shrinking rate parameter accurately, because a wide initial spotlight with a high shrinking rate makes the same predictions as a narrow initial spotlight with a low shrinking rate. Therefore, it has been recommended to calculate a composite measure of the duration of interference as the ratio of the two parameters, sda/dr, to account for the trade-off during model estimation. Although there have not yet been any systematic analyses on the psychometric properties of parameter estimates, correlations of $r = 0.42 - 0.80$ between model parameters across different cue conditions of the Attention Network Test suggest at least moderate to good reliabilities, especially for the interference ratio with correlations of about $r \approx 0.80$. So far, the shrinking spotlight model has not yet been applied in intelligence research, but it would be promising to relate individual differences in the susceptibility to interference (as reflected in the interference parameter) to individual differences in intelligence test performance and working memory capacity to further explore the role of selective attention in cognitive abilities.

An alternative account of performance in the Eriksen flanker task is given by the dual-stage two phase model. This model proposes two distinct processing stages: In the first processing stage, evidence accumulation is affected both by evidence accumulation towards the response associated with the target stimulus and by evidence accumulation towards the response associated with the flanker stimuli. At the same time, an attention-driven parallel evidence accumulation process selects a single stimulus for further processing. If this stimulus selection process terminates before response selection is finished, response selection enters a second stage with the drift rate being solely determined by the selected stimulus. As of yet, model comparison studies have not yet decided which of the two models provides the best account of selective attention phenomena. Both models can be fit to data and subsequently be compared using the R package flankr.

Guidelines for Model Selection

When deciding which cognitive model to use for a specific research question, there are some conceptual and practical issues to be considered in order to select the appropriate model: First of all, the research question has to be specified. Second, the cognitive processes of interest that are to be related to general intelligence for this research question have to be identified. Third, an appropriate model providing a description of these cognitive processes has to be chosen. During this step, theoretical reasons for choosing one model over its alternatives should be considered. Fourth, experimental tasks congruent with the assumptions of the selected model should be selected to allow the valid estimation of model parameters.

In general, discussing these issues during project planning aims to strengthen two important points for the conclusions from the modeling results. On the one hand, researchers should clarify which specific cognitive processes they are interested in and select a cognitive model accordingly. On the other hand, researchers should maximize the fit between the measurement or operationalization of a specific cognitive process (i.e., the task used) and the selected cognitive model.

For example, a group of researchers might be interested in which cognitive processes in simple decision tasks are related to intelligence. Such tasks may require participants to decide whether a number is odd or even, or whether a letter is a vowel or consonant. They decide to use the drift diffusion model to quantify the different cognitive processes associated with binary decision making. However, one of these tasks has an additional switching demand, requiring participants to switch between the number and the letter decision. Because this task is a binary decision task, the drift-diffusion model may still provide suitable estimates for the cognitive processes in such a task. However, this task arguably requires more than one decision: On the one hand the decision which task is to be carried out, and on the other hand the decision corresponding to the task. Thus, this task does not fully fit the conceptualization of the drift-diffusion model as there may not be a single decision process but two. Therefore, researchers should either think about using a different task that has a better fit to the basic assumptions of the drift-diffusion model or search for an alternative model that better fits the task they want to use.

This example reiterates the importance of an explicit and critical decision for a specific cognitive measurement model with respect to the measurement and operationalization that has already been pointed out before. As the developers of cognitive models often suggest a specific task suitable for parameter estimation e.g., he initial model publication is usually a good starting point for finding prototypical tasks that match the model assumptions.

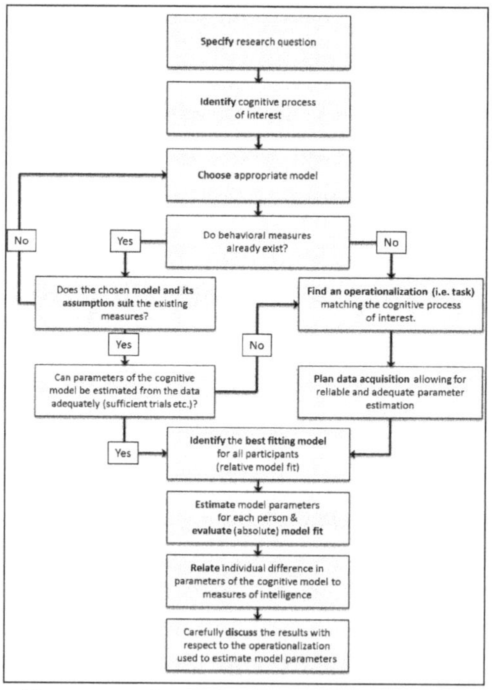

Flowchart illustrating the different planning and decision steps when using cognitive models in intelligence research.

Guidelines for Model Application

After identifying an appropriate model based on theoretical considerations as outlined in the previous topic, we strongly recommend to further plan the application of mathematical models ahead of data collection to ensure the interpretability and trustworthiness of the estimated model parameters. Specifically, three basic steps should be pursued when applying a cognitive model to a specific research question:

1. Researchers should plan their data collection to meet requirements for reliable and stable parameter estimates.

2. Model fit should be carefully evaluated after fitting the model to the empirical data.
3. Model parameters should be adequately related to other individual differences variables of interest such as intelligence test performances.

Design and Data Collection

Reliability and Stability of Estimated Model Parameters

The reliable estimation of model parameters from empirical data usually requires more data points than would be needed if only applying a statistical model to the data. For illustration, compare the description of reaction time distributions in decision tasks by a Gaussian distribution to the description by a diffusion model. When describing performance in a binary choice task by a Gaussian distribution, 20–30 trials are usually sufficient to provide reliable estimates of means and standard errors of the distribution. When describing performance by a diffusion model, however, many more trials are needed because model parameters are not calculated analytically, but are found by fitting them to empirical response time distributions in an iterative process. Hence, a small number of trials will result in an inadequate representation of the full response time distribution and will therefore impair the estimation of model parameters describing distributional elements beyond measures of central tendency.

For the basic DDM (with the four parameters drift rate, boundary separation, starting point, and non-decision time), simulation studies have shown that 100 trials are sufficient to produce relatively reliable estimates of drift rates and that no further increases in parameter reliabilities are gained by increasing trial numbers beyond 500 trials. For other measurement models less prominently used in individual differences research, such systematic simulation studies have not yet been conducted. Therefore, we urge researchers interested in applying less frequently used models to run a simulation study before starting data collection to determine how many experimental trials are needed for a reliable parameter recovery. While a simulation does not guarantee reliable parameter estimates for an experiment in general, it rules out that low reliability is due to noisiness in the parameter estimation process.

Trait, Situation and Task Characteristics of Model Parameters

In addition, it is important to consider to what degree individual differences in model parameters reflect individuals' personality traits or abilities, and to what degree they reflect task-specific characteristics, state-specific characteristics, and unsystematic measurement error. Imagine applying a model of verbal working memory to complex span data: Model parameters such as the individual rate of verbal refreshing or the ability to resist interference from distracting stimuli would reflect both individuals' general abilities in verbal refreshing and inhibition of interference as well as their abilities to maintain memory stimuli in this specific task. Depending on the research question, researchers may be more interested in the general ability to maintain information in working memory as reflected in those parameters across different working memory tasks, or they may be interested in the specific ability to maintain information in working memory in precisely this task.

Usually, intelligence research questions are more likely to concern abilities generalized across specific operationalizations and situations than abilities in specific operationalizations or situations. However, model parameters estimated in a specific task are always going to contain both trait-, state- and task-specific amounts of variance. For example, a latent state-trait analysis of DDM parameters in elementary cognitive tasks revealed that only about 45 percent of the variance in task-specific drift rates was accounted for by the common trait, and that only about 30 to 35 percent of the variance in task-specific boundary separation and non-decision time parameters were accounted for by their respective common traits. Therefore, if a research question using cognitive models in intelligence research concerns performance in certain cognitive processes that is generalizable across specific operations, it may be worthwhile to design a test battery consisting of three or more tasks to which the cognitive model can be applied. Averaged or latent performance in process parameters across tasks will then allow a more precise estimate of individuals' performance in model parameters that is independent of specific task or situation characteristics.

Evaluation of Model Fit

Relative Model Fit: Which Model Provides the Best Account for the Data?

After finishing data collection, but before relating model parameters to intelligence tests or other covariates, it is necessary to evaluate how well a chosen model describes the empirical data and to possibly adjust model specifications to increase model fit. For most cognitive models, these empirical data consist of single-trial accuracies and/or response times, but aggregate measures such as proportion correct for different conditions might also be entered into the analysis. Before the raw data are entered into any kind of model, they should be carefully inspected for extreme values or other distributional properties that violate model assumptions and that may impair or even systematically bias parameter estimation. Once fidelity in these raw values has been established, cognitive models can be fitted to these empirical data. For this purpose, it has to be decided how many and which model parameters will be estimated and which model parameters will be fixed, because they are not expected to be affected by task characteristics or are not of interest for the current research question. Moreover, if experimental tasks contain several conditions, it may be necessary to decide which (if any) parameters are allowed to vary between conditions. It may even be desirable to split data from different conditions into separate data sets for separate model estimations to be able to subsequently model these separately estimated model parameters as latent variables. For this purpose, it may be helpful to reflect on the relationship between model complexity and the stability of parameter estimates: The more parameters of a model are estimated, the more likely it is to provide an accurate account of the data. However, if too many model parameters are estimated relative to the number of experimental trials, the stability of parameter estimates will be impaired.

Therefore, we suggest fitting several models to the empirical data containing different combinations of estimated or fixed parameters that are consistent with the current research question, unless there are strong theoretical reasons to decide on a specific model instantiation a priori. These models can then be compared based on parsimonious fit indices such as the Akaike Information Criterion or the Bayesian Information Criterion, which take into account both model fit and model parsimony, to identify the model making the best trade-off between model fit and model complexity. As mentioned before, this model comparison step may not be necessary when a priori deciding for a specific instantiation of the model.

However, this model comparison approach only addresses one element of model fit evaluation, relative model fit. By identifying the best-fitting specification of the model out of a number of alternative specifications, it is possible to identify the model providing the best description of the empirical data. However, this does not guarantee that the best-fitting model provides a good description of the data.

Absolute Model Fit: How Well Does the Selected Model Describe the Data?

Therefore, in the next step the absolute model fit has to be evaluated to decide if the model can be accepted for all data sets. Absolute model fit is typically ascertained by either (a) statistical tests of model fit, (b) goodness-of-fit (GOF) indices, or (c) graphical inspections of model fit.

Statistical tests of model fit quantify the discrepancy between the empirical data and model predictions by means of a test statistic that is then tested for significance. However, this null hypothesis-testing of model fit contains several problems, as the power of statistical tests is closely tied to the amount of data available. When only a few trials are available, statistical tests may not be capable of rejecting the null hypothesis due to a lack of power, whereas when the trial number is large, statistical tests tend to become overly sensitive and detect even irrelevant deviations between the empirical data and model predictions. To overcome some of the problems associated with null hypothesis testing, it has been suggested to simulate a large number of data sets based on the estimated model parameters, fit the model to each of the simulated data sets, and derive the 95 percent or 90 percent quantile of the resulting distribution of p-values as a critical value for the statistical tests of the originally estimated models. However, models will still be accepted with an unknown error probability.

Goodness-of-fit indices are much more common in individual differences research, where they are used to evaluate the model fit of structural equation models, than in cognitive modeling. GOF indices standardize test statistics and take into account both model complexity and the number of data points. Typically, GOF indices have a fixed value range from 0 to 1 with certain cut-off values that indicate acceptable or good model fit. GOF indices are less frequently used in cognitive modeling, probably because several GOF indices used in structural equation modeling require the comparison of the actual model to a minimally plausible baseline model, which cannot be easily specified for most cognitive models. However, it has been recently suggested to adapt the root mean square error of approximation for the evaluation of cognitive models that can be fitted with a $\chi 2$ -distribution, such as the diffusion model. Note that simulation studies have shown that this approach is only advisable when trial numbers are sufficiently large.

Finally, a third and widespread approach to the evaluation of absolute model fit is to graphically compare the empirical data to model predictions. To graphically inspect model fit, empirical data can be plotted against or overlaid by model predictions separately for each participant or aggregated over participants. This process can be rather time-consuming in larger samples if each participant is inspected individually. Moreover, it is important to be aware of the fact that graphical evaluations of model fit are inherently subjective and may therefore lead to spurious conclusions. Having two independent raters evaluate model fit and discuss their conclusions may therefore increase the objectivity of the evaluation process.

If individual data sets can be identified that do not provide a satisfying model fit, raw data should be inspected for coding errors or outliers that may need to be removed (e.g., extremely fast reaction times with decision behavior close to guessing in a decision task). If model fit remains unacceptable, individual data sets may then need to be removed from further analyses, as it cannot be ascertained that the model parameters characterize the cognitive processes in the task accurately.

Relating Model Parameters to Intelligence Test Performance

Finally, after reliable estimates for the best fitting model have been obtained, the model parameters should be related to measures of intelligence. While this seems straightforward, there are actually two major methodological concerns.

First, extreme values in either parameter estimates or cognitive abilities measures need to be addressed. If extreme values (univariate outliers) are detected in parameter estimates, it is imperative to inspect if any outliers, coding errors, or abnormal distributional properties of the participant's raw data may have contaminated parameter estimation. If this is the case and if these outliers only constitute only a small amount of the data, they should be removed or winsorized and the model fitting procedure should be repeated to see if this treatment has led to more reasonable parameter estimates. If parameter estimates are still extreme or if outliers in raw data cannot be dealt with (e.g., because this participant's distribution of raw data deviates from model assumptions), this participant should be removed from further analyses as model parameters most likely reflect other properties of cognitive processes for this participant than for the rest of the sample. A similar problem is raised by multivariate outliers that may need to be removed based on an inspection of scatterplots or the calculation of the Mahalanobis distance. It goes without saying that information about the number of data points and/or participants removed and a rationale of their removal needs to be included in any description of the modeling results.

Second, researchers usually obtain one or more person-specific estimates for each model parameter of interest across different tasks or experimental conditions, just like they do when using aggregated performance measures such as accuracies or mean reaction times. Then the relationship of these model parameters with intelligence test scores is estimated by means of correlations or structural equation modeling. However, this approach represents a sequential analysis plan that treats the estimated parameters as manifest variables when quantifying the relationship between parameters of the cognitive model and the intelligence measures.

Treating estimated model parameters as manifest variables ignores the uncertainty that these parameters inherit from estimation and leads to an underestimation of standard errors in the second analysis step. In fact, this is the case both for behavioral aggregates, such as mean reaction times or proportion correct, and for model parameters that are estimated from behavioral data or calculated from aggregate performance measures. Although this does not necessarily affect the estimated size of the relation between parameters obtained from cognitive models and intelligence measures, a sequential analysis plan always leads to an overestimation of the statistical significance of the estimated relationships.

A solution to this problem is hierarchical modeling. In hierarchical modeling approaches, parameters of a cognitive model can be estimated simultaneously not only for all participants but across various tasks. Additionally, relationships with third variables, such as intelligence, can be estimated in the same step. On the one hand, such models avoid underestimating the standard errors of the relationship between model parameters and third variables such as intelligence measures by simultaneously estimating the model parameters and their relationship to intelligence (for an example of hierarchical models of the worst performance rule). On the other hand, by assuming that the distribution of model parameters across individuals follows a higher order distribution3 (so called hyper-priors), hierarchical models do not estimate parameters for each individual independently, but instead estimate model parameter for each individual informed by the parameter estimates from all other individuals. Not only does this render the parameter estimation more robust, but it also allows obtaining reliable estimates for the parameters of a cognitive model for each individual with fewer trials.

Although this modeling approach is structurally similar to hierarchical modeling in latent variable models (i.e., SEM), there are some important differences. While hierarchical latent variable models separate general from specific factors in between person variances e.g., hierarchical models in the field of cognitive models distinguish between parameters estimated within a person and the distribution of parameters between persons. In this, hierarchical modeling of cognitive processes is closely related to multi-level modeling separating the within and between person level.

For instance, when applying the diffusion model, parameters of each individual can be estimated independently without assuming a specific distribution of estimated model parameters across participants. While this achieves the highest flexibility in parameter estimation, this approach ignores possible information from the between person level. In contrast, hierarchical modeling assumes that the parameters from each individual stem from a distribution of parameters on the between person level, and thus parameters for each individual are estimated taking information from all other subjects into account. As stated before, this account has two important benefits: (1) hierarchal modeling renders the parameter estimation for each individual more efficient; and (2) parameters and their relationship to third variables like intelligence can be estimated simultaneously, accounting for the uncertainty of parameter estimates and thus adequately reporting the significance of the relationship between parameter estimates and third variables.

A serious complication of hierarchical modeling is that these models typically have to be explicitly specified and translated into code for each application, and that software solutions for parameter estimation are still rare. Nevertheless, hierarchical models do provide the mathematically accurate and sound solution for estimating the relationship between estimated model parameters and intelligence measures. Still, the sequential estimation of model parameters and their relationship to intelligence test scores seems to yield results comparable to hierarchical approaches. In conclusion, while sequential approaches may overestimate the statistical significance of the relationship between model parameters and covariates (biasing inference), they nevertheless provide reasonable and unbiased estimates of the effect size of this relationship. For the future, it would be desirable that the application of cognitive modeling in the field of intelligence research or individual differences in general leads to the development of further simple software solutions or R packages that simplify the use of hierarchical models.

Interpretation of the Results

Regardless of how the relationship between parameters from a cognitive model and intelligence measures is estimated, ultimately this relationship has to be interpreted on a conceptual level. Although parameters of a cognitive model provide more specific information about the cognitive process underlying the behavioral responses, these parameters still have to be interpreted with respect to the operationalization of the cognitive process. For instance, the diffusion model can be estimated in a broad set of tasks, ranging from perceptual judgment tasks (e.g., a random-dot motion task), over elementary cognitive tasks (e.g., Posner or Sternberg task), to even more complex memory tasks. In all of these different tasks, the diffusion model estimates the same set of parameters (i.e., drift rates, boundary separations, and non-decision times). However, this alone does not imply that model parameters estimated in the different tasks can be interpreted the same way. Specifically, the drift rate estimated in a random-dot motion task may represent the speed of perceptual information accumulation towards one response alternative. In a memory recognition task, however, the drift rate would rather be interpreted as the signal-to-noise ratio of the representation in memory. Beyond a theoretical discussion of the similarity of different tasks, statistical methods such as factor analysis or structural equation models can be used to get further information on variance that is shared across different tasks, or that is specific to a task or a situation. However, all in all, the interpretation of parameters of a cognitive model always relies on the specific experimental tasks.

In general, a cognitive model always represents a structural description of the behavioral measures from a specific task. The semantic meaning of the parameters of a model, however, can only be obtained with respect to the context (i.e., the task or materials) they are estimated in. Consider the following equation: $v = x/t$. On its own, this equation is merely a structural description how v can be obtained from x and t. In contrast, if the context of the observations of x as a distance between two points, and t as the time taken to get from one point to the other is known, then v can reasonably interpreted as the average speed of travel. It is just the same with parameters from any cognitive model: Without the context of their estimation they are merely transformations or estimated simplifications of the observed variables. Adding the semantical context of the observations however allows to interpret the parameters in a meaningful way.

All in all, the matter of adequately interpreting parameters of a cognitive model relates to a broader issue, namely validity. On the one hand, there is the question of how far a cognitive model provides a valid description of the cognitive process underlying the behavioral responses in a task. On the other hand, there is the question of how far individual differences in these parameters can be generalized across different tasks and assumed to represent between person variation in a more general and task-unspecific cognitive process. These are hardly problems that can be solved within a single study, but there is a combined effort needed to establish which parameters of cognitive models provide meaningful representations of individual differences in specific aspects of cognitive processing.

For example, attempts to unite psychophysiological and neuroimaging research with cognitive modeling may be particularly informative about issues of validity, as they allow a direct test of the idea that process parameters reflect certain neural correlates. Several studies have already suggested a close link between diffusion model parameter and neural processing correlates in the EEG. In particular, the latency of the N2, which is a neural correlate of visual encoding time, has been shown to be associated with the non-decision time parameter of the diffusion model, and the buildup rate of a positive centroparietral positive potential has been suggested to directly reflect the rate of evidence accumulation captured in the drift rate parameter on a neural level.

Altogether, following certain guidelines and carefully discussing the underlying assumptions and the operationalization when using a cognitive model provides a more explicit approach to measuring individual differences in cognitive processes, and thus represents a decisive improvement compared to the prevailing methods. At the very least, such careful reflection might immunize against the category error that cognitive models are accurate reflections of a latent, unobservable cognitive process. Any (cognitive) model cannot be anything but a simplification of reality that, if successful, captures the most important aspects, but never the entirety of an ontological (cognitive) process. In the same way that a map provides a simplification of a city's layout that is useful for navigation without ever providing a detailed account of the whole city system, cognitive models may refine our understanding of how those unobservable cognitive processes operate and thereby facilitate the measurement of certain process properties. Or, as Box put it: "All models are wrong, but some models are useful".

Measuring Intelligence

Standardization and the Intelligence Quotient

The goal of most intelligence tests is to measure g, the general intelligence factor. Good intelligence tests are reliable, meaning that they are consistent over time, and also demonstrate construct validity, meaning that they actually measure intelligence rather than something else. Because intelligence is such an important individual difference dimension, psychologists have invested substantial effort in creating and improving measures of intelligence, and these tests are now the most accurate of all psychological tests. In fact, the ability to accurately assess intelligence is one of the most important contributions of psychology to everyday public life.

Intelligence changes with age. A three-year-old who could accurately multiply 183 by 39 would certainly be intelligent, but a 25-year-old who could not do so would be seen as unintelligent. Thus understanding intelligence requires that we know the norms or standards in a given population of people at a given age. The standardization of a test involves giving it to a large number of people at different ages and computing the average score on the test at each age level.

It is important that intelligence tests be standardized on a regular basis because the overall level of intelligence in a population may change over time. The Flynn effect refers to the observation that scores on intelligence tests worldwide have increased substantially over the past decades. Although the increase varies somewhat from country to country, the average increase is about three intelligence (IQ) points every 10 years. There are many explanations for the Flynn effect, including better nutrition, increased access to information, and more familiarity with multiple-choice tests. But whether people are actually getting smarter is debatable.

Once the standardization has been accomplished, we have a picture of the average abilities of people at different ages and can calculate a person's mental age, which is the age at which a person is performing intellectually. If we compare the mental age of a person to the person's chronological age, the result is the IQ, a measure of intelligence that is adjusted for age. A simple way to calculate IQ is by using the following formula:

$$IQ = \text{mental age} \div \text{chronological age} \times 100.$$

Thus a 10-year-old child who does as well as the average 10-year-old child has an IQ of 100 ($10 \div 10 \times 100$), whereas an eight-year-old child who does as well as the average 10-year-old child would have an IQ of 125 ($10 \div 8 \times 100$). Most modern intelligence tests are based the relative position of a person's score among people of the same age, rather than on the basis of this formula, but the idea of an intelligence ratio or quotient provides a good description of the score's meaning.

A number of scales are based on the IQ. The Wechsler Adult lntelligence Scale (WAIS) is the most widely used intelligence test for adults. The current version of the WAIS, the WAIS-IV, was standardized on 2,200 people ranging from 16 to 90 years of age. It consists of 15 different tasks, each designed to assess intelligence, including working memory, arithmetic ability, spatial ability, and general knowledge about the world. The WAIS-IV yields scores on four domains: verbal, perceptual, working memory, and processing speed. The reliability of the test is high (more than 0.95), and it shows substantial construct validity. The WAIS-IV is correlated highly with other IQ tests such as the Stanford-Binet, as well as with criteria of academic and life success, including grades, measures of work performance, and occupational level. It also shows significant correlations with measures of everyday functioning among the mentally retarded.

The Wechsler scale has also been adapted for preschool children in the form of the Wechsler Primary and Preschool Scale of Intelligence (WPPSI-III) and for older children and adolescents in the form of the Wechsler Intelligence Scale for Children (WISC-IV).

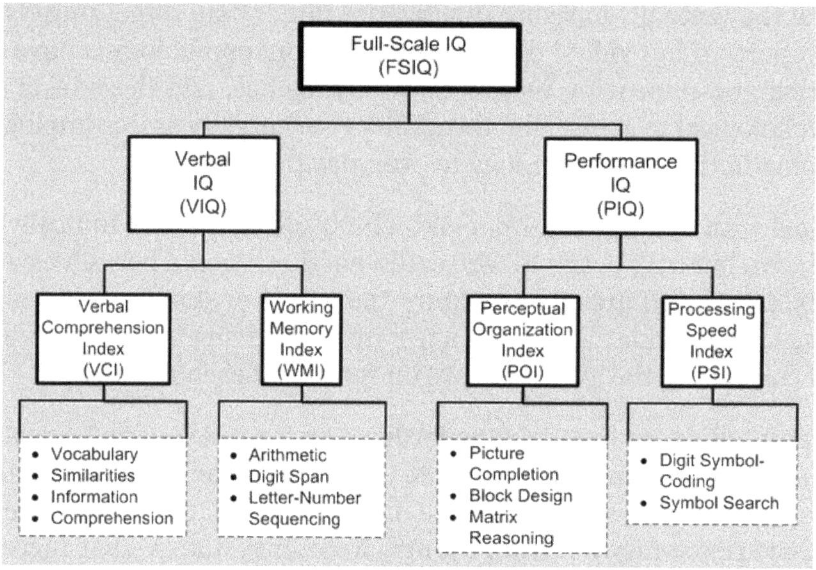

Wechsler Adult Intelligence Scale (WAIS).

The intelligence tests that you may be most familiar with are aptitude tests, which are designed to measure one's ability to perform a given task, such as doing well in undergraduate, graduate, or post-graduate training. Canadian post-secondary institutions request official high school transcripts demonstrating minimum grade admission requirements, while most American colleges and universities require students to take the Scholastic Assessment Test (SAT) or the American College Test (ACT). Post-graduate schools in both countries require the Graduate Record Examination (GRE), Graduate Management Admission Test (GMAT), Medical College Admissions Test (MCAT), or the Law School Admission Test (LSAT). These tests are useful for selecting students because they predict success in the programs that they are designed for, particularly in the first year of the program. These aptitude tests also measure, in part, intelligence. Frey and Detterman found that the SAT correlated highly (between about r = .7 and r = .8) with standard measures of intelligence.

Intelligence tests are also used by industrial and organizational psychologists in the process of personnel selection. Personnel selection is the use of structured tests to select people who are likely to perform well at given jobs. The psychologists begin by conducting a job analysis in which they determine what knowledge, skills, abilities, and personal characteristics (KSAPs) are required for a given job. This is normally accomplished by surveying and/or interviewing current workers and their supervisors. Based on the results of the job analysis, the psychologists choose selection methods that are most likely to be predictive of job performance. Measures include tests of cognitive and physical ability and job knowledge tests, as well as measures of IQ and personality.

The Biology of Intelligence

The brain processes underlying intelligence are not completely understood, but current research has focused on four potential factors: brain size, sensory ability, speed and efficiency of neural transmission, and working memory capacity.

There is at least some truth to the idea that smarter people have bigger brains. Studies that have measured brain volume using neuroimaging techniques find that larger brain size is correlated with intelligence, and intelligence has also been found to be correlated with the number of neurons in the brain and with the thickness of the cortex. It is important to remember that these correlational findings do not mean that having more brain volume causes higher intelligence. It is possible that growing up in a stimulating environment that rewards thinking and learning may lead to greater brain growth, and it is also possible that a third variable, such as better nutrition, causes both brain volume and intelligence.

Another possibility is that the brains of more intelligent people operate faster or more efficiently than the brains of the less intelligent. Some evidence supporting this idea comes from data showing that people who are more intelligent frequently show less brain activity (suggesting that they need to use less capacity) than those with lower intelligence when they work on a task. And the brains of more intelligent people also seem to run faster than the brains of the less intelligent. Research has found that the speed with which people can perform simple tasks — such as determining which of two lines is longer or pressing, as quickly as possible, one of eight buttons that is lighted — is predictive of intelligence. Intelligence scores also correlate at about $r = .5$ with measures of working memory, and working memory is now used as a measure of intelligence on many tests.

Although intelligence is not located in a specific part of the brain, it is more prevalent in some brain areas than others. Duncan et al. administered a variety of intelligence tasks and observed the places in the cortex that were most active. Although different tests created different patterns of activation, as you can see in Figure, "Where Is Intelligence?", these activated areas were primarily in the outer parts of the cortex, the area of the brain most involved in planning, executive control, and short-term memory.

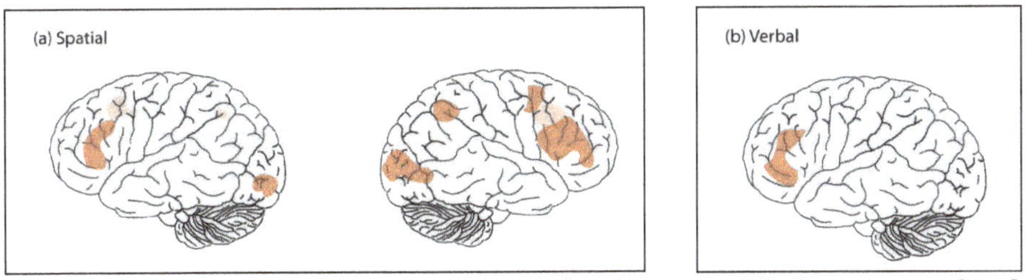

Where Is Intelligence? fMRI studies have found that the areas of the brain most related to intelligence are in the outer parts of the cortex.

Intelligence Nature or Nurture

Intelligence has both genetic and environmental causes, and these have been systematically studied through a large number of twin and adoption studies. These studies have found that between 40% and 80% of the variability in IQ is due to genetics, meaning that overall, genetics plays a bigger role than environment does in creating IQ differences among individuals. The IQs of identical twins correlate very highly (r = .86), much higher than do the scores of fraternal twins who are less genetically similar (r = .60). And the correlations between the IQs of parents and their biological children (r = .42) is significantly greater than the correlation between parents and adopted children (r = .19). The role of genetics gets stronger as children get older. The intelligence of very young children (less than 3 years old) does not predict adult intelligence, but by age 7 it does, and IQ scores remain very stable in adulthood.

But there is also evidence for the role of nurture, indicating that individuals are not born with fixed, unchangeable levels of intelligence. Twins raised together in the same home have more similar IQs than do twins who are raised in different homes, and fraternal twins have more similar IQs than do nontwin siblings, which is likely due to the fact that they are treated more similarly than nontwin siblings are.

The fact that intelligence becomes more stable as we get older provides evidence that early environmental experiences matter more than later ones. Environmental factors also explain a greater proportion of the variance in intelligence for children from lower-class households than they do for children from upper-class households. This is because most upper-class households tend to provide a safe, nutritious, and supporting environment for children, whereas these factors are more variable in lower-class households.

Social and economic deprivation can adversely affect IQ. Children from households in poverty have lower IQs than do children from households with more resources even when other factors such as education, race, and parenting are controlled. Poverty may lead to diets that are undernourishing or lacking in appropriate vitamins, and poor children may also be more likely to be exposed to toxins such as lead in drinking water, dust, or paint chips. Both of these factors can slow brain development and reduce intelligence.

If impoverished environments can harm intelligence, we might wonder whether enriched environments can improve it. Government-funded after-school programs such as Head Start are designed to help children learn. Research has found that attending such programs may increase intelligence for a short time, but these increases rarely last after the programs end. But other studies suggest that Head Start and similar programs may improve emotional intelligence and reduce the likelihood that children will drop out of school or be held back a grade.

Intelligence is improved by education; the number of years a person has spent in school correlates at about r = .6 with IQ. In part this correlation may be due to the fact that people with higher IQ scores enjoy taking classes more than people with low IQ scores, and thus they are more likely to stay in school. But education also has a causal effect on IQ. Comparisons between children who are almost exactly the same age but who just do or just do not make a deadline for entering school in a given school year show that those who enter school a year earlier have higher IQ than those who have to wait until the next year to begin school. Children's IQs tend to drop significantly during summer vacations, a finding that suggests that a longer school year, as is used in Europe and East Asia, is beneficial.

It is important to remember that the relative roles of nature and nurture can never be completely separated. A child who has higher than average intelligence will be treated differently than a child who has lower than average intelligence, and these differences in behaviours will likely amplify initial differences. This means that modest genetic differences can be multiplied into big differences over time.

Spearman Theory

Spearman and General Intelligence

Charles Spearman was one of the researchers who helped develop a statistical technique known as factor analysis. Factor analysis allows researchers to a number of different test items that can measure common abilities. For example, researchers might find that people who score well on questions that measure vocabulary also perform better on questions related to reading comprehension.

Spearman believed that general intelligence represented an intelligence factor underlying specific mental abilities. All tasks on intelligence tests, whether they related to verbal or mathematical abilities, were influenced by this underlying g-factor.

General intelligence can be compared to athleticism. A person might be a very skilled runner, but this does not necessarily mean that they will also be an excellent figure skater. However, because this person is athletic and fit, they will probably perform much better on other physical tasks than an individual who is less coordinated and more sedentary.

Many modern intelligence tests, including the Stanford-Binet, measure some of the cognitive factors that are thought to make up general intelligence. These include visual-spatial processing, quantitative reasoning, knowledge, fluid reasoning, and working memory:

- Visual-spatial processing involves such abilities as putting together puzzles and copying complex shapes.
- Quantitative reasoning involves the capacity to solve problems that involve numbers.
- Knowledge involves a person's understanding of a wide range of topics.
- Fluid reasoning involves the ability to think flexibly and solve problems.
- Working memory involves the use of short-term memory such as being able to repeat a list of items.

Challenges to the Concept of General Intelligence

The notion that intelligence could be measured and summarized by a single number on an IQ test was controversial during Spearman's time and has remained so over the decades since. Some psychologists, including L.L. Thurstone, challenged the concept of a g-factor. Thurstone instead identified a number of what he referred to as "primary mental abilities."

More recently, psychologists such as Howard Gardner have challenged the notion that a single general intelligence can accurately capture all of human mental ability. Gardner instead proposed that different multiple intelligences exist. Each intelligence represents abilities in a certain domain such as visual-spatial intelligence, verbal-linguistic intelligence, and logical-mathematical intelligence.

Research today points to an underlying mental ability that contributes to performance on many cognitive tasks. IQ scores, which are designed to measure this general intelligence, are also thought to influence an individual's overall success in life. However, while IQ can play a role in academic and life success, other factors such as childhood experiences, educational experiences, socioeconomic status, motivation, maturity, and personality also play a critical role in determining overall success.

References

- Theories-of-intelligence: mindvalley.com, Retrieved 2 June, 2019
- Fluid-crystallized-intelligence: thoughtco.com, Retrieved 11 August, 2019
- What-is-emotional-intelligence: verywellmind.com, Retrieved 13 February, 2019
- Defining-and-measuring-intelligence: opentextbc.ca, Retrieved 29 January, 2019
- What-is-general-intelligence: verywellmind.com, Retrieved 1 May, 2019

Permissions

All chapters in this book are published with permission under the Creative Commons Attribution Share Alike License or equivalent. Every chapter published in this book has been scrutinized by our experts. Their significance has been extensively debated. The topics covered herein carry significant information for a comprehensive understanding. They may even be implemented as practical applications or may be referred to as a beginning point for further studies.

We would like to thank the editorial team for lending their expertise to make the book truly unique. They have played a crucial role in the development of this book. Without their invaluable contributions this book wouldn't have been possible. They have made vital efforts to compile up to date information on the varied aspects of this subject to make this book a valuable addition to the collection of many professionals and students.

This book was conceptualized with the vision of imparting up-to-date and integrated information in this field. To ensure the same, a matchless editorial board was set up. Every individual on the board went through rigorous rounds of assessment to prove their worth. After which they invested a large part of their time researching and compiling the most relevant data for our readers.

The editorial board has been involved in producing this book since its inception. They have spent rigorous hours researching and exploring the diverse topics which have resulted in the successful publishing of this book. They have passed on their knowledge of decades through this book. To expedite this challenging task, the publisher supported the team at every step. A small team of assistant editors was also appointed to further simplify the editing procedure and attain best results for the readers.

Apart from the editorial board, the designing team has also invested a significant amount of their time in understanding the subject and creating the most relevant covers. They scrutinized every image to scout for the most suitable representation of the subject and create an appropriate cover for the book.

The publishing team has been an ardent support to the editorial, designing and production team. Their endless efforts to recruit the best for this project, has resulted in the accomplishment of this book. They are a veteran in the field of academics and their pool of knowledge is as vast as their experience in printing. Their expertise and guidance has proved useful at every step. Their uncompromising quality standards have made this book an exceptional effort. Their encouragement from time to time has been an inspiration for everyone.

The publisher and the editorial board hope that this book will prove to be a valuable piece of knowledge for students, practitioners and scholars across the globe.

Index

CPSIA information can be obtained
at www.ICGtesting.com
Printed in the USA
LVHW060901030122
707669LV00002B/285

9 781647 261597